SECOND EDITION

Beer Steward

HANDBOOK

A Practical Guide to Understanding Beer

Chief Editor

Stephen R. Holle

Urban Chestnut Brewing Company

Assistant Editors

Ray Klimovitz
Klimovitz Brewing Consultants

Lars Larson
Trumer Brauerei Berkeley

Karl Ockert
Master Brewers Association of the Americas

Steve Presley
Anheuser-Busch Inc. (retired)

Master Brewers Association
of the Americas

D1233876

Cover image of beer glassware © iStockphoto.com
Cover image of barley © Shutterstock Images LLC

Library of Congress Control Number: 2012938282
International Standard Book Number: 978-0-9787726-3-5

© 2012 by Master Brewers Association of the Americas
Second printing 2013
Third printing 2013

All rights reserved.
No portion of this handbook may be reproduced in any form,
including photocopy, microfilm, information storage and retrieval system,
computer database, or software, or by any means, including electronic
or mechanical, without written permission of the publisher.

Master Brewers Association of the Americas
3340 Pilot Knob Road
St. Paul, MN 55121, U.S.A.

Foreword

Prior to the nineteenth century, brewing was a local industry. Innovations such as trains, bottles, kegs, and refrigeration were not yet available to ship beer long distances and keep it fresh. Consequently, beer drinkers drank the beer brewed within a short distance from their home and were only familiar with a few local styles brewed with regional methods and ingredients. The hometown brews were fresh and affordable, and most drinkers remained blissfully unaware of styles outside their region, country, and continent.

Today, because of improvements in transportation, refrigeration, and protective packaging, beer drinkers can enjoy a wide variety of beer styles and brands from around the world. With the growing demand for an ever-widening list of beers, the job of the beer seller has grown more complicated and demanding. No longer is it adequate to simply hand patrons a "beer" from a short list of brands. Patrons now want to choose from a menu of beers, and they expect each beer to be served fresh, at the correct temperature, in the style-appropriate glass, and with complementary cuisine.

To satisfy these new beer enthusiasts, the beer seller must become a true beer "steward", which is why the Master Brewers Association of the Americas wrote the *Beer Steward Handbook* and is sponsoring the Beer Steward Certificate Program that the handbook supports.

The responsibilities of a beer steward are at least as demanding as a wine sommelier. The list of beer styles is long and has developed over centuries from the endless combination of ingredients and brewing methods from around the world. Beer is a natural product that has a much shorter shelf life than other alcoholic beverages, so the beer steward must be a caretaker who ensures that the customer receives beer that has been diligently cared for from brewery to glass. Serving beer is also an art that requires skill and experience. Unlike other drinks that come only in bottles, beer is also served from serving tanks, kegs, and casks, and each style has its own type of glassware that best expresses the beer's flavors and aromas. Beer drinking is also a visual experience because it is carbonated and served with a foam collar that requires skill and the proper pouring technique associated with each style of beer and glassware.

Beer remains a wholesome natural drink that quenches thirst, refreshes tired bodies, and lifts weary spirits, but its use in cooking, as a partner with food, and as a rich and complex pleasure to be enjoyed like fine wines or spirits is just becoming more fully appreciated. The beer steward is the artisan that safeguards and delivers the promise of taste and quality that the brewery makes when it ships beer from the brewery. In this way, brewers and beer stewards are partners in providing great-tasting beer to their common customers. This is the reason the Master Brewers Association of the Americas created the Beer Steward Certificate Program.

Cheers,
Stephen R. Holle

Acknowledgments

We thank the authors for their time and commitment to sharing their expertise with others. We also thank the following individuals who contributed their time and efforts toward reviewing the chapters in this handbook: Hildegarde Heymann, Department of Enology, University of California-Davis; Florian Kuplent, Urban Chestnut Brewing Company; Ashton Lewis, Paul Mueller Company/Springfield Brewing Company; George Olsen, M.D., Department of Physiology and Pharmacology and Department of Medicine, Oregon Health and Science University; Steven Pauwels, Boulevard Brewing Co.; George Philliskirk, Carlsberg-Tetley Brewing Ltd.; Dave Radzanowski, Radzan Associates; George Reisch, Anheuser-Busch Inc.; Lauren Salazar, New Belgium Brewing Co.; and Fred Scheer, Voith-Meri Environmental Solutions Inc.

Authors

Charles Bamforth, University of California-Davis
Dirk Bendiak, Molson Canada
Art DeCelles, Beer Institute
Roy Desrochers, GEI Consultants Inc.
Rex Halfpenny, *Michigan Beer Guide*
Stephen R. Holle, Urban Chestnut Brewing Company
Dave Hysert, John I. Haas, Inc. (retired)
Laine J. Murphey, M.D., Ph.D.
Gary Namm, Tampa Bay Partners
Karl Ockert, Master Brewers Association of the Americas
Steve Presley, Anheuser-Busch Inc. (retired)
Gregg Smith, North American Brewers Association
Bill White, Better with Beer
    (formerly Labatt Brewing Co., Oland Specialty Beer Co., Interbrew)
Neil Witte, Boulevard Brewing Co.

Stephen R. Holle
Ray Klimovitz
Lars Larson
Karl Ockert
Steve Presley

Contents

Chapter 1: History of Beer 1
Gregg Smith, Rex Halfpenny, and Stephen R. Holle

Chapter 2: Overview of Brewing 13
Stephen R. Holle and Steve Presley

Chapter 3: World Beer Styles 43
Rex Halfpenny, Gregg Smith, and Stephen R. Holle

Chapter 4: Beer Freshness 91
Bill White

Chapter 5: Serving Beer 101
Bill White

Chapter 6: Beer and Food 119
Gary Namm and Stephen R. Holle

Chapter 7: Ingredients 131
Stephen R. Holle, Dave Hysert, and Dirk Bendiak

Chapter 8: Draft Beer 157
Neil Witte and Stephen R. Holle

Chapter 9: Beer Flavor 175
Roy Desrochers and Karl Ockert

Chapter 10: Beer and Health 189
Charles Bamforth and Laine J. Murphey

Chapter 11: Beer and Regulation 199
Art DeCelles

Appendix A: Summary of the Modern Brewing Process 207
Appendix B: Ideal Gas Pressure 209
Appendix C: Beer Flavor Wheel 211
Appendix D: Beer Institute Advertising and Marketing Code 213

Glossary 221

Index 229

Chapter 1:
History of Beer

Gregg Smith, Rex Halfpenny, and Stephen R. Holle

Man has been brewing beer since the dawn of civilization, and beer's influence on human development is far reaching. Beer has played an important role in human health by being a nutritional part of man's daily diet and a safe source of drinking water when people first crowded into cities. The brewing industry has been an economic engine that has created employment and produced wealth. Over time, political powers have competed for control of the brewing industry because its wealth provided a source of taxes and ultimately greater political influence. Because of beer's importance in the public diet and of consumers' abuse of alcohol, beer also led governments to enact early social controls on food and public health. As a source of wealth and trade, brewing also spurred important commercial and industrial innovations, such as pasteurization, food packaging, microbiology, refrigeration, transportation, branding, and advertising. Because the consumption of beer occurs often with food and at social gatherings, beer is closely entwined in human culture. In summary, because of beer's enduring influence on nutrition, commerce, technology, culture, politics, and health, its relevance extends far beyond its role as a tasty beverage that daily quenches the thirst of countless people worldwide.

> "Directly and indirectly, the [U.S.] beer industry employs approximately 1.9 million Americans, paying them almost $62 billion in wages and benefits. The industry pays over $41 billion in business, personal and consumption taxes, including $5.4 billion in excise taxes and $5.7 billion in sales, gross receipts, and other taxes."
>
> (Beer Institute and National Beer Wholesalers Association, 2009)

The following pages describe how the look and taste of beer evolved as brewers gained further knowledge of fermentation and perfected brewing techniques. Early beer was warm, hazy, uncarbonated, and often made at home, in contrast to the type of beer that dominated the twentieth century, which was cold, clear, effervescent, and mass produced. However, in the twenty-first century, brewers seem prepared to expand a trend born in the last 2 decades of the twentieth century by looking back into history to resurrect previously forgotten styles and father a new birth of stylistic diversity through an ever-growing number of specialty breweries.

Ancient History

Fermentation is a part of the natural decomposition process that sustains and renews life. It has always existed; man simply learned to control fermentation for his own benefit. The discovery of alcohol undoubtedly happened at different times and places across the globe and with various fermentables, including grapes (wine), fruit (cider), honey (mead), and of course grain (beer).

It is impossible to know where or when the first beer was made. Early man probably ate some grain that had begun to germinate and discovered that it was sweeter and softer to chew when making a liquid porridge. When allowed to sit, the porridge fermented from naturally occurring airborne yeast. In thick versions of this porridge, fermentation caused the dough to "rise". When this "leavened" dough was baked, the resulting loaves were lighter and better tasting. In watery versions of the porridge, man discovered beer. In this way, the early development of bread and beer were closely related and why many cultures treated both bread and beer as food staples.

Archaeological discoveries in the Fertile Crescent of modern Iraq indicate that Sumerians grew grain for brewing around 4,000 B.C.E., making them history's first recorded beer drinkers. One of the earliest descriptions of brewing is in the Sumerian "Hymn to Ninkasi" (goddess of brewing), which described beer made from barley, dates, and loaves of bread. Beer was widely consumed by all classes and was an important part of Mesopotamian life, culturally and commercially. One-half of the wheat and barley from this area may have been used in brewing, and beer was so common that it was often a form of barter.

Figure 1.1. A mural painting depicting beer brewing in Kenamun's tomb (New Kingdom, Thebes). (Reprinted from Ishida, 2005)

How Did Sumerians Brew and Drink Beer?

"Kiln-dried malt in Sumeria was pounded and sieved, and the crushed malts stored or made immediately into dough for oven baking. The small loaves were known as bappir. Various aromatics may have been incorporated into the loaves....

The loaves were crumbled, mixed with water, and heated, that is, they were mashed. After cooling, date juice or maybe honey may have been added. Some say that the mix was boiled, but there is little evidence for this. It is likely that fermentation was triggered by yeast naturally seeded from additions of fruit, but it was likely soon realized that a more reliable trigger to fermentation was the addition of a portion of the previous brew [which contained yeast].

After fermentation, the mixture was transferred to another vessel to clarify and then the liquid was drawn off and poured into jars for storage and transportation. Despite the clarification stage, the finished product was far from "bright," hence, the preference for drinking through straws, which were made literally of straw or, for the successively higher walks of life, [of] copper, silver, or gold."

(Bamforth, 2008, pp. 26-27)

Mesopotamians were not the only ancient civilization brewing beer. Ancient Egypt was another important center of brewing because, like Mesopotamia, Egypt was a major producer of grain. The Egyptian hieroglyph for a meal is the combination of the two hieroglyphs for beer and bread. Our modern word for "cash" may have derived from the Egyptian word "kash" for beer, since beer was often used to make payment for goods and services. The pharaoh Ramses operated a brewery that provided 10,000 hL of beer annually to temple employees, and Cleopatra (69–30 B.C.E.) may have been the first ruler to tax beer and initiate a source of revenue that still funds many governments today. Hieroglyphs of the Egyptian beer-brewing process have been found (Figs. 1.1 and 1.2).

The reason the long history of brewing in Egypt and the Middle East is largely unrecognized today is because the spread of Is-

Figure 1.2. Line drawings of the beer-brewing process depicted in Kenamun's tomb. The colored items indicate beer-brewing ingredients and tools. (Reprinted from Ishida, 2005)

lam in the eighth century brought brewing to an end because of its prohibition of alcohol. The brewing of beer was also known and practiced by the Chinese as described in manuscripts from 2000 B.C.E.

Rome

Romans and Greeks lived along the Mediterranean, where the climate and latitude was conducive to the growth of grape vines. Vinifera grapes used in wine thrive in a temperate climate that roughly exists between the 30th and 50th parallels, from the Mediterranean shores to central Europe. Where grapes thrived, people made wine, and the Greeks and Romans were avid drinkers of wine, as they remain to this day. There is historical evidence that the upper classes found wine far superior to beer, but Romans drank beer and knew about brewing through their conquests of Egypt, the Middle East, and Germania. Even though the Romans brought their grape vines to central Europe, they also engaged in brewing. At the fortress Castra Regina, built in A.D. 179 (in present day Regensburg, Germany), the Romans provisioned their 6,000 troops with beer from a sophisticated brewery that included a mash tun and kettle.

In spite of the immense popularity of wine, beer became a part of Roman culture, especially on the northern frontier and among the working classes that could not afford wine. Even the Roman name for beer reflected its importance in the Roman diet. *Ceres* was the god of agriculture and *vis* meant "strength"; thus, the Latin word for beer, *cerevisiae*, meaning "the strength-giving drink from the goddess Ceres". To this day, *cerveza* remains the name for beer in Spanish, and *Saccharomyces cerevisiae* is the scientific name for brewer's yeast, meaning "sugar fungus of beer"!

Because grain grows in so many areas of the world and under various growing conditions, it is more widespread and costs less to produce than grapes. There are many types of grain that grow in different parts of the world that can be used to make beer. Millet grows in Africa, corn (maize) in the Americas, rye in Russia, rice in China, and wheat and barley in Europe. This availability and the stability of grain in storage make the ingredients in beer affordable. Because grain is cheaper than grapes, throughout history, beer has often been the drink of the masses and wine the drink of the affluent. This association endures to this day, and some people unfairly view the high price of wine as an indication of its higher quality in comparison to beer.

Middle Ages

With the fall of the central government in Rome, western society entered into a chaotic period that saw a decline in trade and learning. With no central government to collect taxes, issue currency, provide defense, or maintain roads, commerce and wealth declined. Land-holding lords banded together for mutual protection under a land-based system of feudalism. Monarchs granted land estates to vassals who, in turn, managed the king's possessions and pledged military support and loyalty to their lord. Serfs worked the land and filled their lord's military ranks as soldiers in exchange for food, shelter, and protection.

Land rights were not the only privileges monarchs could bestow upon their subjects. Important commercial activities such as brewing were also doled out by the king in exchange for service. The emperor Charlemagne insisted that each of his estates include a brewery, the beer of which he consumed along with other products of the estate as he traveled his realm. The Catholic church in Rome was the lone centralized organization in western Europe, and monarchs soon recognized the church's ability to assist in governing the realm. Rulers appointed bishops as judges, tax collectors, and other civil servants. In exchange, the church often received feudal privileges, including the right to brew and sell beer.

During this time, monasticism arose within the church. St. Benedict (A.D. 480–547) is recognized as the founder of Christian monasticism that was based on a pledge of piety and self-sufficiency through manual labor. The monasteries supported themselves by raising crops and livestock, making their own clothes, and of course brewing beer. The feudal right to brew beer became especially important as these monasteries became inns where travelers and pilgrims could rest, eat, and find beer. The discipline and education of the monks allowed them to become accomplished brewers. The tenth and eleventh centuries saw the expansion of monasticism, with many monasteries becoming important commercial brewing centers that brought wealth to the church and laid the foundation for modern brewing science.

Although the cooperation of feudal monarchs and the church was necessitated by chaotic times, the relationship was not without conflict. Nobles coveted the power the church had to appoint rulers and administer civil justice and especially the wealth it had acquired through vast land holdings and the privilege to sell beer on which the church paid no tax! As the power of feudal kingdoms increased through the course of the Middle Ages toward becoming strong centralized states, the influence of the church waned, as did its monopoly over brewing.

Events such as the Reformation and the conflicts it spawned (e.g., Thirty Years War) caused the closing of many monasteries, some of which were taken over by the state or purchased by commercial enterprises. The Weihenstephan Monastery in Bavaria, which opened in A.D. 725 and began brewing in 1040, was taken over by the state in 1803. Today, Weihenstephan is still the location where the Bavarian State Brewery brews commercially and the University of Munich operates one of the world's premier brewing colleges.

Other monasteries sold their brewing operations to commercial brewers whose breweries still operate under the name of the original monastic order. There are three well-known breweries in Munich that still carry the names Paulaner, Franziskaner, and Augustiner. Other brands bearing the name of past affiliations with monastic breweries also exist in Belgium, e.g., Augustijn, St. Bernardus, and St. Sixtus. Even though their numbers are greatly diminished, there are still monastic orders brewing beer for their own use and for commercial sale to support their various Christian missions. Monasteries Andechs and Weltenburg in Bavaria are popular destinations where visitors can eat hearty meals and drink beer brewed by the monastery. Perhaps the best known brewing order is the Trappists, with six brewing monasteries in Belgium: Achel, Chimay, Orval, Rochefort, Westmalle, and Westvleteren.

Renaissance and the Rise of Commercial Breweries

Most commoners in the Middle Ages brewed their beer in their home. Like cooking and baking, brewing was primarily done by women, who were called alewives and brewsters. At some point, brewers began to boil the wort, at first to better extract the flavors from "gruit", made up of various botanicals such as sweet gale, mugwort, yarrow, juniper, and heather, and then later to dissolve the bitter acids of hops when it became the primary flavoring in beer. Gruit extraction may have also led to the separation of brewing into two distinct processes: mashing and boiling. Brewers realized that they could control the alcoholic strength of beer through the rinsing of the grain during mashing, with the first worts being the strongest and subsequent rinsings producing decreasing levels of wort strength.

Brewers also found that brewing systems with separate mash tuns and copper kettles that were heated by specialized ovens produced better beer. Consequently, cities created public baking ovens and brewing facilities to improve the quality of the two products, protect public health, prevent residential fires, and gain better control of the wealth (i.e., taxes) that these two important enterprises provided. Technological advances in metallurgy produced bigger and better brewing vessels. Even mundane advances in barrel-making and transportation helped expand markets for brewers. These developments laid the groundwork for large-scale commercial brewing.

As medieval economies developed, trade and wealth increased, allowing workers to escape the agrarian economy of feudalism. Laborers and business owners specialized in the production of specific goods, such as beer, and accumulated capital to purchase the specialized tools to produce them. Guilds were important trade groups that advanced the skills of its members and battled nobles for increasing commercial and political freedoms to conduct commerce. Just as monarchs were taking back influence from the church, they were losing it to the increasing power and wealth of the merchant class who supported the realm through taxes—some of which came from brewers.

What Was Beer Like in the Middle Ages?

In its most basic form, early medieval brewing included malt dried by the sun that was crushed, mixed with hot water, flavored with gruit, and inoculated with the yeast-containing sludge from a previous brew. The whole mash was left to ferment for a few days, with the beer separated from the spent grain and yeast by straining. The milky pale, slightly effervescent beverage was drank within a few days before it could sour.

Archeological evidence indicates that Germanic tribes were using large bronze kettles by the beginning of the Christian era and that Roman settlements in the same area employed kilns, mash tuns, and fermenters. Because kilns dried malt with direct heat from wood-burning fires, the malt acquired a smoky taste with a color neither as light nor as dark as modern pale or roasted malts, respectively, and beer flavored with gruit would have stood in sharp contrast to modern hopped beer.

Because of the lack of sanitation and the inability to pitch pure strains of brewer's yeast, the beer may have had increased fruity esters and spicy phenols in addition to moderate tartness from wild yeast and various acid-producing bacteria. However, with the wide use of hops by the end of the Middle Ages, even the sourness could have been managed. Hops also would have allowed for increased stability for longer maturation periods, during which the beer in pitch-lined casks could have undergone visible clarification through the gravitational settling of haze and noticeable carbonation through the entrapment of carbon dioxide in secondary fermentation. The tart taste of a barrel-aged Belgian West Flanders red ale or the smoke flavor from German *Rauchbier* ("smoked beer") may be reasonable examples of common beer flavors from the Middle Ages.

The new class of commercial brewers prospered when consumers bought beer, as did rulers when they taxed the profits. No one benefited when bad beer affected public health or reduced consumption. Therefore, nobles and city rulers took increasing interest in regulations that protected the quality of beer. Perhaps the most famous is the Bavarian *Reinheitsgebot* ("Purity Law") of 1516 that guarded against the adulteration of beer by limiting its ingredients to water, hops, and barley malt (yeast had not been discovered). These ingredients remain the basic tenant of the law, which is still incorporated into modern German brewing regulations, making the *Reinheitsgebot* the oldest food and consumer protection law in the world.

Colonial America

In colonial America, as in Europe, beer was an important part of a healthful lifestyle because of the polluted condition of water in human settlements. Drinking beer simply helped people avoid waterborne illnesses. The Pilgrims' choice of Plymouth Rock as their landing site in Massachusetts in 1620 was out of necessity because of the depletion of food, and especially beer, as noted by Pilgrim William Bradford.

> So in the morning, after we had called on God for direction, we came to this resolution—to go presently ashore again and to take a better view of two places which we thought most fitting for us; for we could not now take much time for further search or consideration, our victuals being much spent, especially our beer, and it now being the 19th of December. (G. Smith, *Beer in America: The Early Years—1587-1840: Beer's Role in the Settling of America and the Birth of a Nation*, p. 10)

To preserve their health, one of the first structures the Pilgrims erected in Plymouth Colony was a brewery, as it was in many early American settlements. The tavern was another important building, for it became not only a provider of beer and food but also a community meeting place to exchange ideas, conduct business, administer government, and promote trade and commerce.

The course of American democracy is tied closely to taverns since patriots and the Founding Fathers often planned the course of independence over tankards of beer. Samuel Adams and John Hancock met at the Green Dragon Tavern to organize the raid known as the Boston Tea Party in 1773 to show opposition to the British tax on tea. Much of the behind-the-scenes work at the Constitutional Convention in Philadelphia 1787 occurred in taverns such as The George, Black Horse, and City Tavern. Even the compromise for a bicameral legislature consisting of the House and Senate is said to have been worked out in the Indian Queen Tavern by Roger Sherman of Connecticut and John Rutledge of Virginia.

Because beer was safer and more nourishing than water, it became a daily part of the colonists' diet, and most everyone drank it. Workers consumed it with breakfast, and employers supplied beer during the day for laborers. Even the Continental Congress passed a resolution in November 1775 that soldiers in the Continental Army should receive one quart of beer or cider each day. Samuel Adams, Thomas Jefferson, Benjamin Franklin, and George Washington were all home brewers.

The first commercial brewery in colonial America opened in New Amsterdam (New York City) in 1623 as the Red Lion Brewery. The growth of breweries and taverns across the colonies continued as each community saw a need for fresh beer and a meeting place for their citizens. Massachusetts went so far as to enact a law to encourage the establishment of at least one tavern per town. In 1640, Harvard University established a brewery to provide a daily ration of beer to its students. Students at that time could even pay a portion of their tuition with malted barley. The first student strike in the country occurred at Harvard University when there was not enough beer. As the fledgling industry began to grow, the national government imposed an import beer tax in 1789 to protect domestic brewers.

Development of Modern Beer

With the beginning of the nineteenth century, the Industrial Revolution was already underway. Industrial technology was transforming brewing from low-tech local concerns operated with back-breaking labor to mechanized factories run with steam power, hydraulics, and coal-fired furnaces. Railroads and faster ships allowed breweries to expand their markets where they could deliver their increased volume of production. Improvements in sanitation and packaging increased the shelf life of beer and simple instruments such as the thermometer (1794) and hydrometer (1843) allowed for greater product consistency. These developments transformed beer from a dark, inconsistent, murky beverage to a sparkling, effervescent, golden liquid. The brewers that pioneered these changes became wealthy "beer barons" and some of the best known industrialists of their age, including names such as Busch, Coors, Schlitz, Miller, and Pabst.

Direct-heated kilns created inconsistent results and were capable of producing only amber-colored malts with hints of smoke flavor. In 1817, Daniel Wheeler patented the drum roaster, capable of producing dark coffee-colored malt that led to the popularity of stout and porter. In 1818, the indirect hot-air kiln was developed, which allowed for smokeless drying and the production of pale, delicate-flavored malt that would, in part, give birth to the world's most popular beer style, the pale-colored pilsner. Carl Enzinger developed a filter in Germany in 1878 to remove haze, and clear glassware began replacing the ceramic and metal mugs so brewers could show off the sparkling brilliance of their new filtered beers.

Advances in microbiology, particularly by Frenchman Louis Pasteur who, in 1868, identified yeast as the organism that fermented sugar and Emil Hansen who, at the Carlsberg brewery in Denmark, developed a method to isolate single pure strains of yeast, allowed for predictable fermentations that produced consistent flavors free from the influence of wild yeast and other microbes. Pasteur's process of heating liquids inside bottles (pasteurization) also killed microbes that could spoil packaged beer, thus extending shelf life.

There were also other inventions that preserved freshness. German Carl von Linde created a system to dispense draft beer under pressure of carbon dioxide that protected beer from staling oxygen and airborne microbes and preserved its effervescence. Simple inventions such as bottle caps and inexpensive homogenous bottles allowed for efficient, sanitary bottling that improved the transportability and availability of beer. Finally, von

Linde's invention of artificial refrigeration allowed for consistent fermentations that could be conducted independent of seasonal temperatures, and it preserved the freshness of beer after it was packaged. It also allowed the spread of lager brewing, which was originally concentrated in northern cities such as Milwaukee, Chicago, New York, and St. Louis (where ice from lakes could be harvested to chill beer in well-insulated caves and cellars), to warmer regions of the United States.

These advances in malting, fermentation, brewing equipment, microbiology, refrigeration, packaging, and transportation created more consistent beers with much longer shelf lives that could be distributed over much greater distances. They also helped transform the American beer market from a vast group of localized colonial breweries producing a wide variety of medium- to dark-colored ales to one in the twentieth century consisting primarily of a smaller number of large national breweries producing pale-colored lagers.

It can be argued that beer was transformed more extensively in the short span of the nineteenth century than in all the time that preceded it. The innovations that created national, and even global, markets for these new industrial breweries would have further influence on the character and sale of beer in the twentieth century, as the age-old influences of politics, wealth, and religion would continue to affect the production and consumption of beer, especially in the United States.

Consolidation, Prohibition, and Consumerism

The number of breweries in the United States peaked at about 4,000 in 1870. The next 100 years was a period of consolidation. Innovations in production allowed brewers to produce ever increasing volumes of beer that they could ship on railroads that now spanned the continent. Competition was no longer local but regional and even national. Inefficient local brewers who lacked the capital to invest in modern equipment and advertising could not compete with the large breweries. Many small brewers went out of business or were swallowed up through mergers. By the end of World War I, the number had declined to approximately 1,500.

Another result of consolidation was the loss of diversity.

Figure 1.3. The Anheuser-Busch brewhouse in the 1880s. (Reprinted from Halcrow, 1987)

As local breweries closed, the individual styles they brewed also disappeared. The loss of regional styles was also exacerbated by the popularity of the new mild-tasting, pale lager that German immigrants brought to the United States in the mid-1800s. Brewers satisfied the nation's craving for the clean-tasting, thirst-quenching lagers by producing brands that would appeal to a broad range of beer drinkers. In fact, Anheuser-Busch of St. Louis created Budweiser in 1876 to be "... a light-colored lager with a drinkability and taste what would appeal to the masses..." (*Anheuser-Busch Companies Inc. 2001 Annual Report*) (Fig. 1.3). The next blow to diversity would be the convergence of political and religious forces that culminated with the implementation of national Prohibition in 1920.

Throughout the nineteenth century, there was a growing movement among certain religious and reform groups to address what was seen as the moral decay in American society, especially the abuse of alcohol and the great number of saloons tied to breweries that sold alcohol. Groups such as the Anti-Saloon League and Women's Christian Temperance Union pushed for the total prohibition of alcohol, even though some prohibitionists in the early 1800s did not always object to beer but focused their attentions on stronger forms of alcohol such as whiskey. Already by 1907, Kansas, Maine, North Dakota, Georgia, Oklahoma, Mississippi, North Carolina, Tennessee, and West Virginia were dry. With the start of World War I, voices calling for a national prohibition increased, drawing on support to conserve grain for the war effort and on suspicions of the loyalty of German-Americans who dominated the brewing industry. Although World War I ended in November 1918, the Eighteenth Amendment was passed in 1919 with the provision for it to be implemented 1 year after passage, on January 23, 1920. Congress then voted into law the Volstead Act, which gave the government the power to enforce Prohibition.

Understandably, Prohibition was disastrous for U.S. brewers. Of the approximate 1,500 breweries before Prohibition, only 353 reopened upon its repeal in 1933, and times were tough for the survivors. A whole generation came of age during Prohibition without a taste for beer, and many of the remaining beer drinkers could no longer afford it because of the Great Depression.

The next 5 decades was a period of ongoing consolidation. With the expanding interstate highway system to distribute beer and with television networks to market it, the selling of national brands became even more profitable. For the same reasons that a small number of national brands dominated other consumer goods, such as soft drinks, coffee, white bread, and hamburgers, beer sales became concentrated in a few national breweries producing relatively similar pale lager beers. Perhaps created by consumers' postwar focus on health and weight, demand turned to lighter-bodied beers with decreasing levels of bitterness. Marketing experts developed new strategies to meet changing consumer preferences that were manifested in low-calorie "light beers" and "dry beers" that would be remarketed as "low-carbohydrate" beers in the twenty-first century. By 1978, the United States had only 89 brewing plants owned by 41 brewing companies, with the five largest manufacturers producing approximately 75% of the beer.

By the 1980s, the "craft beer" movement had emerged, which reversed the trend of consolidation and expanded the diversity of beer styles. In 1978, President Carter signed legislation to permit home brewing, and these amateur brewers soon became the entrepreneurs who pioneered the formation of many new microbreweries and brewpubs in the 1980s and 1990s. Craft brewers revolted against the homogeneity of the past and resurrected forgotten American beer styles, copied Old World styles, and created new ones. Ale yeast, specialty malts, and loads of hops differentiated craft beers from the American standard lagers of the large national breweries. By 2007, there were approximately 1,400 breweries in the United States (almost the same number as before Prohibition) producing sales of about $100 billion annually. Although craft beers made up only 6% of these sales, craft beer sales have shown increases every year since. Some craft brewers who started brewing in 1980 grew tremendously over the years (Figs. 1.4 and 1.5). In the span of 2 decades, the U.S. beer market transformed itself from one of the most homogeneous beer markets in the world to one of the most diverse, dynamic, and innovative.

Figure 1.4. Early days for craft brewing pioneer Sierra Nevada Brewing Company, circa 1980, in Chico, California. (Courtesy Sierra Nevada Brewing Co.)

Figure 1.5. Sierra Nevada Brewing Company in 2010. (Courtesy Sierra Nevada Brewing Co.)

Selected References

Bamforth, C. 1998. Beer: Tap Into the Art and Science of Brewing. Insight Books, Plenum Press, New York.

Bamforth, C. 2008. Grape vs. Grain: A Historical, Technological, and Social Comparison of Wine and Beer. Cambridge University Press, New York.

Beer Institute (BI) and National Beer Wholesalers Association (NBWA). 2009. beerservesamerica.org. BI, Washington, DC. NBWA, Alexandria, VA.

Dornbusch, H. D. 1997. Prost! The Story of German Beer. Brewers Publications, Boulder, CO.

Halcrow, R. M. 1987. A look at the brewing industry in America 100 years ago. Technical Quarterly Master Brewers Association of the Americas 24:121-128.

Hardwick, W. A., Jr. 1999. World history of brewing and its development in the Americas. Pages 1-32 in: The Practical Brewer, A Manual for the Brewing Industry, 3rd ed. J. T. McCabe, ed. Master Brewers Association of the Americas, St. Paul, MN.

Holle, S. 2005. Craft beers: What sets them apart? All About Beer 25(6):32-35.

Holle, S. R., and Schaumberger, M. 1999. The Reinheitsgebot—One country's interpretation of quality. Brewing Techniques 7(1):34-41.

Hornsey, I. S. 2003. A History of Beer and Brewing. Royal Society of Chemistry, Cambridge, U.K.

Ishida, H. 2005. Two different brewing processes revealed from two ancient Egyptian mural paintings. Technical Quarterly Master Brewers Association of the Americas 42:273-282.

Ogle, M. 2006. Ambitious Brew: The Story of American Beer. Harcourt, Inc., Orlando, FL.

Smith, G. 1998. Beer in America: The Early Years—1587-1840: Beer's Role in the Settling of America and the Birth of a Nation. Siris Books, Brewers Publications, Boulder, CO.

Chapter 2:
Overview of Brewing

Stephen R. Holle and Steve Presley

Beer is a fermented beverage made from grain. While barley is by far the most common type, many grains are used for brewing, including wheat, rye, corn, rice, sorghum, millet, and other starchy seed-producing grasses. Because this main ingredient in beer is so widespread and affordable, beer, like bread, is found in nearly every culture in which farming is practiced.

Fermentation is a natural process that mankind has used for millennia to produce many kinds of food, including sauerkraut, cheese, and even chocolate. Yeast is the fermentation microbe in beer that converts grain-derived sugar to alcohol. Innumerable yeast strains are found across the globe, and over time, brewers domesticated certain strains that were best suited

Figure 2.1. Beer comes in all kinds of colors, flavors, and aromas directly shaped by the ingredients and brewing methods used. (© iStockphoto.com)

to make beer in their regions. Each region also developed its own brewing techniques, selected indigenous flavoring ingredients, and adapted to the unique local water supply. These endless combinations of grain, yeast, flavorings, water, and brewing techniques make beer not only one of the most ubiquitous beverages but also one of the most diverse in style (Fig. 2.1).

The quality of water, malt, and hops can vary from year to year. Unlike wine drinkers, who often embrace the flavor variances from vintage to vintage, beer drinkers typically expect their brands to taste the same year in and year out. Therefore, the commercial brewer must not only develop a recipe but also have the skill to manage a complex process and produce a consistent product even though the inputs are constantly changing.

This chapter leads readers through some common methods to brew beer. Not every brewing method is discussed, nor are readers expected to gain the knowledge of a professional brewer. Rather, the chapter exposes readers to the main processes of modern brewing so that they can understand and better identify why the beer in their glass tastes the way it does.

In its basic form, modern brewing can be broken down into the following 10 steps.

1. Malting—preparing raw grain for brewing through controlled germination and drying
2. Mashing—converting starch to sugar to create a sugary liquid called sweet wort
3. Wort Separation—separating dissolved sugar from the residual grain
4. Boiling—stabilizing the wort with heat and extracting bitterness from the hops
5. Wort Clarification and Chilling—removing wort solids and cooling to fermentation temperature
6. Fermentation—yeast converting sugar to alcohol and carbon dioxide and creating flavor compounds
7. Conditioning—allowing time for beer flavors to mature
8. Filtration—removing suspended yeast and haze (*optional process not used in all beers*)
9. Packaging—filling containers (cans, bottles, kegs, or serving tanks)
10. Pasteurization—protecting beer from spoiling (*optional process not used in all beers*)

A diagram and brief explanation of the brewing process is in Appendix A. The reader may find it helpful to refer to this diagram while reading the following narrative.

Malting

For most fermented beverages, nature supplies the sugar that yeast converts to alcohol. Examples include grape juice for wine, apple juice for cider, and honey for mead. In contrast, the raw grains used in brewing store their sugar as unfermentable starch, so brewing requires an extra step to convert the grain starch to sugar. This conversion process starts with malting the grain, most commonly barley (Fig. 2.2).

The conversion of starch to sugar is a fundamental process for plants and animals. A seed stores energy in the form of sta-

Figure 2.2. Barley, the main ingredient in making beer, grows in North America in the Midwest, western United States, and western Canada. Spring varieties are most common, which are harvested each summer. (Courtesy S. Presley)

ble complex carbohydrates until it is time to release that energy to the sprouting plant. When the seed is ready to sprout, naturally occurring enzymes in the kernel converts the starch to sugar. Humans also use enzymes in saliva in the mouth to begin starch conversion that is then completed by enzymes in the gut. This is why a starchy cracker may become sweet tasting when chewed. Malting is essentially controlled germination to produce enzymes that convert starch to sugar in the mash and soften the kernel for milling. A seed contains two primary parts, the embryo (or germ) that produces a new plant and the starchy endosperm that feeds the sprout until it is mature enough to feed

Figure 2.3. Grain enters the steeping tank in the malt house and is mixed with water. Steeping wakes up the barley kernel and start its germination. (Courtesy Weyermann Specialty Malting Company)

itself through photosynthesis. To sprout in nature, the seed must have moisture, warmth, and oxygen. These conditions are the signals to germinate, which initiates enzyme production, followed by conversion of the starchy endosperm to sugar. The kernel also softens as the enzymes break down the structural gums and proteins that surround the starch.

Likewise, malting begins by steeping grain in a tank of relatively warm water accompanied by aeration (Fig. 2.3). After about 2 days of steeping, the moist kernels are transferred to a chamber where they are allowed to germinate (Fig. 2.4). After the kernels have germinated for 3–5 days and a sufficient degree of softening (modification) has occurred, the malt is transferred to the kiln. Hot air forced through the grain bed slowly dries the malt until the moisture content is reduced to 5% or less. Drying arrests germination, removes cucumber and grassy flavors, further softens the kernel, and stabilizes the grain for storage.

Unkilned malt tastes raw and vegetable-like. Heat drives off most of these unwanted flavors and develops additional pleasant ones in the same manner that roasting improves the taste of nuts and coffee beans. During kilning, the combination of protein and sugar in the malt with heat also produces a browning reaction that creates flavor and color compounds called melanoidins. Melanoidins are also present in other foods, such as caramel and bread crust. Varying the levels of moisture, heat, and time during kilning or roasting creates a wide range of malt flavors and colors.

Just like coffee beans, the level of heat applied to the malt helps determine its color and the intensity of its flavor. Light kilning at 185°F (85°C) produces a pale-colored and neutral-tasting malt that is used for brewing pale-colored beers, such as American standard lagers. More intense kilning at 221°F (105°C) produces amber malts rich in caramel flavors and toasty aromas that are desirable for brewing brown ales and copper-colored *Märzen* lagers. Roasting at high temperatures for longer periods creates dark acrid malt with chocolate and coffee flavors that is used in black porters and stouts (Fig. 2.5).

Figure 2.4. Top, After steeping, the wet barley is transferred to germination beds where it begins grow. **Bottom,** Germinating barley transforms itself from seeds to plants. During the transformation, or modification, the seed goes from hard and steely to soft and crumbly, making it easier to mill and brew at the brewery. (Courtesy Anheuser-Busch InBev)

High levels of heat destroy (denature) malt enzymes, which renders dark malts that are useless in converting starch to sugar. Brewers use a darker malt to achieve color and flavor changes in their beer. When doing so, they must ensure that they use enough paler malt, with its enzymes still active, to convert the starches in the dark malt into sugars. The same condition exists when a brewer uses a portion of unmalted grain, such as rice or corn, which contains starch but no enzymes.

Malting is a costly and time-consuming process in comparison to the significantly less time needed for the preparation of the raw materials used in wine and cider production. Once malted, barley becomes an ingredient that is stable and capable of being stored without any deterioration in quality and usability for an extended period of time. This stability is one reason why beer is such a common and affordable drink. Beer does not have to be produced immediately after harvest before the fruit rots, as is required with grapes and apples. Brewers not only can store malt to produce fresh beer year-round but they can also transport it inexpensively. For this reason, a brewer thousands of miles from Germany can still produce a fresh authentic German-style lager with malts and hops transported from Germany. Affordable access to quality ingredients helps put brewers on a relatively level playing field, where the brewer's skill becomes a major factor in determining the quality of the beer.

Mashing

The brewing process utilizes a series of cooking vessels and is done in the brewhouse; this is the "brewmaster's kitchen". Brewhouse vessels in a large brewery (Fig. 2.6), a craft brewery (Fig. 2.7), and a brewpub (Fig. 2.8) vary. The vessels in all three accomplish the same operations but in a different scale.

Figure 2.5. Drum roaster discharging crystal malt. Some specialty grains are heated in large roasters, which helps develop characteristic colors and flavors. (Courtesy Great Western Malting Co.)

Figure 2.6. Brewhouse vessels in a large American lager brewery: mash tuns, lauter tun, brew kettles, and tanks. (Courtesy Anheuser-Busch InBev and S. Presley)

Figure 2.7. Brewhouse vessels in a regional craft ale brewery: British-style mash tun with mash mixer inlet (Steele's Masher), brew kettle, whirlpool tank, and hop-back (hop jack). (Courtesy BridgePort Brewing Company)

Figure 2.8. Brewhouse vessels in a pub: small combination mash/lauter tun and combination brew kettle/whirlpool tank. (Courtesy Rock Bottom Brewery)

Mashing is the combining of brewing-quality hot water and crushed malt to activate dormant malt enzymes that convert starch to sugar. Before mashing begins, the malt is coarsely crushed in a mill to make the inner parts of the starchy endosperm accessible to malt enzymes and water (Fig. 2.9). Otherwise, much of the potential sugar would remain in the spent grain as unconverted starch. However, care must be taken not to grind the malt too finely. If too much flour is created or the grain husks are finely shredded, the lautering process described later will be impeded. Finely shredded husk can also contribute to the leaching out of an increased amount of harsh-tasting phenols, which can have a direct impact on the resultant beer's flavor and appearance.

After milling, the malt and hot water are mixed in an insulated mash tun. The mash, as this combined mixture is called, is held for 30–60 minutes, during which time the starch conversion to sugar occurs (Fig. 2.10). Mashing can be accomplished by holding the mash at one temperature, by heating the mash through a range of temperatures, or by removing a small portion of the mash to a separate cooker, boiling it, and returning it to the main mash to increase the overall mash temperature. The time needed to complete mashing and the choice of mashing technique is dependent on the malt quality, beer style, economics, brewing system, and brewer's preference. Mashing cycles can be anywhere from 2 to 8 hours long.

Starch is a series of long chains of individual sugar mole-

Figure 2.9. The brewing process begins with milling the grain through the malt mill. This four-roll mill grinds 1 ton of malted grain per hour into an assortment of husk, grist, and flour. (Courtesy BridgePort Brewing Company)

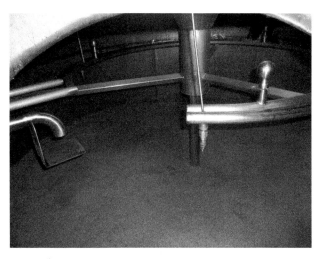

Figure 2.10. Freshly mashed grain rests in the mash tun for 2–8 hours until the sugary liquid, called sweet wort, is drawn off and the husk-laden spent grain is left behind. (Courtesy BridgePort Brewing Company)

cules. Enzymes in the malt called beta amylase and alpha amylase produce sugar by cleaving sugar molecules off these starch chains. Maltose consists of two sugar molecules and is the primary wort sugar. Single-molecule glucose is the second most numerous type of sugar in wort. Brewer's yeast is generally capable of converting sugars up to three molecules in size (known as maltotriose) to alcohol. More-complex sugars of four or more molecules are called dextrins. Dextrins are unfermentable by brewer's yeast and add body and sweetness to the beer. Enzyme starch-converting efficiency is time and temperature dependent. The length of time a mash is held at conversion temperature determines the amount of fermentable and nonfermentable sugars developed.

Beta amylase is useful in cleaving small fermentable sugars from the end of starch chains, while alpha amylase cleaves unfermentable dextrins and some fermentable sugars from the starch units. Beta amylase works optimally between 140 and 150°F (60 and 65°C) and alpha amylase works optimally between 158 and 167°F (70 and 75°C). Consequently, long, low-temperature mashes (140°F/60°C) produce an abundance of maltose, which is highly fermentable, because of beta amylase. Worts of this type produce beers with elevated alcohol content, thinner body, and lower residual sweetness. Short, hot mashes limit beta- and alpha-enzyme activity and produce worts that lead to beers that are lower in alcohol content, full bodied, and sweet.

The cool maritime climate in Great Britain is conducive to growing barley that is easily converted in the brewhouse. For this reason, English brewers developed a simple, single-temperature infusion mashing technique that occurs in a combination mashing/lautering vessel. A single mash temperature of 150–153°F (65–67°C) is used because both beta and alpha amylase enzymes are active at this compromise temperature. Because of its simplicity and low equipment costs, brewpubs frequently use single-temperature infusion mashing.

In earlier times, before maltsters could produce highly modified malt and soft, friable, low-protein kernels, more-intensive mashing techniques were developed to break down gums, proteins, and starches that the maltsters of the day could not. The undermodified malt was hard and contained few enzymes. Brewers discovered that boiling a portion of the malt would break down its starchy endosperm, making it more accessible to the action of the sugar-producing enzymes. The boiled mash, or decoction, is combined with the regular mash to raise its temperature to a point more conducive to the limited amount of enzymes present. Brewers using this method employ from one to three decoction mashes to achieve a rising series of mash temperature rests that are designed to be at the optimum points for enzyme activity. This multistage process is called decoction mashing.

Decoction was most common in continental Europe in earlier times when less-modified malt was produced. Even though improved barley varieties and malting techniques produce well-modified malts on the Continent today, decoction mashing is still widely used in Germany, where brewers continue to follow the time-honored tradition to produce beers that benefit from it. Because extended boiling of the mash creates dark, caramel-tasting melanoidins, many such brewers prefer decoction for malty, caramel-colored beers. However, debate now exists whether decoction mashing is really necessary to produce amber beers because of improved techniques that produce these same melanoidins during malting. Because

Figure 2.11. The sweet mash is rinsed, or sparged, leaving spent grain in the lauter tun and sweet wort in the brew kettle. (Courtesy Newlands Systems Inc.)

decoction mashing consumes a lot of time and energy, many breweries have chosen simpler mashing techniques for economic and time-saving reasons.

A hybrid of infusion and decoction mashing is step mashing in which a heated mash tun raises the entire mash through multiple temperature rests or steps. Because multiple-temperature mashing is efficient in producing high extract yields (i.e., lots of sugar) and provides great flexibility in working with a variety of malts and beer styles, it is the most common technique used in the modern brewhouse. The interior of a small lauter tun containing grain after all the extract has been removed is shown in Figure 2.11.

Wort Separation

The sugary liquid resulting from mashing is called sweet wort. The sugar that has been dissolved in the mash water, along with small amounts of protein, minerals, and other trace elements, is called extract. After mashing, the grain is transferred to a lauter tun to separate the cloudy wort from the residual grain particles.

A lauter tun is a vessel with a perforated false bottom (like a screen) that sits a few centimeters (inches) above the vessel's actual bottom (Figs. 2.12 and 2.13). For single-temperature infusion mashing used in the British ale style or tradition, mashing and lautering is usually conducted in the same vessel, called a mash tun (Figs. 2.14 and 2.15). Grain husks provide permeability to the grain bed that sits on top of the false bottom. This is why the grain milling process carefully crushes the kernels to prevent damaging the husk. The wort is drawn through the grain bed and exits as a clear, turbid-free liquid. To recover as much of the extract from the grain as possible, hot brewing sparge water (about 172°F/78°C) is added to the top of the lauter tun. The water percolates through the grain bed and rinses sugar from it. The brewer typically adds water at

Figure 2.12. Large lauter tuns sometimes measure 30 feet or more in diameter. (Courtesy Anheuser-Busch InBev and S. Presley)

Figure 2.13. The inside of a large lauter tun has cutting knives that help keep the mash bed from channeling so that the sweet wort runoff is not disturbed. (Courtesy Anheuser-Busch InBev and S. Presley)

Figure 2.14. A British-styled mash tun uses an inlet mixer called a Steele's Masher to mix the grain with hot water. These mash tuns are typically narrower and have deeper beds than lauter tuns. This mash tun is in a regional ale brewery. (Courtesy BridgePort Brewing Company)

Figure 2.15. British-style mash tuns use a floating mash bed and do not need rakes; this system is commonly used to make ales. Inside the mash tun, the arm at the bottom is used to push out spent grain. (Courtesy BridgePort Brewing Company)

the same rate that the out-flowing wort is piped to the wort kettle. Lautering time ranges from 1 to 2 hours. The protein-rich spent grains left over from mashing are removed and used as cattle feed (Fig. 2.16). As the volume and temperature of sparge water increases, the more efficient the process is in rinsing sugar from the grain. However, there is a limit. Excessive heat (>172°F/78°C) and too much water, together or individually, can extract many undesirable elements that cause harsh flavors or beer haze. Too much water also dilutes the brew's sugar content, which reduces the beer's alcohol content.

All other brewing parameters remaining constant, the more water used with a given amount of grain, the lower the alcohol content of the beer because of dilution of the fermentable sugars that produce alcohol. Many beer drinkers falsely believe that the color of beer indicates its alcohol content. Color is determined primarily by the intensity of the malt color, the amount of colored malt used in the mash, and the duration of the wort boiling stage. While many beers high in alcohol (e.g., barley wine and *Doppelbock*) are dark, the color simply reflects the style. In fact, the draft version of a well-known Irish stout has a relatively low alcohol content at 4.1% alcohol by volume (ABV) compared with many domestic pale lagers that are in the area of 5.0% ABV.

Figure 2.16. Spent grains from a mash tun are pulled from a side door into a tote for removal and sale as nutritious cattle feed. (Courtesy Newlands Systems Inc.)

Boiling

The wort collected from the lauter tun is directed to the wort kettle, where it is boiled for 1–2 hours (Fig. 2.17). The duration of the boil is dependent upon the type of kettle, beer style, and composition of the wort. Boiling wort serves the following purposes: sterilizes the wort; dissolves bitter hop alpha acids; drives off unwanted flavor volatiles with escaping water vapor; denatures malt enzymes, which arrests the conversion process; concentrates the sugar (extract) content of the wort; increases wort color by caramelizing sugars; and coagulates protein for improved beer clarity.

Figure 2.17. The sweet wort collected in the brew kettle is boiled and bittering hops are added at this stage. (Courtesy BridgePort Brewing Company)

Sterilizes the Wort

Boiling sterilizes the wort by killing microbes in the water or attached to the grain that might later cause off-flavors. For this reason, beer was an important part of the medieval diet because it rendered contaminated water safe to drink. Even today, beer is a preferred drink in areas without potable water.

Dissolves Bitter Hop Alpha Acids

Hops are the most common flavor ingredient used in beer and the only one allowed by law for beer brewed and sold in Germany under their Purity Law, known as the *Reinheitsgebot*. Hop alpha acids, which contribute bitterness as a counterbalance to the sweet malt, are not soluble in cold wort. Boiling transforms the structure of the alpha acids through a process called isomerization that makes them soluble. Hops became the dominant flavoring agent not only for their bittering properties but also for their ability to protect beer from bacterial spoilage.

Hops added early in the boil provide the majority of bitterness in beer. The longer they are boiled, the greater the amount of bitter acids that are isomerized. Hops also contain aromatic oils, common in certain beer styles, such as American pale ales. These aromatic oils are easily volatized by heat, so oils in the bittering hops rarely survive in beer. Therefore, brewers may make one or more late hop additions within the last 10 minutes of the boil to give the beer an aromatic hop character. Because of the short boiling time, late-addition hops contribute little bitterness to the beer. To contribute aroma, hops may also be added in the hopback (or hop jack), whirlpool, fermenter, or even the cask for production of English real ale (also known as cask-conditioned ale).

Drives Off Unwanted Flavor Volatiles

Although the majority of a malted grain's vegetable notes are removed in the kilning process, several undesirable vegetable-like compounds are carried over into and develop in the wort. The predominant compound in this group is dimethyl sulfide (DMS). DMS is a sulfur-based compound created by heat from a precursor formed during malting. DMS has an aroma described as canned creamed corn or cooked cabbage and is considered offensive at high levels. Although heat initially creates DMS, boiling volatizes and drives it off in the escaping water vapor (steam). The presence of DMS in beer is an indicator of an insufficient boil or of unwanted beer spoilers. Grassy-flavored aldehydes produced during malting are also volatized by boiling.

Denatures Malt Enzymes

Heat ends enzymatic activity by denaturing the malt enzymes and thereby fixes the amount of fermentable sugar and unfermentable dextrins in the wort, arresting the conversion process.

Concentrates the Wort

Boiling concentrates the sugar (extract) content of the wort by evaporating water. This is one tool the brewer uses to remove some of the excess water added in the lauter tun and to establish the extract content of the wort to produce the desired alcohol content of the beer. Long boils are common for some strong beers because the increased concentration of wort sugars increases the alcohol potential of the beer.

Increases Wort Color

As in malting, the combination of sugar, heat, and protein creates melanoidin flavor compounds and darker wort color by caramelizing the wort sugars. For this reason, amber beers are sometimes boiled longer than pale ones.

Coagulates Protein

Heat coagulates malt proteins, which form large flocs that drop out of suspension due to their decreased solubility, improving beer clarity. (Boiling has the same effect on malt protein as it does on the whites of a hard-boiled egg.) If this protein were left in the wort, it could contribute to beer haze and off-flavors.

Wort Clarification and Chilling

Clarification

At the end of the boil, the wort contains solids such as spent hops, flocs of protein, and even a small amount of husks washed out of the lauter tun. Three ways in which this solid residue (trub) is removed is by whirlpool action, filtration in a hopback, or settling in a large, flat vessel called a coolship.

The brewer creates a whirlpool by pumping the boiled wort in a circular motion either in the kettle or in a separate whirlpool vessel (Fig. 2.18). As the wort flows in a circular motion, the trub is drawn to the center. When the wort stops spinning, the trub settles in a compact cone in the center. The clear wort is then drawn from the bottom or side of the vessel. The whirlpool technique is sometimes referred to as the "teacup effect" because the trub acts similar to how tea leaves in a stirred cup of tea collect in the cup's center.

An ancient, time-honored technique used by ale brewers to clarify the wort, while also increasing its floral hop notes, is to filter it through a vessel filled with whole hops, called a hopback or hop jack. The hops act as a filter to hold back the trub and spent hops as the wort flows through them. An additional benefit of this method is that the fresh hops contribute aromatic oils to the wort (Fig. 2.19).

A very old clarification and chilling technique uses a coolship, which is simply a wide

Figure 2.18. After the wort has boiled, it is pumped to the whirlpool tank to separate the hops and sediment (trub) prior to cooling. The trub pile can be seen after the wort has been drawn off. Note that the inlet nozzle points at an angle so the wort turns as it fills the tank. (Courtesy Newlands Systems Inc.)

Figure 2.19. Hopbacks are sometimes used to capture whole hops from the brew kettle and also to add fresh flavorful hops prior to cooling. (Courtesy BridgePort Brewing Company)

shallow pan into which the wort is pumped and stands a few centimeters (inches) deep. The shallow depth causes a rapid settling of the trub. An added benefit is the cooling of the wort through the rapid dissipation of heat across the large surface area. The downside of the coolship is that it also exposes the cooled wort to the ambient air, which may contain a variety of bacteria and wild yeast. In Belgium, for the production of lambic beers, brewers still employ a coolship for this very reason. Lambics are acidic beers produced by spontaneous fermentation. The term spontaneous refers to the naturally occurring airborne microflora (wild yeast and bacteria) that inoculate the wort as wind blows across the coolship. These microflora produce a wide range of alcohols and acids that give lambic beer its unique tart flavor.

Chilling

Because the high temperature of the wort leaving the whirlpool or hopback would kill brewer's yeast, the wort must be cooled to fermentation temperature before inoculation. A wort chiller contains a series of metal plates (Fig. 2.20). Hot wort flows in a thin broad stream between plates. On the opposite side of these plates, chilled water or a chilled glycol–brine solution flows in the opposite direction to carry away the heat. This is a quick process (20–45 minutes depending on the brew size and cooler capacity) that delivers a uniform wort discharge temperature that the brewer can regulate based on the desired temperature for delivery into the fermenter. The drop in temperature also decreases the solubility of additional protein, known as cold trub. Cold trub settles in the bottom of the fermenter and may or may not be removed based on the beer style or preference of the brewer. Its removal is common for the production of delicate-flavored beers.

Figure 2.20. From the whirlpool tank or hopback, the hopped wort is cooled quickly to fermentation temperatures using an enclosed wort chiller. Hot water generated from this process is used on the next brew. (Courtesy Anheuser-Busch InBev and S. Presley)

Fermentation

The Latin name for brewer's yeast is *Saccharomyces cerevisiae*. When roughly translated, it means "sugar fungus of beer". Yeast feeds on sugar for sustenance and reproduction. The waste product of their feeding is almost equal parts of ethyl alcohol (ethanol) and carbon dioxide, with lesser amounts of important flavor compounds in the form of esters, aldehydes, phenolic compounds, fusel alcohols, and acids. In addition to sugar, yeast requires other nutrients, including amino acids, vitamins, minerals, and oxygen. Fortunately, properly constituted wort (especially from malted barley) supplies all of these nutrients in adequate quantities, except oxygen, which is usually dissolved into the wort with sterile air or oxygen in route to the fermenter. When yeast is added (pitched), the process of converting wort to beer begins. At this point, it is called young (*ruh*) beer until it completes fermentation and flavor maturation.

Yeast strains are classified in two broad categories: top-fermenting ale yeast and bottom-fermenting lager yeast. The primary difference is the ability of lager yeast to ferment at low, near freezing, temperatures even though primary fermentation takes place at ±50°F (10°C). Ale yeast typically ferments near room temperature (59–77°F/15–25°C) and becomes dormant below 48°F (9°C). While both lager and ale yeast work throughout the entire volume of the fermenter, lager yeast is typically harvested for reuse from the bottom of the tank at the completion of fermentation and ale yeast is traditionally harvested by skimming the frothy head of yeast that rises to the top as fermentation progresses. Today, fermentation temperature is the primary defining difference between ale yeast (top fermenting) and lager yeast (bottom fermenting) because modern fermentation in cylindroconical tanks (tall cylinders with a sharp-angled conical bottom/outlet) forces both yeast types to the bottom for collection after fermentation (Figs. 2.21 and 2.22). At

Figure 2.21. Cooled wort fills the fermenter vessel, commonly a vertical cone-bottom tank. This fermenter is in a pub brewery. (Courtesy Rock Bottom Brewery)

low temperatures, yeast metabolism slows and the amount of metabolic by-products is greatly reduced, particularly fruity-tasting esters and fusel alcohols (as opposed to more neutral-tasting ethyl alcohol). Consequently, the flavor of ale is often described as fruitier than the mellow flavor of lager. Prior to advances in brewery hygiene and artificial refrigeration, lager beer was also prized for its flavor stability. Fewer microbes are active at low temperatures, so lager was less likely to be influenced by off-flavors from competing wild yeast and other microbes. Both ale and lager yeasts are equally valued by brewers for the variety of unique beer styles that each produces.

Brewers typically use a single yeast strain (even a proprietary strain) because of the specific flavor it imparts to the beer. Brewers must be diligent in the fight against invading microbes that might produce off-flavors or spoil the beer if allowed to grow. Unlike winemakers, who employ sulfites to control unwanted microbes, brewers rarely use any type of additives to protect their beer. Their two main defenses against spoilage microbes are the boiling of the wort to ensure its sterility and the use of strict hygiene practices throughout the process. Consequently, on the cold side of the wort chiller, sanitation becomes very important because heat is no longer there to protect against wild yeast or bacteria. In the fermentation cellar, every surface in contact with the beer must be cleaned and sanitized. In fact, in some small, nonautomated breweries, the brewer may spend as much time cleaning as brewing.

Modern breweries generally employ enclosed stainless steel fermenters because of the protection they afford against outside microbes, their durability, and the ease with which they can be cleaned and sanitized. The fermenters are placed in a climate-controlled room or the tanks themselves have cooling jackets. Yeast metabolism and the flavors produced are highly affected by temperature. Therefore, a key to consistent beer taste is a consis-

Figure 2.22. Fermentation cellar in a regional craft ale brewery. Each tank receives two brews that take 7 days to ferment and cool. (Courtesy BridgePort Brewing Company)

tent temperature from one batch to another. Because trub and dead yeast cells drop out of suspension during fermentation, modern fermenters are also designed for the easy collection and removal of this sediment before it can affect the taste of the beer. Finally, modern design and construction methods used for these stainless steel tanks provide for the hygienic recovery of yeast for reuse in subsequent fermentations and for the sanitary transfer of the beer to its next phase of the process.

Excellent beer can also be produced in traditional, open-top fermenters (Fig. 2.23). When using such vessels, the brewmaster must not only see to it that the wort is properly aerated and a sufficient quantity of healthy yeast is pitched but also that the wort is protected from airborne microbes by isolating the fermenting room. With this combination, the yeast quickly multiplies and consumes nutrients used by competing microbes. As with all wort fermentations, it produces what is called the krausen head, a dense layer of foam and yeast with carbon dioxide that rises to and covers the top of the fermenter (Fig. 2.24). In the case of coolship use, this thick, dense head provides a protective layer that separates the wort from the ambient atmosphere. Additionally, the bitter hop alpha acids afford some protection, and once fermentation starts, yeast also produces acids that lower the beer's pH to inhospitable levels for other microbes. In this way, yeast effectively crowds out other microbes so they have little chance to multiply. Open fermentation is still used for some traditional English ales and many Bavarian wheat beers (Fig. 2.25).

Figure 2.23. Traditional open fermentation at an ale brewery, where the fermentation is exposed and each stage monitored by the brewer. (Courtesy Sierra Nevada Brewing Co.)

In distilling and winemaking, the selection of individual yeast strains receives less attention than it does in beer making. In these processes, the emphasis is on efficient alcohol production. The flavors imparted by yeast to distilled spirits and wine typically do not receive the same focus as they do in brewing. Good evidence of this fact is the two major categories of beer, ale and lager, which are defined by yeast type. Furthermore, many styles, particularly ales, are clearly identifiable by their yeast

Figure 2.24. Fermentation foam protects from possible airborne microbes that might spoil the beer. (Courtesy BridgePort Brewing Company)

Figure 2.25. Open fermentation of Bavarian-style *Weizen* beer. The rocky heads clean themselves away as they fall down the fermenter chute. (Courtesy New Glarus Brewing Company)

character. In fact, a brewer may as easily recognize the yeast strain as the hops or malt in a beer since it is felt that 50–60% of a beer's flavor is developed or created by its yeast.

Clean yeast slurries for re-pitching can be harvested from the bottom of the fermenter or skimmed from the top. Brewers go to great lengths to care for their yeast because unhealthy yeast performs poorly and does not produce consistent flavors. Brewing is often compared with baking, and historically, bread and beer are certainly closely connected. Both employ a skilled artisan who uses yeast to convert grain into a more-refined product. Brewers make wort, but yeast makes beer. Consequently, yeast is more than just a simple ingredient. The brewer must raise and care for the yeast and feed it with properly constituted wort to produce consistent-tasting beer. When the yeast becomes old and tired, new vital yeast is propagated, and the old is discarded.

Conditioning

Although moderately high temperatures may shorten ale fermentation times when compared with lager fermentation times, the primary fermentation time for both ale and lager yeasts is about 1 week, during which time most of the sugar is converted to alcohol and carbon dioxide. Fermentation also produces a large number of flavor compounds. Some of these flavors are desirable and some are undesirable. Although the work of making alcohol is largely finished after primary fermentation, the yeast must still clean up and mellow young beer flavors, particularly buttery-tasting diacetyl, green-apple-tasting acetaldehyde, and various sulfur notes. For this maturation process (also called lagering, aging, or conditioning), the beer is usually transferred to a conditioning tank, where it may rest for several weeks (Fig. 2.26).

Because ales condition at higher temperatures, the yeast is more active and conditioning time is usually less than 2 weeks. Many ales are fermented and aged in the same tank. Lager beers often condition at 30–41°F (–1 to 5°C) and the yeast activity is slower, so more time is required, perhaps 2–6 weeks. Strong beers, i.e., ones with higher alcohol levels, may require even longer maturation times. Cold lagering accelerates clarification because haze particles are less soluble at low temperatures and settle out. Lager brewers claim the cold also produces mellower flavors.

In addition to maturing a beer, cold conditioning facilitates the removal of haze-forming particles. Haze is caused by suspended yeast or tannin–protein complexes. Clarification for removal of these particles can be accelerated with various aides added to the conditioning tank. These aides are insoluble and flavor neutral and are left in the tank when the beer is transferred or removed later by filtration. Clarification aids attract one of these haze precursors and then settle out of solution. Bentonite clay and silica hydrogel attract protein. The infrequently used enzyme papain degrades protein to smaller, non-haze-forming molecules. Gelatin and a form of plastic flakes known as polyvinyl-polypyrrolidone (PVPP) attach to tannins. Isinglass, a traditional British fining agent, is a nearly pure form of collagen that attracts yeast, protein, and lipids. A less-expensive agent made from seaweed is often used in conjunction with the more-expensive isinglass to remove protein.

The cold-conditioning phase can also be used to naturally carbonate beer. During primary fermentation, carbon dioxide is vented to prevent the rupturing of the tank. In larger breweries,

Figure 2.26. After fermentation, the beer is pumped to these horizontal conditioning tanks to settle and clarify. Some beers may undergo a secondary fermentation to naturally carbonate. (Courtesy BridgePort Brewing Company)

the vented gas is collected and cleaned for reuse later in the process. However, if a small amount of fermentable sugar is carried over into a pressure-capable conditioning tank, the carbon dioxide produced from this secondary fermentation can be contained in the vessel and thereby carbonate the beer. Traditional brewers make claims shared by some makers of sparkling wine that natural carbonation produces a finer, more stable bubble. Another practice used to naturally carbonate beer is krausening. Krausening is a traditional method that adds 10–15% volume of fermenting beer to the *ruh* beer in a conditioning tank to produce carbonation that is retained in the beer under pressure. Finally, many breweries simply vent carbon dioxide from fermentation and force carbonate to the proper level from carbon dioxide tanks before packaging.

Much of the character of wine and whiskey is contributed by the barrels in which they are aged. Wood is porous and an excellent breeding ground for microbes. The sulfites in wine and the high alcohol content in whiskey guard against these spoilage microbes. Beer lacks these protections, so, when the use of wooden barrels and casks was still common, the wood was usually coated with hot pitch to sanitize the inside and create a hygienic inert barrier between the wood and the beer. However, some beer styles are purposely aged in exposed wood. Lambics and Flemish red and brown ales are examples in which

Figure 2.27. Oak barrels are stacked in a small specialty brewery specializing in sour ales. Used wine casks, bourbon barrels, and port pipes are favored to age and flavor super-specialized Belgian-styled ales. (Courtesy Cascade Brewing)

the wild yeast and acid-producing bacteria living in the porous wood are desirable to create the beer's refreshing sour character. American brewers have also grown fond of aging some stouts and barley wines in old bourbon barrels so the flavor of bourbon is imparted to the beer (Fig. 2.27).

Filtration

Prior to packaging, many beers are filtered to remove the haze caused by suspended yeast and protein–tannin complexes (Fig. 2.28). Although not necessarily a true indicator, clear beer has nonetheless been identified with quality, especially after glass drinking vessels became economical in the nineteenth century. In spite of this perception, normal protein-caused beer haze is essentially tasteless and can create a slight mouthfeel desirable in some styles. Its removal is done primarily for visual reasons. The removal of yeast can have some flavor benefits since yeast eventually starves, decomposes, and releases various flavor components and enzymes that can change the character of beer. (Hopefully, the beer will be consumed when fresh and yeast autolysis will not be a problem in unfiltered beer.) Live yeast, however, is an oxygen scavenger that can reduce staling from oxygen that enters into the package upon filling. Filtration can also damage beer if done improperly. Any oxygen intrusion during the filtration process can damage freshness since the oxygen-scavenging yeast has been removed. Extremely tight filtration can also remove flavor and color as well as protein, which contributes to body and head retention.

Finally, a variety of beer styles are not filtered. Cask-conditioned ales, artisanal beers, and many styles of wheat beer are common examples. Unfiltered beers may simply rely on natural sedimentation or fining agents to clear the beer. Other styles may be defined by turbidity and embrace the fact that they are unfiltered. In Germany, unfiltered beer is often labeled *Naturtrüb*, meaning "naturally turbid".

Figure 2.28. After conditioning and prior to packaging, the beer may be filtered. This is a plate-and-frame filter using paper filter sheets that trap yeast and sediments still in the beer. (Courtesy Anheuser-Busch InBev and S. Presley)

Packaging

After filtration, the clear (bright) beer is usually held in a bright-beer tank, where carbonation can be adjusted, the beer can be blended with other batches to improve consistency, or priming can be added (priming is described later). From here, the beer can be dispensed into bottles, cans, kegs, casks, and serving tanks. The only potential difference in the beer as it is filled into these various containers is a lower carbonation level in beers for kegs, casks, and serving tanks than that in bottled and canned beers.

Several keys to successful packaging are 1) strict hygiene to avoid contamination, 2) low air pickup to prevent staling, and 3) constant pressure and temperature to minimize carbon dioxide loss through foaming. Each time beer foams prior to packaging, the protein that supports a sturdy head loses its capacity to create future foam in the glass. Foam may also contribute to particulate haze after it collapses.

Bottles

Bottle are filled by evacuating the air and filling the bottle with carbon dioxide to remove oxygen and pressurize the bottle to prevent foaming (Fig. 2.29). The tolerance for air pickup is low (usually <0.05 parts per million [ppm]) because even a small amount of air in filtered beer can cause stale flavors. The beer is fobbed (caused to foam) by jetting a minute high-pressure stream of hot water into the neck or pinging the bottle to release some carbon dioxide from suspension. The bottle is capped on the foam to keep oxygen from the headspace. After crowning, the bottle is rinsed, labeled, and packed in cartons.

Many small brewers are now using microbottling machines to package their beer into 22-ounce bottles called bombers. This has allowed them to enter the package market with

Figure 2.29. Beer is bottled in high-speed lines that evacuate the air from the bottles to extend shelf life. Bottles are commonly rinsed, filled, and crowned at speeds exceeding 250 bottles per minute. These bottles are leaving the bottle filler. (Courtesy New Glarus Brewing Company)

Figure 2.30. Microbottling allows smaller breweries into the bottled beer market. The process with small, mobile microbottlers is more labor intensive but avoids the capital expense of the high-speed lines. (Courtesy Green Bottling)

less capital expense (Fig. 2.30). Glass is a good packaging material because it is completely inert and easily sanitized. It is moderately effective at guarding the beer from the harmful effects of light, and brown glass is better than green or clear glass. Glass is breakable and heavy; therefore, it is expensive to ship. For this reason, plastic polyethylene terephthalate (PET) bottles are gaining popularity for their ruggedness and light weight. However, plastic is not impermeable and allows oxygen penetration and carbon dioxide loss. Therefore, the plastic bottle interior must be covered with an impervious coating. Even with the coating, the plastic provides a less-protective barrier than that of glass.

Cans

The canning process is similar to bottling but the can is closed by placing a lid on the can as a stream of carbon dioxide flows over the opening to expel air. The lid is secured by a seamer that mechanically crimps the lid over the walls of the can.

Aluminum cans are light and economical to ship. They also offer complete protection from light. To protect the beer from the aluminum, the interior is spray coated with a flavor-neutral, impervious lining.

Kegs

Stainless steel kegs are first cleaned with detergent, sanitized with steam or chemical sanitizers, and then filled and pressurized with carbon dioxide. Filling the keg under pressure is similar to bottling. Kegs usually experience lower oxygen pickup than bottles and cans because the headspace where oxygen accumulates is smaller relative to the volume of beer. Kegs are typically not pasteurized since it is impractical. Instead they are kept cold after leaving the brewery and consigned for consumption within several weeks. For these reasons, draft beer may be fresher than beer in bottles or cans, provided the retailer is following good draft dispense practices.

Casks

Casks are the traditional package for English ales. Although originally made from pitched-lined wood staves, stainless steel casks are now commonly used. Casks are filled with fully fermented, unfiltered, and uncarbonated beer. Sugar, called priming, is added to the cask along with hops and isinglass. The yeast carried over from the fermenter (remember, the yeast has not been filtered out) ferments the sugar and produces natural carbonation, although some new vigorous yeast may be added. The cask is filled gently to avoid excessive oxygen pickup, but the yeast in the cask helps scavenge oxygen. Hops are added to produce aromatics but no bitterness. The isinglass clarifies the beer.

Figure 2.31. Cask-conditioned beers are racked directly from the fermenters to casks, which act as conditioning vessels. This 11-gallon firkin was set on a stillage rack to settle and then tapped. (Courtesy BridgePort Brewing Company)

Traditionally, the casks are cellared at the pub for at least 1 week, during which time the ale carbonates, the hops give up their aromatic oils, and the isinglass clears the haze and yeast. Because sediment of yeast, hops, isinglass, and trub rests at the bottom of the cask, the pub owner must handle the casks carefully to avoid rousing the sediment (Fig. 2.31).

Cask beer is served at cellar temperature and with less carbonation than that of most commercial beers. It is also not dispensed under pressure. When the cask has conditioned properly, it is attached to a pump called a beer engine (Fig. 2.32). The bartender then pumps the beer by hand to the tap, which also entrains it with air (especially when a sparkler is used). Because air is about 80% nitrogen, which forms very small stable bubbles, the beer in a glass filled by a beer engine has a stable creamy head and a smooth mouthfeel. Nitrogenated beers with widgets are essentially replicating the effects of a beer engine. Because the void left by the dispensed beer is replaced with unpressurized air, cask beer has a short shelf life of 2 days or less before it goes stale and flat. Although frowned upon by purists, some systems use nitrogen or carbon dioxide to fill the headspace as the cask is emptied to extend shelf life.

Figure 2.32. Cask beer is typically served using a beer engine but can also be tapped and served by gravity right on the bar. (Courtesy BridgePort Brewing Company)

After World War II, cask ale started falling out of favor in the United Kingdom as cold spritzy lagers gained popularity at the expense of what some drinkers considered flat warm ales. However, cask ale (sometimes called real ale) has made a comeback, largely due to the movement known as the Campaign for Real Ale (CAMRA).

Bottle Conditioning

Classic champagne is a sparkling wine that receives its sparkle from carbon dioxide produced by yeast after the addition of a "dosage" of sugary syrup and wine into the bottle as it goes into conditioning storage. Many bottled beers are also carbonated in a similar fashion. The typical process involves filling the bottle with fully fermented, unfiltered beer to which an exact amount of sugar (known as priming) has been added. When fermented by yeast, the sugar produces the desired level of carbonation. The sugar can come from two sources. One source may be wort or young, not fully fermented, beer. The other source may be simple sugar. The yeast carried over from the fermenter (or new yeast added with the priming) converts the sugar to carbon dioxide, which is trapped in the capped bottle. Bottle conditioning is especially common for Trappist-style Belgian ales and Bavarian wheat beers. With Trappist ales, the beer is usually carefully decanted off the sediment when poured. With Bavarian wheat beers, the sediment is usually resuspended and poured with the beer into the glass, where it adds a smooth bready character to the beer's flavor. Bottle-conditioned beer is often identified on the label as unfiltered or *mit Hefe*, meaning "with yeast" in German.

Serving Tanks

Brewpubs have simplified their packaging process. They do not pasteurize because of the high equipment costs, space needs, and the fact that they rarely fill cans or bottles, except for carryout. Also, the beer will likely be consumed quickly before spoilage can occur. If spoilage did occur, the brewer could simply remove the tainted beer—something brewers who sell through third-party pubs or stores have a more difficult time controlling.

Brewpubs usually serve beer from serving tanks for reasons of simplicity, cost, and freshness (Fig. 2.33). When the beer is fully conditioned, the beer is transferred to a serving tank. After fermentation, the beer contains no oxygen, and if the transfer to the conditioning tank is done with care, the pickup of staling oxygen is greatly minimized. Some pubs may also allow their beers to naturally clarify and carbonate, further avoiding air pickup during filtration and carbonation. Because brewpubs usually brew in small batches that are quickly consumed, beer in brewpubs can be consumed at the peak of freshness.

Figure 2.33. Many brewpubs avoid the handling and labor of kegs by putting their beer into serving tanks that directly serve the bar. The tanks are typically in a refrigerated room and hold five to ten kegs worth of beer each. (Courtesy Rock Bottom Brewery)

Pasteurization

Prior to advancements in hygienic packaging, refrigeration, and especially pasteurization, beer was a local industry because beer spoiled quickly or was too costly to ship. If beer drinkers wanted fresh beer, they had to live in fairly close proximity to a brewery. A few days bumping along in the sun on the back of a wagon was a favorable environment to encourage the growth of beer-spoilage microbes that would have invariably been present in the beer. It was a Frenchman, Louis Pasteur, who discovered that heating packaged food protected it by killing the spoilage microbes inside. The same principle of pasteurization that renders milk stable also applies to beer. However, pasteurization was applied to beer many years before it was used for milk production.

Tunnel pasteurization is the typical method for pasteurizing beer. Bottles and cans move through the pasteurizer on a conveyor, where they are sprayed with increasing levels of hot water to gradually heat the beer to about 140°F (60°C). After pasteurization, the bottles and cans are cooled to prevent damage to the beer's flavor. The effectiveness of pasteurization is dependent on temperature and time. The hotter the spray and the longer the beer is heated, the higher the microbial kill rate. While the microbial stability of the beer may increase with increasing time and temperature, the potential impairment of freshness also increases. Heat accelerates the staling effects of oxygen, so it is especially important to limit the uptake of oxygen when filling cans or bottles that will be pasteurized. Because of the potential harmful effects of pasteurization, the high cost of equipment, or both, some brewers simply choose not to pasteurize.

Another form of pasteurization used for kegged beer, but sometimes also for bottles, is flash pasteurization. In this version, a heat exchanger rapidly heats and then cools the beer in transit to the kegging or bottling line. The thermal impact on the beer is the same, except that it occurs before the beer is packaged.

An alternative to pasteurization is aseptic filtration, which does not kill the microbes but rather traps them before they enter the package. While aseptic filtration avoids heat damage, it introduces another point for air entry into the beer and may potentially strip the beer of body, color, and flavor. The term "draft" is sometimes applied to bottles or cans that are aseptically filtered because, like traditional kegs, they are not pasteurized.

Production of Specialty Beers

The preceding sections described some typical processes employed in modern breweries to produce commercial beer. However, certain specialty brewing techniques are also worth describing because they produce many well-known substyles and specialty beers.

Light, Low-Carbohydrate, and Dry Beers

Light Beer

In the United States, light beer is generally a term for a beer that contains fewer calories than those of its parent brand. Because most of the calories in beer come from alcohol, the low calorie content of light beer dictates that the beer also has a reduced alcohol content. In general, light beer is typically 4.0% ABV with 85–125 calories or less in a 12-

ounce serving versus ~5.0% ABV and ~150 calories in the regular beer. The lower caloric content is typically achieved by simply diluting the beer with water after filtration. Most light beer formulas also have higher fermentability than that of regular beers, which produces a dryer and less full-bodied finish. While the term "light" is primarily applied to beer low in calories, these beers are also typically lighter in body, color, and bitterness.

Low-Carbohydrate Beer

The popularity of the Atkins and South Beach diets, which promote low carbohydrate intake to lose weight, has created consumer interest in beers low in carbohydrates. The majority of the calories in beer comes from alcohol and unfermentable sugars (i.e., dextrins). These unfermentable sugars are the source of carbohydrates in beer. Therefore, low-carbohydrate beer mashes are designed to produce a large percentage of fermentable sugars and few unfermentables. The low level of residual sugar also creates a dry finish. In the United States, low-carbohydrate beer must contain less than 7 grams of carbohydrates per 12-ounce serving. The Brewers Association style guidelines limit the carbohydrate content to 3 grams. A typical North American standard lager has about 12 carbohydrates per 12-ounce serving.

A Blurred Line of Separation

In reality, the distinction between light and low-carbohydrate beers is often hard to distinguish. Most low-calorie beers also have low levels of residual carbohydrates in order to achieve a lighter flavor. Most low-carbohydrate beers also have fewer calories in order to minimize the level of residual carbohydrates. Low-carbohydrate and dry beers are brewed in similar ways, except that the dry beer is likely to have a higher starting gravity that produces a higher alcohol content.

Dry Beer

Dry beer is a hybrid style brewed with an alcohol content similar to that of standard beer but with a reduced level of carbohydrates. This dichotomy is achieved through a mashing process that produces normal-strength wort with a very high percentage of fermentable sugars that are converted to alcohol. Because there are few unfermentable carbohydrates remaining in the beer, it lacks sweetness and it has a "dry" finish.

Ice Beer

Alcohol freezes at a lower temperature than water. If beer is chilled to a temperature several degrees below freezing, some of the water forms ice crystals but the alcohol does not. When these ice crystals are removed by filtration or skimming, the water is separated from the alcohol, thereby increasing the beer's alcohol content. The cold also reduces the solubility of polyphenols and proteins in beer, which makes them more easily removed during filtration. Their removal produces a beer with a softer, rounder palate. Some brewers allow the ice to melt before filtration, using the freezing process only for the more efficient removal of the harsh-tasting polyphenols and protein. These beers are often brewed with a higher starting alcohol content to match the strength of ice beers that have their ice removed. The most common ice beers brewed in North America have an alcohol content of 5.5–6.0%.

Non-Alcoholic Beer

Non-alcoholic beer contains less than 0.5% ABV. To reduce the alcohol content, brewers employ three different processes: restricted alcohol formation, membrane separation, and evaporation.

Restricted Alcohol Formation

This process stops fermentation before a large portion of the fermentable sugar is converted to alcohol. The beer is then aged, filtered, and adjusted by dilution to the 0.5% alcohol limit. This method differs from the other two methods, which remove the alcohol from fully fermented and aged beer.

Membrane Separation

In membrane separation, fully fermented and aged beer passes across a submicron cellulose filter that separates the alcohol from the beer. After separation, the alcohol content is also adjusted with dilution water.

Evaporation

Alcohol has a lower boiling point than water. When beer is heated, the alcohol forms vapor at a lower temperature than water. In this way, the alcohol is removed in the escaping vapor. However, excessive heat damages beer's flavor. In a vacuum, the boiling point of a liquid is reduced and vapor forms at a lower temperature. For non-alcoholic beer production, a vacuum is used with relatively low heat to flash off the alcohol from the fully fermented and aged beer into a collection vessel for discharge. This evaporation technique is basically a reverse form of distillation. After evaporation, the alcohol content is also adjusted with dilution water.

Gluten-Free Beer

Gluten-free beer is brewed for persons with celiac disease, an intestinal disorder in which the inability to absorb gluten (a cereal grain protein) triggers a damaging immune response. Gluten-free beer is brewed like standard beer, except the gluten-containing wheat and barley are replaced by nongluten grains, usually malted sorghum and unmalted rice or corn.

Malt Liquor

Malt liquor is a lager beer brewed in a manner similar to that of a standard lager but with more alcohol (usually higher than 5.5% ABV). Compared with American standard lagers, malt liquors have a higher gravity and, consequently, a higher alcohol content. Higher-alcohol malt liquors are brewed for a higher degree of fermentability and are characterized by having a smooth, warming impact on the palate.

Flavored Malt Beverages

Flavored malt beverages (FMB) are beer-based drinks flavored with ingredients not traditionally used in beer. Although made from beer, flavored malt beverages usually have little or no resemblance to it. The base beer (usually referred to as clear malt base) is either a low-hopped American standard lager or an unhopped beer stripped of its color and flavor by either ultrafiltration or by contact with decolorizing carbon. Commercial "flavor houses" supply custom flavors specified by the brewery, which are added to the beer just prior to packaging. There is a diverse range of flavored malt beverages, with fruit flavors being very popular, particularly the citrus flavors used in drinks such as "hard" lemonade. Flavored malt beverages are just one type of flavored alcohol beverage (FAB), which also includes flavored drinks made from wine or distilled spirits.

Organic Beer

To be organic, 95% of a beer's ingredients (excluding water) must be produced using sustainable, chemical-free farming methods in soil that has been free of toxic pesticides and fertilizers for a minimum of 3 years. The ingredients cannot be genetically modified. If only 75–95% of its ingredients meet these criteria, the beer can only be labeled "made with organic ingredients". The farmer and the brewer must be certified by USDA inspectors as organic producers before the beer can be labeled "organic".

All types of beer can qualify as organic. Organic ingredients do not have a perceivable impact on the appearance, composition, or flavor of beer. Brewers who use organic ingredients are showing support for sustainable farming methods and supplying beer to consumers who also want to support these methods.

High-Alcohol Beer

Beer high in alcohol requires wort with a high concentration of fermentable sugar and yeast that can withstand a high level of alcohol.

High-Sugar Extract

The amount of fermentable sugar in the wort determines the alcohol potential of the beer. Therefore, high-alcohol beers require a greater amount of malt and mashing techniques that produce increased levels of fermentable sugars. Brewers may also fortify the wort with malt syrups or sugar to boost alcohol potential. Evaporating water during the kettle boil concentrates the sugar content of wort but does not increase its fermentability.

Alcohol-Tolerant Yeast

Alcohol is a waste product that is toxic to yeast. When the alcohol concentration reaches a certain level, the yeast stops fermenting. To produce high-alcohol beers, brewers initially pitch larger quantities of yeast and ozygen or sterile air to start fermentation and then add more healthy yeast when the initial yeast population loses vitality from alcohol stress. The subsequent addition of yeast may be that of a more-alcohol-tolerant strain, particularly wine yeast used for champagne. The initial yeast strain provides the desired flavor profile for the style. The second yeast finishes fermentation. A prolonged fermentation and conditioning times may be required for the yeast to complete fermentation.

The maximum alcohol concentration that yeast can tolerate is 14 or 15% by volume. To achieve higher alcohol levels, the beer would require fortification with a distilled spirit, removal of water (as with ice beer), or distillation, in which case the beer is transformed into a distilled spirit, such as whiskey or vodka.

Whiskey

Wine is to brandy as beer is to whiskey. That is, brandy is distilled wine and whiskey is distilled beer. In fact, all distilled spirits made from mashed grain, including vodka, gin, and whiskey, start as a wort like that made for beer. While wort produced for whiskey is not hopped, it is produced from mashed grains and then fermented to produce the base alcohol distilled into whiskey. Bourbon whiskey is made predominantly from corn, and Irish and Scotch whiskeys are made predominantly from malted barley. Scotch whiskey also carries the distinction of using malt dried by burning peat, which adds a hint of peat-flavored smoke to the liquor. Wine drinkers readily identify the relationship of wine to fine premium brandies, such as cognac, but beer drinkers rarely connect beer to premium barrel-aged, single-malt scotch. However, the close relationship of beer and whiskey is recognized by one of the world's largest professional technical organizations representing both brewers and distillers—the Institute of Brewing and Distilling (IBD), located in London, England.

Sake

Sake is often called rice wine, but it is more akin to beer since it is a fermented beverage made from grain. Sake does not undergo traditional mashing. Unmalted rice is polished to remove fats and protein and then steamed to break down the starch. Koji mold is added to the steamed rice, which converts the starch to fermentable sugars. Yeast is added to the mash that ferments the sugars simultaneously with the conversion of starch to sugar. This parallel process continues for about 30 days until fermentation is complete. The mash is then pressed to release the clear liquid, which is filtered and aged before serving. Typical sake contains about 15% ABV.

Selected References

Bamforth, C. 1998. Beer: Tap Into the Art and Science of Brewing. Insight Books, Plenum Press, New York.

Bamforth, C. W. 2002. Standards of Brewing: A Practical Approach to Consistency and Excellence. Brewers Publications, Boulder, CO.

Holle, S. R. 2003. A Handbook of Basic Brewing Calculations. Master Brewers Association of the Americas, St. Paul, MN.

Hough, J. S. 1994. The Biotechnology of Malting and Brewing. Press Syndicate of the University of Cambridge, Cambridge, U.K.

Lewis, M. J., and Young, T. W. 1996. Brewing. Chapman and Hall, London, U.K.

McCabe, J. T., ed. 1999. The Practical Brewer, 3rd ed. Master Brewers Association of the Americas, St. Paul, MN.

Ockert, K., ed. 2006. MBAA Practical Handbook for the Specialty Brewer: Vol. 1—Raw Materials and Brewhouse Operations; Vol. 2—Fermentation, Cellaring, and Packaging Operations; Vol. 3—Brewing Engineering and Plant Operations. Master Brewers Association of the Americas, St. Paul, MN.

Chapter 3:
World Beer Styles

Rex Halfpenny, Gregg Smith, and Stephen R. Holle

Before the world was connected by modern transportation systems that could deliver raw materials and finished products across the globe, beer styles developed in isolated areas based on regional grains, yeast varieties, and cultural tastes. Countries and regions also specialized in unique means of production that best suited the local ingredients and conditions. As the globe became more closely connected and advances in packaging made the beer trade global, consumers and brewers recognized that beer existed in a variety of styles beyond their local borders. Eventually, these differences were recognized as "styles" associated with specific countries and regions.

For this reason, the following discussion of beer styles is organized into four sections based on brewing traditions from the areas that have been the source of many commercial beer brands sold around the world.

- Belgium and France
- England, Scotland, and Ireland
- Germany and Continental Europe
- North America

North America is included, not because it is a prolific originator of beer styles, but because its brewers have embraced beer diversity with an ardent passion that has resurrected many forgotten styles or expanded the boundaries of others. The world's classic beer styles are organized by these regions of origin to reflect the importance that climate, agronomy, politics, and culture have had in the development of beer styles.

Beer styles are not static. They are evolutionary. Sometimes they evolve by conscious choice and other times because of technological advances. Furthermore, any attempt to compartmentalize beer by rigid definitions is wrought with inadequacies. Even limiting the classification of styles to specific regions is deficient because it is too narrow. While a beer style may trace its ancestry back hundreds of years, today it may be different in nuance or by quantum leap from its predecessor. Therefore, the purpose of the following classifications is not to define how a beer must look and taste but to build a platform in which to compare and contrast beers, describe their character, and understand how brewers create different styles.

The North American Brewers Association (NABA) generously allowed the use of their beer style guidelines in this chapter (www.northamericanbrewers.org/node/10). Organizations such as NABA, Brewers Association, and Beer Judge Certification Program (BJCP) establish style guidelines to recognize and preserve the diversity of beer styles and to promote brewing excellence by supporting competitions in which brewers test the quality of their beer against their peers. When NABA descriptions do not match the styles presented in this chapter, other sources are cited.

World Beer Styles

- Belgium and France
  - Farmhouse ales
    - *Bière de garde*
    - *Saison*
  - Trappist and abbey ales
    - *Dubbel*
    - *Tripel*
  - Belgian strong ales
    - Golden strong ale
    - Dark strong ale
  - Belgian sour ales
    - Flanders sour ales
    - Lambics
      - Lambic (unblended)
      - *Gueuze* (blended)
      - Fruit lambics
      - *Faro*
  - Other Belgian ales
    - *Wit*
    - Belgian blond ale
    - Specialty ales
- England, Scotland, and Ireland
  - English bitter
    - Ordinary bitter
    - Special bitter
    - Extra special bitter
  - Pale ales
    - English pale ale
    - American pale ale
    - Belgian pale ale
  - India pale ales
    - English India pale ale
    - American India pale ale
    - Double/imperial India pale ale
  - Brown ales
    - English mild
    - English brown ale
    - American brown ale
  - Porters
    - Brown porter
    - Robust porter
    - Baltic porter

- o Stouts
  - Dry (Irish) stout
  - Sweet stout
  - Oatmeal stout
  - Imperial (Russian) stout
  - Foreign extra stout
  - American stout
- o Irish red ale
- o Scottish ales
  - Scottish light (60/-)
  - Scottish heavy (70/-)
  - Scottish export (80/-)
- o Strong ales
  - Scotch ale
  - English old ale
  - English barley wine
  - American barley wine
- Germany and continental Europe
  - o Continental lager beers
    - Vienna lager
    - *Märzen*/Oktoberfest
    - Munich *Dunkel*
    - *Schwarzbier*
    - Pilsner
      - □ Bohemian pilsner
      - □ German *Pils*
    - *Dortmunder* export
    - Munich *Helles*
    - International pale lagers
    - *Rauchbier*
      - □ *Rauchbier*
      - □ *Steinbier*
      - □ Style variations
    - Bock beers
      - □ Bock
      - □ *Maibock/Heller Bock*
      - □ *Doppelbock*
      - □ *Eisbock*
  - o German ales
    - Bavarian *Weizen* (Bavarian wheat beer)
      - □ *Hefeweizen*
      - □ *Kristall Weizen*
      - □ *Dunkelweizen*
      - □ *Weizenbock*
    - Rye beer

- Other German ales
  - □ *Kölsch*
  - □ *Alt*
  - □ *Berliner Weisse*
- North America
  - o North American lagers
    - American standard lager
    - American light lager
  - o North American ales
    - California common
    - Cream ale
    - American *Hefeweizen*

Belgium and France

The southern half of Belgium, known as Wallonia, shares a strong cultural tie, a common language, and a soft border with France. The northern half of Belgium, Flanders, borders Holland, where its residents speak Flemish, Belgium's dialect of Dutch. Although the two regions are divided by language and culture, they are united by a love of beer and a proud brewing tradition. Belgium is a young country, only independent since 1832. The region is at latitudes where both grains and hops are grown. For centuries, different cultures invading the area have left their impact on brewing. This convergence of cultures and brewing traditions accounts for the wide diversity of brewing techniques and ingredients used by Belgian brewers, who produce an incredibly large number of unique beer styles.

Nevertheless, like most of the world, Belgium's indigenous styles have experienced the same pressures from globalization and consolidation that have forced the closure of hundreds of small breweries. Today, pale lagers represent the majority of beer enjoyed in Belgium; however, large and small Belgian breweries still produce a significant number of special indigenous styles that are closely tied to the old traditions of farmhouse ales, monastic brewing, and spontaneous fermentation. Moreover, traditional Belgian and French ales are enjoying renewed popularity, especially in the United States, where brewers are producing many examples of classic Belgian styles.

There are many characteristics of Belgian ales that set them apart. Although Belgium is not known as a wine-producing region because of climate (too far north) and politics (Napoleon destroyed vineyards in southern Belgium because French wine was considered *supérieur*), the influence of French winemaking is clearly visible. Wooden barrels for aging beer, beers approaching wine in alcoholic strength, corked 750-milliliter bottles, and spontaneous fermentation demonstrate historic connections to wine. Many beer styles are unfiltered and then bottle conditioned for a refermentation in the bottle like champagne. Because the yeast is not disgorged as with champagne, the beer is carefully decanted off the lees, leaving the yeast in the bottle, except in certain examples, such as *wit*.

There are other characteristics that also define Belgian beer. Many styles are unfiltered and slightly turbid, although sufficient aging may produce exceptionally bright beers through the natural settling of haze. Belgians have also continued the medieval practice of flavoring beer with botanicals besides hops and of intentionally brewing sour beers.

Belgian ales are noted for their distinct fermentation-driven flavors (e.g., spicy phenols, fruity esters, warm fusel alcohols) from exotic yeast strains and other nonyeast microbes. High fermentation temperatures (85°F/30°C) and elevated alcohol levels also contribute to the high concentrations of yeast flavors in some Belgian ales. Strong beers may be cellared for further development of esters, mellowing of tannins, and aging of alcohols, as is used in wine and sherry production. In other words, for Belgian breweries, almost anything goes in producing a wide range of flavorful and unique-tasting ales.

Farmhouse Ales

Bière de Garde

Bière de garde is an artisanal style from northern France originally brewed by farmers in late winter or early spring and cellared for consumption during the summer and harvest seasons; thus, *bière de garde*, a "beer that has been kept or stored". Because the beer was brewed during colder months, it fermented and matured at low temperatures, which created a smooth character with fewer fruity flavors than that of other Belgian ales brewed in warmer months. Pale pilsner is typically the base malt with Vienna or Munich malt added to create a golden to light brown color and slightly sweet, toasty malt flavor. Long boils can create deeper color and additional caramel flavors. *Bière de garde* has a decided malty character but is fairly well attenuated for a medium-dry, malty finish. Adjuncts of raw grain and sugar are sometimes used to boost the alcoholic character without adding body or sweetness. *Bière de garde* is highly carbonated, unfiltered, and bottle conditioned. As with many Belgian ales, hop flavor is modest, and bitterness is present at levels sufficient to balance the malt without creating a decidedly bitter character. Because of the artisanal conditions under which it was originally brewed, modern examples may still exhibit earthy, musty, and rustic notes, especially those packaged in corked bottles.

As with wine, the French associate products with a region and look to the local ingredients to create the character of that region's products. *Bière de garde* is simply considered a provision beer, so the parameters defining this style are quite broad and commercial examples are quite diverse. Therefore, guidelines defining the style must be applied loosely and not considered as all encompassing.

In earlier times when farms operated largely with manual labor, farmers provisioned their workers with food and beer produced on the farm. Farmers brewed low-alcohol beers that were refreshing and less intoxicating and served young and fresh before they could sour. These modest beers of 3–4% alcohol by volume (ABV) were called *bière faible* ("weak beer"), *petite bière* ("small beer"), or *bière de table* ("table beer"). Because of the higher alcohol content of *bière de garde* (6–8% ABV), it could be stored over the summer. It could then be consumed after the supplies of fresh, weaker beer ran out since brewing often ceased during the summer when high temperatures increased the number and vigor of beer-spoilage microbes.

With the modernization of farming and the availability of affordable commercial brands, the need for farmers to brew their own beer faded away, and remaining examples of the style dwindled after World War II. Small brewers seeking a specialty niche in a market dominated by pale lagers resurrected *bière de garde* to capture the growing demand for unique local products. *Bière de garde* is an example of an artisanal style that is no longer brewed for its original purpose. Although brewing methods of commercial producers do not exactly replicate the original beers brewed on the farm, these small artisanal brewers strive to capture the essence of the brewing traditions so that this unique style is preserved.

Bière de Mars is the name for another provision beer, usually brewed in December and January and stored for at least 2 months to condition. Because the malt and hops were at the height of freshness at this time, the beer was particularly prized for its fine quality. Since the beer was ready for consumption in March, it became known as a spring beer (*bière de printemps*) or March beer (*bière de Mars*) for the first month of spring. *Bière de Mars* is similar to *bière de garde* but may be maltier and more hop accented.

Examples: Jenlain (amber), Jenlain Bière de Printemps (blond), St. Amand (brown), Ch'Ti Brune (brown), Ch'Ti Blonde (blond), La Choulette (all three versions), La Choulette Les Sans Culottes (blond), Saint Sylvestre 3 Monts (blond), Saint Sylvestre Bière Nouvelle (brown), Castelain (blond), Jade (amber), Brasseurs Bière de Garde (amber), New Belgium Biere de Mars.

Saison

Saison is another farmhouse provision beer like *bière de garde*, but it is associated with the French-speaking Wallonia region of southern Belgium. *Saison* means "season" in French, and the seasonal farm workers who consumed this beer during harvest were known as *les saisonniers*. In general terms, *saison* is typically lighter in color, less malty, fruitier, spicier, and dryer than *bière de garde*. Like *bière de garde*, the style parameters can be quite loose. The color may range from pale yellow to light brown. Pilsner malt and unmalted wheat and oats contribute the pale color. In darker versions, Vienna and Munich malts may be used. French six-row pilsner malt, which is high in phenolic husks and protein, may add a rustic, earthy character and protein haze that also adds mouthfeel to this otherwise highly attenuated beer. The dry finish is accentuated by a modestly bitter finish contributed by noble German hop varieties or by the earthy varieties Fuggles and Styrian Goldings that enhance the rustic character. Mixed yeast strains fermented at high temperatures produce a character spicier than that of *bière de garde*, which may be accented by other herbs, including anise, sage, green peppercorn, cumin, coriander, and orange peel. *Saison* is unfiltered, bottle conditioned, and highly carbonated to produce a thick, dense, rocky head. Hop aromas are typically minimal to modest, but citrus and spicy pepper aromas are often contributed by the yeast or added spices, if any. *Brettanomyces* yeast, if present, adds rustic barnyard notes and acidity that lends to the citrus character and a dry, thirst-quenching finish.

Examples: Saison Dupont Vieille Provision, Fantôme Saison d'Erezée Printemps, Saison de Pipaix, Saison Regal, Saison Voisin, Lefebvre Saison 1900, Ellezelloise Saison 2000, Silly Saison.

	Bitterness (IBU)[a]	Alcohol (% ABV)[b]	Color (SRM)[c]
Bière de garde	25–30	4.4–7.9	6–16 (golden to light brown)
Saison	20–30	4.0–7.0	4–16 (yellow to light brown)

[a] IBU = international bitterness unit.
[b] ABV = alcohol by volume.
[c] SRM = standard reference measure.

Trappist and Abbey Ales

In the late seventeenth century, a new order of monks, Order of Cistercians of the Strict Observance, formed at La Trappe Abbey in Normandy, France. It was a reform movement dedicated to the rule of St. Benedict, which included the belief "for then are they monks in truth, if they live by the work of their hands". These self-sufficient monks worked not only to support their needs but to produce cheese, bread, and beer, which they sold to finance their mission work.

Today, Belgium has six Trappist monasteries that still brew and sell beer: Achel, Scourmont (Chimay), Orval, Rochefort, Westmalle, and Westvleteren. (Koningshoeven is a seventh Trappist brewery in the neighboring Netherlands.) As in medieval times, the industrious monks became well known for the quality of their beer, leading secular brewers to also use the Trappist name on their labels. In 1962, the monasteries won a trademark battle that reserved the appellation *Trappistenbier* only for the monasteries. When the beer is brewed under the direct supervision of a Trappist monk, the beer may be labeled "authentic Trappist product" or simply "Trappist" beer. If a secular brewer produces a Trappist-style beer, it may only be called an "abbey-style" or "abbey" beer. So favorable is the public's identification with abbey beer that many secular breweries license monastic names for their abbey ales (e.g., Abbaye de Leffe by InBev).

While a variety of Trappist and abbey beer styles exist, *dubbel* ("double") and *tripel* ("triple") are two of the best known. The exact historical origin of these names is not clear. One possible explanation is based on the parti-gyle method of mashing in which the mash/lauter tun received three separate charges of water that were allowed to fully drain before the next charge was added. The extract content of the wort would become progressively weaker with each new charge. Because the extract strength of the last wort runnings (e.g., 7.5% sugar) was roughly one-half the extract strength of the second runnings (15%) and one-third the extract strength of the first runnings (22.5%), the designations of single, double, and triple were assigned to the three separate beers from the same mash.

Dubbel

Caramel, Munich, and aromatic malts, along with caramelized sugar syrups added to a pilsner malt base, provide *dubbel* with its copper to light brown color. Long wort boils that concentrate the wort can also add color and caramel flavors. Roasted flavors are not typical, since roasted malts are associated with British styles in Belgium. Hop aroma is typically subdued or not perceived, and bitterness is modest to simply balance malt sweetness. Sugar may be used to elevate the alcohol content and contribute a dry finish. *Dubbel* is a fermentation-driven beer whose malt character may range from malty sweet (but not cloying) to dry and vinous, especially in aged examples. Yeast strains that produce fruity esters and spicy phenolic compounds often contribute intense fermentation flavors, which may be further intensified with high fermentation temperatures. *Dubbel* is traditionally unfiltered and is bottle conditioned in corked 750-milliliter bottles. Aromas and flavors include malt; caramel; chocolate; and dark fruits, such as raisin, plum, cherry, and date; as well as a host of other fruity esters, spicy clove phenols, and higher alcohols. Because of its heightened alcohol content, *dubbel* can be cellared, which intensifies the dark fruit flavors and adds other sherrylike flavors from the oxidation of alcohols to aldehydes.

Examples: Westmalle Dubbel, St. Bernardus Pater 6, La Trappe Dubbel, Corsendonk Abbey Brown Ale (Pater), Grimbergen Dubbel, Affligem Dubbel, Chimay Première (Red), Pater Lieven Bruin, Duinen Dubbel, St. Feuillien Brune.

Tripel

Tripel is higher in alcohol content and lighter in color and may be more highly carbonated than *dubbel*. The Westmalle Monastery is credited with popularizing this golden-colored style in the 1930s. *Tripel* may have been brewed in response to the growing popularity of pale lager beers. *Tripel* is unfiltered and bottle conditioned in corked 750-milliliter bottles. Because it is highly carbonated, many examples produce a thick rocky head of creamy foam. Pilsner malt and occasionally unmalted wheat create a pale golden color. White sugar is sometimes used to contribute the pale color, add alcoholic strength, and produce a semidry finish, although some examples may be semisweet. Yeast produces fruity esters, especially banana and citrus, along with nutmeg-, pepper-, or clovelike phenols. Herbs, such as coriander along with orange peel, may contribute the fruity citrus flavors. Fuggles and Styrian Goldings hops add an herbal earthy character but still play a supporting role to the crisp malt, fruit, and spice flavors.

Examples: Westmalle Tripel, La Rullés Triple (Bière de Gaume), St. Bernardus Tripel, Chimay Cinq Cents (Triple), Watou Tripel, Val-Dieu Triple, Affligem Tripel, Grimbergen Tripel, La Trappe Tripel, Witkap Pater Tripel, Corsendonk Abbey Pale Ale (Agnus), St. Feuillien Triple.

	Bitterness (IBU)	Alcohol (% ABV)	Color (SRM)
Dubbel	18–25	6.0–7.5	10–16 (copper to light brown)
Tripel	20–35	7.0–10	3–6 (yellow to gold)

Belgian Strong Ales

Belgium's artisanal and Trappist brewers are well known for their many strong ales, and there are several possible explanations why these "big" beers became so prevalent. Because of the popularity of French wines, Belgian brewers may have developed strong beers as a winelikc alternative. Also, for a period following World War I, Belgium enforced a law prohibiting the sale of spirits in public places. Brewers may have sought to fill the spirit void by producing high-alcohol beers. Finally, small brewers who were unable to compete with large breweries producing pale lagers may have turned to higher-alcohol beers to create a niche market for their specialty beers.

In France, fine wines from exceptional vineyards are labeled *grand cru*, which is translated as "exceptional growth". Belgian brewers who wish to indicate the release of a special beer may also label them *grand cru* to indicate the high quality of the malt and hops in addition to increased alcohol levels, which further intensify the flavor of these premium ingredients.

Golden Strong Ale

The Moortgat Brewery is credited with creating the golden strong ale style when it introduced *duvel* ("devil" in Flemish) in 1971 to compete with the popular pilsner styles. This ale exhibits a complex array of yeast-derived, fermentation-driven aromas and flavors, including a mix of light fruity banana and apple esters and clovelike phenols. Pilsner malt provides a pale color and a clean malty background, while sugar elevates the alcohol content and produces a dry pilsnerlike finish that is accentuated by assertive bitterness and earthy herbal hop aromas from Saaz and orange citrus from Styrian Goldings hops. The result is a clean, crisp, and complex beer that can be surprisingly easy drinking, disguising the alcoholic strength to the uninitiated. Golden strong ale is highly carbonated, is usually bottle conditioned, and requires careful pouring to contain the long-lasting, thick, rocky white head in the glass. This beer resembles *tripel* but tends to be dryer, paler, less fruity, and crisper.

Examples: Duvel, Hapkin, Lucifer, Brigand, Judas, Delirium Tremens, Dulle Teve, Piraat, Eau Bénite.

Dark Strong Ale

Dark strong ale is very similar to *dubbel* but can be more intense in color, flavor, and alcohol.

Examples: Westvleteren 12 (yellow cap), Rochefort 10 (blue cap), St. Bernardus Abt 12, Gouden Carolus Cuvée van de Keizer Blauw/Blue (Grand Cru of the Emperor), Achel Extra Brune, Rochefort 8 (green cap), Chimay Grande Réserve (Blue), Abbaye des Rocs Grand Cru, Gulden Draak, Kasteelbier Bruin-Brune (Bière du Chateau Donker).

	Bitterness (IBU)	Alcohol (% ABV)	Color (SRM)
Golden strong ale	20–30	7.0–11.0	3–6 (yellow to deep gold)
Dark strong ale	20–35	7.0–11.0	7–20 (amber to brown)

Belgian Sour Ales

While sour ales represent a small minority of beers today, sourness was certainly a more common and accepted flavor in beer prior to the Industrial Revolution, at which time single-strain yeast propagation, hygienic brewing protocols, refrigeration, sanitary packaging, and pasteurization allowed brewers to largely engineer sourness out of beer. These techniques have been so effective that sourness is generally considered a flaw today, leaving only small pockets of brewers, especially in Belgium, to carry on the tradition of brewing sour ales. However, renewed interest in sour beers has reinvigorated the style in Belgium and led a growing number of American brewers to develop sour beers as well.

Belgian sour ales fall into two major categories: Flanders sour ales and lambics. The sour beers of Flanders undergo a mixed fermentation with brewer's yeast during primary fermentation and with acid-producing wild yeast and bacteria during a long aging period. Lambics are not inoculated with brewer's yeast but are allowed to "spontaneously" ferment with wild airborne yeast and bacteria and then mature in oak barrels that also harbor acid-producing microbes. These techniques are rooted in medieval brewing traditions and likely produce beers that resemble the barrel-aged styles brewed during earlier centuries.

Flanders Sour Ales

Flanders red and brown ales take their name from the Flanders region in the north of Belgium where the Dutch variant Flemish is spoken. These sour ales are mashed in conventional fashion to produce worts rich in fermentable sugars.

However, the wort is pitched with a mixed strain of brewer's yeast and acid-producing bacteria and wild yeast.

Red ale of West Flanders is transferred off the lees from primary fermentation into re-used oak barrels that contain microbes ensconced in the wood grains and crevices from previous brews. The development of acids and other fermentation-driven flavors takes place from the growth of these residual microbes in the barrel during the aging period, which may last from 18 months to 3 years. The brown ale of East Flanders differs from the red ale primarily because the beer is aged in stainless steel tanks instead of in wood. Brewers of Flanders ales typically blend the aged beer with young beer before leaving the brewery in a practice closely linked to the blending practices in England (see Porters and English Old Ale styles discussed later in this chapter). Historically, publicans blended inexpensive young beer with a small amount of more-expensive aged beer to give their patrons a more flavorful and complex mixture. Today, the brewery may blend sweeter, less-acidic young red ales to balance the intense tartness of the older beer or blend fully aged barrels to achieve product consistency. Rodenbach produces an unblended, barrel-aged red ale with a slightly higher alcohol content that it labels Grand Cru. *Lactobacillus* bacteria contribute a clean tartness to the beers and *Brettanomyces* yeast contributes an earthy, horsey sourness. Because oak barrels are not airtight, *Acetobacter* bacteria that convert alcohol to acetic acid in the presence of oxygen often contribute a vinegary tartness to red ale. This tartness is not found in brown ale, which is conditioned in sealed stainless steel tanks.

Flanders ales are typically brewed with a majority of the malt being pilsner malt and specialty malts, such as caramel, Vienna, and Munich, for color and caramel-biscuit flavors and possibly along with cooked adjunct grains. Fermentation begins with Belgian ale yeasts, which produce alcohol along with fruity esters and spicy phenols. The acid-producing microbes pitched along with the brewer's yeast continue their work during aging. Consequently, the acidity of the beers increases over time, especially due to the slow-acting *Brettanomyces* yeast. Slow oxidation during aging also produces vinous and sherry flavors and dark fruit flavors, such as raisin, plum, prune, fig, date, and black cherry. The long aging in the presence of multiple microbes produces a dry, tart finish. Hop bitterness is very low and hop aroma is not perceived. Barrel aging may contribute rustic notes and a very mild tannic character due to the use of reused barrels. Barrels require some attention to maintain consistent flavors, which may include periodic rinsing, cleaning, and scraping. One Belgian brewer reportedly scrapes the vats to expose new wood to contribute higher levels of vanilla and tannic oak flavors.

Bottle-conditioned examples of the style are rare. In fact, filtration and pasteurization are frequently employed to stabilize the flavor, which would otherwise continue to change in the presence of the microflora used in aging. Some versions are also sweetened to balance acidity, and without pasteurization, these beers would eventually ferment to dryness (not to mention the risk of exploding bottles!). East Flanders brown ale is used as a base for fruit beers but should not be confused with fruit lambics. Fruit can be added to the finishing tank and allowed to ferment to dryness, or fruit juice can be added to the bottle, which is pasteurized to preserve sweetness.

Red ale and brown ale are quite similar, but connoisseurs like to make distinctions. Brown ale is typically darker, maltier, more bitter, and higher in alcohol and has cleaner acidity.

Examples of West Flanders Red Ale: Rodenbach Klassiek, Rodenbach Grand Cru, Bellegems Bruin, Verhaege Duchesse de Bourgogne, New Belgium La Folie, Verhaege Vichtenaar, Panil Barriquée, Mestreechs Aajt.

Examples of East Flanders Brown Ale: Liefmans Goudenband, Liefmans Cuvee-Brut (formerly Kriek), Liefmans Frambozen, Liefmans Odnar, Liefmans Oud Bruin, Ichtegem's Oud Bruin.

	Bitterness (IBU)	Alcohol (% ABV)	Color (SRM)
Flanders red ales[a]	15–25	5.0–5.5	14–17 (copper to light brown)
Flanders brown ales[a]	15–25	4.0–8.0	15–20 (reddish brown to brown)

[a] Beer Judge Certification Program (BJCP) style guidelines.

Lambics

Lambic brewing employs the most primitive form of yeast inoculation—spontaneous fermentation. Because the air is full of microscopic organisms, lambic brewers transfer the hot kettle wort to shallow metal pans, where the large surface area allows the wort to cool overnight. These pans (called coolships) are often located on the top floor of the brewery, where the windows are opened, allowing the wind to deposit airborne wild yeast and other microflora into the wort. Lambic breweries are located along the river Zenne that runs through Het Pajottenland, of which Brussels is the major city. The coolship rooms are usually made of wood so "house character" microbes can live in the pores and cracks. As many as 200 different microorganisms may inoculate the wort. Because the types and mixture of microbes vary from location to location, each brewery has its own fermentation character.

Lambic is typically made with pilsner malt and unmalted wheat or maize to produce a pale wort, although some red-tinted lambics are produced with portions of Vienna, Munich, or caramel malts. A lambic grist is mashed in an unusual way that produces a cloudy, milky wort containing unconverted starch. Starch is undesirable in conventional brews because brewer's yeast cannot ferment it. Starch is beneficial in a lambic fermentation because it becomes food for a number of microbes (particularly *Brettanomyces* yeast) that continue to ferment over the long aging period. Old hops with little bittering potential are boiled in the wort because they still contain antibacterial properties (i.e., beta acids) that protect the beer from certain *Lactobacillus* bacteria strains that produce undesirable flavors. Fermentation and maturation occur in a single oak barrel that has been reused and also contains microbes that further inoculate the wort. Lambic is not brewed in the summer because certain unwanted microbes are plentiful and active during hot weather. Fermentation progresses in ordered sequence. Initially, *Saccharomyces* yeast produces alcohol until the simple sugars are consumed. Then, lactic acid producers, such as *Pediococcus* and *Lactobaccillus* bacteria, become active. In conventional fermentations, the young beer is racked off the cold trub and yeast to avoid the off-flavors they can impart, but lambic undergoes primary fermentation and conditioning in the same barrel. Slow-acting microbes, especially *Brettanomyces* yeast, feed on starch, trub, and the decomposing yeast. *Brettanomyces* yeast and other flora may create a biological film, called a pellicle, that protects the lambic from oxidation in the same way that flora protects sherry aged in a solera.

Lambic may continue to condition for up to 3 years. The long conditioning time and the multitude of organisms completely ferment the wort to dryness to further accentuate lambic's sourness, which is accompanied by a host of other flavors, including earthy, horse blanket, and barnyard flavors from *Brettanomyces* yeast as well as fruity apple, pear, and banana esters, vanilla oak tannins, and spicy clovelike alcohols. The flavors in lambic are often described as winelike.

Lambic and *gueuze* are protected by an *Appellation d'Origine Contrôlée*, which the European Union recognized in 1998. (An *Appellation d'Origine Contrôlée* is an official regional designation. No producer outside of the appellation may describe their product with the appellation name, i.e., champagne, bordeaux, and burgundy.) Any 100% spontaneously fermented beer that is aged in wooden barrels and meets the following criteria may include *oude* or *ville* on the label as an indication of an authentic traditional lambic product. The criteria are the following.

- Minimum starting gravity of 12.7°Plato (12.7% sugar by weight)
- Maximum pH of 3.8
- Maximum color of 25 European Brewing Convention (EBC) (~12.5 standard reference measure [SRM])
- Maximum bitterness of 20 international bitterness unit (IBU)

Lambic (Unblended)

Lambic is unblended beer derived from a single barrel and is sometimes referred to as straight lambic. It can be served young or as an aged version 2 or 3 years of age. Young lambic was originally a less-expensive alternative served straight from the cask, without the expensive practice of aging and blending that produces *gueuze*. Because lambic comes from unpressurized wooden barrels, the beer is almost flat. Young lambic may be less acidic and horsey than older versions since *Brettanomyces* yeast character increases with age. Lambic is infrequently bottled, making the availability of it outside the Senne Valley or Belgium rare. Old lambic is more frequently bottled from the remnants of unused lambic after blending or is the selection of an especially high-quality barrel that is bottled unblended as special *cuvée* as would an outstanding vintage in winemaking.

Examples: Cantillon Grand Cru Bruocsella, Boon, Drie Fonteinen, Lindemans, Timmermans, Girardin. Although straight lambic is often hard to find outside of Brussels.

Gueuze (Blended)

Gueuze is a blend of 1-, 2-, and 3-year-old lambics. The *Appellation d'Origine Contrôlée* requires that the weighted average age of the lambics must be at least 1 year, the oldest at least 3 years, and the mixture must have undergone refermentation on the yeast. Such examples of *gueuze* may carry the *oude* or *ville* distinction on the label. The young lambic provides the fermentables that create the secondary fermentation and carbonation. The 2- and 3-year-old lambics contribute the complex flavors that the blender must marry to produce the desired flavor. Although the brewer typically does the blending, a blender may purchase beer from a number of brewers and blend them in the same tradition that a *négociant* blends wine from various vintners, although this practice is declining since the number of lambic brewers has declined. Belgians see this process of blending and bottle conditioning as parallel to the process by which sparkling wine is produced in the nearby Appellation of Champagne in France. Because *gueuze* is bottled, it is more widely distributed than straight lambic and more highly carbonated.

Examples: Boon Oude Gueuze, Boon Oude Gueuze Mariage Parfait, De Cam Geuze, De Cam/Drei Fonteinen Millennium Geuze, Drie Fonteinen Oud Geuze, Cantillon Gueuze, Hanssens Oude Gueuze, Lindemans Gueuze Grand Cru (Cuvée René), Girardin Gueuze 1882 (black label), Mort Subite Gueuze (unfiltered), Oud Beersel Oude Geuze.

<u>Fruit Lambics</u>

 Fruit lambics are simply *gueuze* to which pureed fruit or fruit juice has been added to make up at least 10%, but not greater than 30%, of the final product. The sugar in the fruit produces a secondary fermentation, which may take place in stainless steel tanks rather than in oak barrels. If the sugars are allowed to fully attenuate, the beer produces a dry finish but with fruitiness to balance the acidity. If fermentation of the sugars is arrested by pasteurization, the beer takes on a fruity sweetness. Some of the most traditional fruits are raspberries (*framboise*) and especially cherries (*kriek*) but other fruits are also used, including peach (*pêche*), apple (*pomme*), black currant (*cassis*), grape (*druif*), and strawberry (*aardbei*). The color of the fruit can influence the hue of this normally pale style. Because fruit flavors tend to subside over time, fruit lambics are intended to be consumed young. Fresh fruit is preferred for flavor and for the natural yeast and other bacterial flora on the skin. Juice provides more-consistent color than raw fruit and is easily dosed at bottling, followed by pasteurization. Although probably more common in past decades, bartenders may also blend fruit syrups with *gueuze* at the time of serving. Enthusiasts of traditional lambic frown upon the use of fruit as a compromise to appease the modern love of soft drinks. In fact, the popularization of pale lagers and soft drinks sharply reduced the demand for lambic, which forced the closure of many lambic breweries during the twentieth century. While interest in the style is rebounding, lambic producers are still a small club.

Examples: Boon Framboise Marriage Parfait, Boon Kriek Mariage Parfait, Boon Oude Kriek, Cantillon Fou' Foune (apricot), Cantillon Kriek, Cantillon Lou Pepe Kriek, Cantillon Lou Pepe Framboise, Cantillon Rosé de Gambrinus, Cantillon Saint Lamvinus (merlot grape), Cantillon Vigneronne (muscat grape), De Cam Oude Kriek, Drie Fonteinen Kriek, Girardin Kriek 1882, Hanssens Oude Kriek, Oud Beersel Oude Kriek, Mort Subite Kriek.

Faro

Faro is *gueuze* to which brown sugar and sometimes spices are added at the café. If *faro* is bottled at the brewery, it is pasteurized to prevent refermentation and maintain sweetness.

Other Belgian Ales

Wit

Wit ("white") beer is traditionally brewed with 50% unmalted wheat, pilsner malt, and occasionally small amounts of other grains, such as oats. *Wit* is unfiltered, allowing the unmalted/unkilned wheat to contribute a very pale color to the beer and a protein-starch haze that casts a "white" milky hue for which the style is named. *Wit* has a low level of bitterness and hop aroma. It uses nonhop botanicals to flavor the beer, especially crushed coriander seeds and dried Curaçao orange peel, which provide the signature citrus character. Other flavor descriptors include fruity and spicy, especially peppery. *Wit* is effervescent and builds a luxurious white foam collar. Although it finishes dry, this unfiltered ale possesses a medium body and creamy mouthfeel due to the yeast and protein haze. *Wit*, also known as *bière blanche* in French, is a popular summer quencher that should be enjoyed young and fresh.

During its peak of popularity in the 1800s, some 30 breweries in the Hoegaarden and Leuven areas were making *wit*. Nevertheless, because of changing consumer tastes, demand declined, and the last *wit* brewer in Hoegaarden stopped production in 1960. In 1966, Pierre Celis opened a *wit* brewery because he missed his local beer. His Hoegaarden *wit* helped revive the style, and he eventually sold the brewery to InBev, which still brews the Hoegaarden brand. Celis took the profits to the United States, opened a new brewery in Texas, and created Celis White, which helped expand the popularity of *wit* and other Belgian styles in the United States.

Examples: Celis White, Hoegaarden, St. Bernardus Blanche, Sterkens White Ale, Unibroue Blanche de Chambly, Wittekerke, Boulevard Zōn, MillerCoors Blue Moon, Anheuser-Busch InBev Shock Top, New Belgium Mothership Wit.

Belgian Blond Ale

Belgian blond ale is a modern style developed in part to compete with popular golden lagers, yet it is typically slightly higher in alcohol than most pale lagers. Belgian blond ale has a honey-malt sweetness with spicy phenols and fruity esters, characteristic of Belgian yeast strains. It is light to deep golden in color with substantial body and mouthfeel. High carbonation produces a thick white head of foam. The mild malty sweetness is balanced by hops and alcohol, making this style one of the easiest drinking of all the Belgian styles. Bittering hops stand in the background but contribute a dry semisweet finish that enhances drinkability.

Examples: Leffe Blond, Affligem Blond, La Trappe (Koningshoeven) Blond, Grimbergen Blond, Val-Dieu Blonde, Brugse Straffe Hendrik Blond, Brugse Zot, Pater Lieven Blond, Troubadour Blond.

	Bitterness (IBU)	Alcohol (% ABV)	Color (SRM)
Wit	10–20	4.0–5.3	2–3 (straw [turbid])
Belgian blond ale[a]	20–30	6.0–7.5	4–6 (light to deep gold)

[a] Beer Judge Certification Program (BJCP) style guidelines.

Specialty Ales

The preceding style categories are helpful in providing consumers with a broad indication of how Belgian beers taste. However, Belgian beers are highly idiosyncratic and attempts to tightly define any Belgian beer by rigid rules are always lacking. Belgian brewers experiment and constantly extend the boundaries of known beer styles. Beers that are created with new recipes or ingredients are often labeled "specialty ales" because they do not fit within the defined rules or simply to indicate that the beer is not one of the widely distributed pale lagers. For beers labeled "special", the brewer often makes up the rules and creates whatever the imagination can invent.

England, Scotland, and Ireland

Like those of Belgium, the classic styles of the British Isles are top-fermented ales, but British ale yeast typically plays a lesser flavor role than Belgian yeast. Hop bitterness and aroma are prominent in many British styles, along with the British affinity for caramel and dark-roasted malt and barley and strong fermentation flavors are not emphasized. Unlike the Belgians whose brewing traditions remained closely tied to small abbey and artisanal breweries, the British leaped headlong into the Industrial Revolution in pursuit of modern techniques to brew beer more efficiently and consistently. For example, by the end of the nineteenth century, the highly mechanized Guinness Brewery in Dublin was the largest in the world.

Like the Germans, their industrial competitor on the continent, the British also provided important technological advances that were applied to brewing to make it more efficient and the beer more consistent. Unlike the Germans, who embraced the *Reinheitsgebot* that strictly controlled the ingredients in beer, Britain's revenue authority enacted the Free Mash Tun Act. It allowed a variety of adjuncts, including unmalted oats, wheat, barley, corn, and sugar. Also, it began the gradual reduction in alcohol content since the new tax rates increased with increasing wort strength. When the act was passed in 1880, wort strength averaged 14°Plato (14% sugar). One hundred years later, it declined to 10°Plato, meaning the alcohol content declined from approximately 6 to 4% ABV. Although strong ales, especially barley wines and Scotch ale, remain traditional British styles, they do not match the availability of strong ales in Belgium.

The British also resisted the transition to cold fermented lagers that swept across much of the globe in the late nineteenth and early twentieth centuries. However, lager styles have gained market share in the United Kingdom, especially following World War II. To defend against the invasion of cold effervescent lagers dispensed from maintenance-free kegs, the Campaign for Real Ale (CAMRA) formed in the 1970s to preserve the availability of traditional unpasteurized, cask-conditioned ales.

The American craft beer movement of the late twentieth century embraced the resurrection of British ale styles as a means to increase beer diversity in the U.S. market, which was saturated with lager brands. Over time, American brewers selected indigenous ingredients, especially intense spicy-citrusy North American hop varieties such as Cascade, to put their own imprint on British styles. Quite frequently, Americans have pursued more assertive interpretations of British styles by adding high levels of hops and alcohol. The most powerful examples of these new styles are often labeled with the prefix "double" or "imperial".

English Bitter

Bitter is a generic name for a number of traditional English ales. The name "bitter" indicates ale brewed with a distinct hop character but not extreme bitterness, although bitterness is certainly a characteristic of this style. There are three types of bitter—ordinary, special or best, and extra special bitter—that represent an increasing order of bitterness and alcohol content, respectively.

Bitter is the British style most commonly served as hand-pumped "cask-conditioned" or "real" ale. Real ale fully ferments before it is transferred to an unpressurized cask, where sugar priming is added. The cask is then sealed with a wooden bung to trap the carbon dioxide created during the secondary fermentation. Hops may be added with the priming to provide hop aroma, along with finings to clarify the beer. The cask "conditions" in the cellar of the pub for a few days to several weeks until it is ready to be served. Real ale is served at low cellar temperature (~50–55°F/10–13°C) with a carbonation level roughly one-third lower than that of a typical pale lager. The higher temperature allows for better appreciation of the malt and hop aromas, and the lower carbonation level reduces the bite of carbonic acid, which allows for a smooth finish. British drinkers differentiate cask ales from keg beer, which is served colder and under constant gas pressure to maintain a higher level of carbonation. It is this contrast between cask and keg beer that causes the uninitiated to refer to real ale as warm and flat, which is untrue. Real ale is simply less chilled and less carbonated.

English bitter is noted for fruity and floral esters contributed by English yeast strains and English-style hops that impart delicate floral or earthy herbal notes. Some British yeasts may impart a light buttery note (diacetyl) that the British find desirable at very low levels to add roundness and complexity to the beer. Bitters should be delicately flavored so that they exhibt "moreishness", that is, they leave the drinker wanting another pint.

Ordinary Bitter

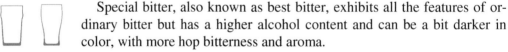

Ordinary bitter is a session beer, meaning it is lower in alcohol and easily enjoyed pint after pint over the course of a long "session" of drinking and conversation in a pub. Ordinary bitter is light to dark amber in color, is light to medium bodied, has moderately high bitterness, and has mild caramel sweetness from a small charge of crystal malt in a base of pale malt. Aromas include fruity esters and moderate to little hop aroma. Carbonation levels are usually low, especially in the cask, but bottled versions may be slightly more carbonated.

Examples: Fuller's Chiswick Bitter, Adnams Bitter, Young's Bitter, Greene King IPA, Tetley's Original Bitter, Brakspear Bitter, Boddington's Pub Ale.

Special Bitter

Special bitter, also known as best bitter, exhibits all the features of ordinary bitter but has a higher alcohol content and can be a bit darker in color, with more hop bitterness and aroma.

Examples: Fuller's London Pride, Adnams SSB (Suffolk Special Bitter), Young's Special, Shepherd Neame Master Brew, Greene King Ruddles County, Black Sheep Best Bitter.

Extra Special Bitter

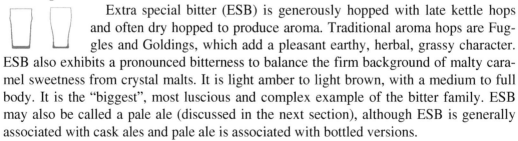

Extra special bitter (ESB) is generously hopped with late kettle hops and often dry hopped to produce aroma. Traditional aroma hops are Fuggles and Goldings, which add a pleasant earthy, herbal, grassy character. ESB also exhibits a pronounced bitterness to balance the firm background of malty caramel sweetness from crystal malts. It is light amber to light brown, with a medium to full body. It is the "biggest", most luscious and complex example of the bitter family. ESB may also be called a pale ale (discussed in the next section), although ESB is generally associated with cask ales and pale ale is associated with bottled versions.

Examples: Fuller's ESB, Adnams Broadside, Shepherd Neame Bishops Finger, Young's Ram Rod, Marston's Pedigree.

	Bitterness (IBU)	Alcohol (% ABV)	Color (SRM)
Ordinary bitter	20–35	3.0–4.0	6–12 (light amber to red/brown amber)
Special (best) bitter	30–45	4.1–4.8	6–17 (light amber to light brown)
Extra special bitter	35–55	4.9–5.8	6–17 (light amber to light brown)

Pale Ales

Pale ale was originally known as the bottled version of ESB, especially ales intended for export. A discussion of pale ale as a distinct style is helpful because, outside of the United Kingdom, pale ale is the most recognizable name for Britain's famous amber-colored ale. Furthermore, pale ale, like the name "bitter", has spawned a series of related styles in progressive degrees of hop flavor, bitterness, and alcoholic strength: pale ale, India pale ale (IPA), and even double/imperial IPA. American craft brewers especially have championed the pale ale style, which they have employed as the vehicle to reignite an appreciation of hops and especially of *über* hoppy beers that test the boundaries of maximum hop-driven aroma and bitterness.

The name "pale ale" is misleading in today's market containing numerous examples of extremely pale beers, especially light-colored lagers. Pale ales are actually amber colored but, in the eighteenth century when the name was termed, these beers were in fact much paler than the prevailing beer of choice, porter.

One of the world's most famous brewing centers, Burton-on-Trent, is considered the focal point for pale ale because of its uniquely hard water, which is low in carbonate and high in sulfate, thus well suited for beers of low color and high hopping rates. Even today, brewers outside Burton adjust their water chemistry to reproduce the characteristic pale ale flavor associated with Burton-on-Trent.

English Pale Ale

English pale ale is characterized by biscuity maltiness, caramel maltiness, or both, with a yeast character that can be neutral to slightly fruity. This ale typically has moderate to high levels of hop aroma and bitterness. English hops often present an earthy herbal character but may also have fruity, floral, and even spicy notes.

Examples: Samuel Smith's Old Brewery Pale Ale, Bass Pale Ale, Whitbread Pale Ale, Black Sheep Ale, Morland Old Speckled Hen, Greene King Abbot Ale.

American Pale Ale

American pale ale is typically more full bodied and aromatic than its British cousin. American versions tend to emphasize "impact", while the British versions emphasize "balance" and "drinkability". The American preference is toward all-malt beers that are full bodied and malty in comparison to the lighter-bodied English ales that may take on a biscuitlike character and a dryer finish, owing in part to the body-lightening effects from the frequent use of adjuncts. American pale ales often use American hops (especially Cascade) that have citrus, resinous pine, or cedar notes as compared with the floral or earthy herbal character of English hops.

Examples: Sierra Nevada Pale Ale, Stone Pale Ale, Great Lakes Burning River, Anderson Valley Poleeko Gold Pale Ale, Deschutes Mirror Pond Pale Ale, Full Sail Pale Ale, Three Floyds X-Tra Pale Ale, Firestone Pale 31, Rock Bottom Hop Bomb, Firestone Pale Nectar.

Belgian Pale Ale

Belgian pale ale is born from British influencc, especially the English ales brought to British troops stationed in Belgium. Belgian pale ale is not a term that the Belgians are likely to use but one used by Americans to describe certain styles that resemble British pale ale, which the Belgians might simply refer to as specialty ales.

Belgian pale ale is light to dark amber, but unlike British pale ale, the Belgian version is more malt driven, with hops playing only a background role. The primary malt flavors are toast and biscuit, with light fruity and floral yeast aromas. British or German noble hop varieties provide spicy aromas and moderate bitterness. Belgian pale ale is quite balanced, with medium body and carbonation.

Examples: De Koninck, Speciale Palm, Dobbel Palm.

	Bitterness (IBU)	Alcohol (% ABV)	Color (SRM)
English pale ale	25–45	4.4–5.3	3–14 (yellow to brown amber)
American pale ale[a]	30–50	4.4–6.3	3–17 (yellow to light brown)
Belgian pale ale[b]	20–30	4.8–5.5	6–14 (light amber to brown amber)

[a] Combines ranges for North American Brewers Association (NABA) American pale ale and American strong pale ale.
[b] Beer Judge Certification Program (BJCP) style guidelines.

India Pale Ales

English India Pale Ale

English IPA is a stronger, hoppier version of pale ale. The style was developed to provision English troops and colonists in India. IPA was brewed with higher alcohol and bitterness levels to prevent spoilage during long, hot ocean voyages. George Hodgson of the Bow Brewery, London, is credited with creating the style in the late 1700s. Burton-on-Trent brewers later became the dominate producers because of the unique gypseous water suited for the style.

Today, this full-bodied beer is brewed to satisfy consumers who appreciate the marriage of intense malt and hop flavors that is displays. All the character of pale ale is present but it is bolder because of the higher levels of alcohol, bitterness, and hop aroma. (Unfortunately, in the United Kingdom, the term "IPA" is sometimes used to brand some British ales [notably Greene King IPA and Deuchars IPA] with alcohol levels of around 3.8%, which should more appropriately be classified as ordinary bitters.)

Examples of true IPA: Meantime India Pale Ale, Freeminer Trafalgar India Pale Ale, Fuller's India Pale Ale, Ridgeway Bad Elf, Samuel Smith's India Ale.

American India Pale Ale

American IPA is a popular American craft beer style characterized by the liberal use of American hops to produce higher levels of bitterness and aroma compared with those of the English versions. The mash consists of a majority of pale two-row barley malt with small amounts of caramel malts to contribute a yellow to amber color. American versions may be more malt accented than British versions, with a slightly caramel-sweet finish (but not cloying) to balance the bitterness. Generous amounts of late-kettle or dry hops may contribute intense aromas of pine, citrus, and spice to American IPAs. A viscous mouthfeel from the elevated original gravity and the higher level of alcohol balances this style's intense hop-driven flavors.

Examples: BridgePort India Pale Ale, Bell's Two Hearted Ale, AleSmith IPA, Russian River Blind Pig, Stone I.P.A., Three Floyds Alpha King, Great Divide Titan IPA, Bear Republic Racer 5 India Pale Ale, Victory HopDevil Ale, Sierra Nevada Celebration Ale, Anderson Valley Hop Ottin' IPA, Dogfish Head 60 Minute IPA, Founders Centennial IPA, Anchor Liberty Ale, Harpoon I.P.A., Avery India Pale Ale.

Double/Imperial India Pale Ale

Double/imperial IPA is a stronger, more intensely flavored, hop-driven version of American IPA. It is an American innovation borne from a love of hops and the intense flavors of high-alcoholic fermentation that produces fruity esters and higher alcohols. Double IPA may have more hop bitterness, flavor, and aroma than nearly any other style of beer. The beer has a firm semisweet caramel malt background required to balance the intense hop bitterness that would overwhelm a lower-gravity beer. Brewers have borrowed the terms "double" and "imperial" from other strong beer styles, such as *Doppelbock* and imperial stout.

Examples: Russian River Pliny the Elder, Three Floyd's Dreadnaught, Avery Maharaja, Bell's HopSlam Ale, Stone Ruination IPA, Great Divide Hercules Double IPA, Surly Furious, Rogue XS Imperial India Pale Ale (I2PA), Moylan's Hopsickle Imperial Ale, Stoudt's Double IPA, Dogfish Head 90 Minute Imperial IPA, BridgePort Hop Czar, Victory Hop Wallop.

	Bitterness (IBU)	Alcohol (% ABV)	Color (SRM)
English IPA[a]	45–70	5.6–7.5	6–17 (gold to reddish brown)
American IPA	45–85	5.6–7.5	3–14 (yellow to brown amber)
Double/imperial IPA	65–100	7.5–11.0	6–15 (gold to copper)

[a] IPA = India pale ale.

Brown Ales

Before the use of coke and indirect-heated kilns made pale malt widely available, most ales were brown. In England, the term "brown" ale appears to have been used to describe any range of dark beers until the moniker became more specifically used to describe classes of brown beer, such as mild and brown ales, in the nineteenth century that were separate from porters and stouts. Brown ales were typically associated with the working class because they were less expensive than pale ales, which were brewed with costly pale malt. As new technology improved malt quality and lowered its price, brown malt was replaced by a pale malt grist with small amounts of high-color crystal and black malts for color. At one time, brown ales were widely popular but their working class image slowly eroded their appeal as the population evolved from blue collar to white collar jobs. The new affluent middle class workers were drawn to the more upscale image of pale ale, and the popularity of brown ale declined, although certain well-known examples, such as Newcastle Brown Ale, remain popular. The American craft beer movement helped reawaken interest in the style in the United States, and brown ales brewed with new American interpretations have gained wide popularity, especially among brewpubs.

English Mild

English mild is moderately bitter, low in alcohol, and malt driven. It was a popular thirst quencher for coal miners and factory workers in the nineteenth century. At that time, "mild" was a term used to describe any ale of various alcoholic strength that was served young and not as a blend of new and old (often soured) cask ales by the publicans. Eventually, mild came to be identified specifically as young, fresh, unblended brown ale. Because of taxes levied on the original gravity of the wort and shortages during wartime, the alcohol level in mild declined over time. Today, many examples are less than 4% ABV. Like bitter in alcohol content and drinkability, mild is also almost exclusively served as cask ale in pubs.

Mild is made from a majority of pale malt with additions of dark crystal, roasted malts or dark sugar that create luscious caramel, toffee, biscuit, and nutty flavors with hints of roast. The finish can range from slightly sweet to dry. The color ranges from light amber to dark brown, with a medium body and modest hop bitterness.

Examples: Manns Brown Ale (bottled, but not available, in the United States), Harveys Nut Brown Ale, Woodeforde's Norfolk Nog.

English Brown Ale

English brown ale is higher in alcohol than mild. Unlike mild, which is traditionally served from the cask, English brown ale is often bottled since Newcastle of northern England created a bottled version of brown ale in 1927. The color ranges from light to dark brown, often with reddish or garnet highlights in the darker examples. Like mild, the emphasis is on malt, which may exhibit itself as somewhat sweet, with notes of caramel, toffee, biscuits, and coffee. Nutty flavors have given rise to the "nut brown ale" moniker. Brown ales from northern England may be dryer, nuttier, and more bitter then are the sweet, fruity brown ales from southern England.

Examples: Harveys Nut Brown Ale, Woodeforde's Norfolk Nog, Newcastle Brown Ale, Samuel Smith's Nut Brown Ale, Riggwelter Yorkshire Ale, Wychwood Hobgoblin.

American Brown Ale

American brown ale is usually higher in alcohol, original gravity, and bitterness than English brown ale. British examples are more likely to use sugar, burnt sugar, or other adjuncts to create a dryer beer, so American examples are sometimes sweeter, maltier, more full bodied, and higher in alcohol. American hops used at higher levels often produce more bitterness and aroma. Some American brewers have even latched on to the "nut brown" descriptor and included nuts in their recipes.

Examples: Bell's Best Brown Ale, Smuttynose Old Brown Dog Ale, Big Sky Moose Drool Brown Ale, North Coast Acme California Brown Ale, Brooklyn Brown Ale, Lost Coast Downtown Brown, Left Hand Deep Cover Brown Ale.

	Bitterness (IBU)	Alcohol (% ABV)	Color (SRM)
English mild	10–24	2.8–4.0	6–20 (light amber to medium brown)
English brown ale	15–25	4.1–5.9	17–26 (light brown to dark brown)
American brown ale	25–45	4.1–6.3	17–26 (light brown to dark brown)

Porters

Porter is a dark ale whose origin is credited by some to Ralph Harwood of the Shoreditch Brewery in London. In 1722, Harwood reportedly developed a single beer for dispense at the pub to replace the popular practice of combining several beers in a mug according to the customer's taste. A popular mixture at the time was "three threads", which combined pale ale, new brown (mild) ale, and stale/sour brown ale. Harwood's goal was to produce a beer that was properly aged at the brewery and could be served to the customer's taste without the time-consuming task of mixing. Instead of a long, costly aging process for every batch, only a small portion of the beer would age and then it would be blended with young beer to provide the desired mature flavor. (The aged beer likely had a sour character from *Brettanomyces* yeast, which at the time was a desirable character in well-conditioned beer.) The blended beer was often called "entire" because it came from only one "entire" butt, a cask that contained 108 imperial gallons. This rich, full-bodied, nutritious beer was especially popular among London workers, such as porters, from whence the name comes.

Porter is often considered the first industrial beer and one of the first beers to gain national and international popularity as it spread from London across the British Isles to Ireland (where it gave rise to another dark ale, stout), to the American colonies (where it was the favorite beer of George Washington), and even to Russia (where it ultimately became imperial Russian stout). Ironically, this style that dominated the British market at one time ceased to be brewed in Britain in 1974, when Guinness stopped brewing its porter. Porter's fall from favor may have been connected to changing consumer tastes away from the robust roasted flavors and sour undertones of porter to the milder flavors from pale malt and lager yeast. In an attempt to lower costs, brewers also increased the use of adjuncts, especially burnt sugar and molasses in place of black malt, which altered the traditional flavor. Finally, stouts, which had once represented strong versions of porter, fell in strength because of alcohol taxes and wartime shortages until it replaced porter as a medium-strength dark ale. In 1978, two small British breweries started brewing porter again. The influence of Campaign for Real Ale (CAMRA) and interest by American craft breweries in style diversity helped further revive the popularity of porter, with many commercial examples available today on both sides of the Atlantic.

Brown Porter

Brown porter is the style's historical version, with roots in brown ale but brewed and conditioned at the brewery and sold ready to drink. Brown would have been the color of early porters made from common brown malt before the development of dark-roasted malt. Today, brown porter may use dark crystal, chocolate, and other roasted malts but should not have the dark, coffee, and burnt character of black malt or roasted barley. Brown porter is medium to deep brown with a light to medium body and a low to medium sweetness that is accented by malt notes of caramel, toffee, and chocolate. Hop bitterness should balance the malt and provide a bitter character without being too assertive.

Examples: Fuller's London Porter, Samuel Smith Taddy Porter, Burton Bridge Burton Porter, RCH Old Slug Porter, Nethergate Old Growler, Hambleton Nightmare Porter, Harvey's Tom Paine Original Old Porter, Salopian Entire Butt English Porter, St. Peter's Old-Style Porter, Shepherd Neame Original Porter, Original Flag Porter.

Robust Porter

Robust porter is a more-modern version of brown porter that is made with a portion of dark-roasted malt or barley to create a nearly opaque black color. In 1817, Daniel Wheeler invented the cylindrical roasting drum that produced highly roasted black malts. Brewers learned they could produce the desired dark porter color by using a small amount of roasted black malts mixed with pale malt. Although pale malt was more expensive than brown malt, it contained more extract and the desired wort gravity could be achieved more cheaply using less malt. The color, bitterness, and alcohol levels are generally higher than those of brown porter and the malt character has more dark-roasted flavors, including toffee, chocolate, and coffee, without an intense acrid burnt finish. Robust porter may have fruity esters and spicy flavors, including licorice, with a dry to semisweet finish.

Examples: Great Lakes Edmund Fitzgerald, Meantime London Porter, Anchor Porter, Smuttynose Robust Porter, Sierra Nevada Porter, Deschutes Black Butte Porter, Boulevard Bully! Porter, Rogue Mocha Porter, Avery New World Porter, Bell's Porter, Great Divide Saint Bridget's Porter.

Baltic Porter

As porter's popularity grew in the eighteenth and nineteenth century, English brewers began exporting to Scandinavia, Russia, and German and Slavic states along the Baltic Sea. Many of these shipments were higher in alcohol and hops to withstand the voyage (see Imperial Stout below). Because of the porter's popularity, local brewers began brewing similar beers to meet domestic demand. Early Baltic porters were largely top-fermenting ales in the British style, but as lager brewing took hold on the Continent, many German and Slavic brewers converted to cold bottom fermentation. Porters on the Continent drifted in character toward dark lagers, such as *Schwarzbier* and bock, having a smooth, clean, rich maltiness that stops short of the intense dark-roasted character of English versions. Brewers in Scandinavia have tended to remain with top fermentation and more of the traditional English character. Alcohol levels may range from modest to high, with stronger versions (sometimes named imperial porters) acquiring complex fruity esters and spicy alcohols that combine with the dark malts to give impressions of molasses, chocolate, licorice, black currants, and other dark fruits. Modest sweetness is common, with enough bitterness to balance the malt without dominating the beer's other flavors.

Examples: Sinebrychoff Porter (Finland), Okocim Porter (Poland), Żywiec Porter (Poland), Baltika 6 Porter (Russia), Carnegie Stark Porter (Sweden), Aldaris Porteris (Latvia), Utenos Porter (Lithuania), Stepan Razin Porter (Russia), Nøgne Ø Porter (Norway), Neuzeller Kloster-Bräu Porter (Germany), Southampton Imperial Porter (United States).

	Bitterness (IBU)	Alcohol (% ABV)	Color (SRM)
Brown porter	20–30	4.4–5.9	19–26 (medium to deep brown)
Robust porter	30–45	5.0–6.5	26+ (deep brown)
Baltic porter[a]	20–40	5.5–9.5	17–30+ (light brown to black)

[a] Beer Judge Certification Program (BJCP) style guidelines.

Stouts

Stout is generally recognized as descended from porter because the term "stout" was often used to describe stronger versions of porter, known as stout porter. Over time, the term "porter" was dropped and stout porters became known simply as stout. Today, stout is the name for a variety of very dark to opaque black ales with a roasty, malt-driven flavor from dark-roasted specialty malts that impart bold, bittersweet chocolate and coffee notes or from roasted barley that gives a dryer, more-subtle acrid roast character. Stout is also closely identified with Ireland and the Guinness Brewery, which was once the largest brewery in the world and very influential in introducing the world to this style of black ale.

Numerous variations of the style also developed that display various degrees of sweetness, alcohol, and specialty ingredients. Today, there are dry stout, sweet stout, oatmeal stout, foreign stout, imperial (Russian) stout, and many other examples that include special ingredients, such as oyster stout, coffee stout, vanilla stout, and fruit stouts. Ageing in oak whiskey barrels has become popular in recent years, adding to the diversity and complexity of this style.

Dry (Irish) Stout

Dry stout is synonymous with Irish stout and is widely recognized around the world through the international success of the Guinness Brewery's signature beer. Dry stout gets its dark color from unmalted roasted barley, which lends a very dry, mild acrid roast character that is a benchmark flavor defining the style.

Although flavorful, the "stout" moniker is oxymoronic for dry stouts in terms of alcohol content and calories. Dry stout is typically brewed with a modest starting gravity (±10.5°Plato) and is highly attenuated to produce a dry-finishing beer modest in alcohol content (e.g., ±4.2% ABV) and calories. Two centuries ago, the typical alcohol level may have been twice that of the modern level. In fact, the slow evolution of dry stout to a session beer due to alcohol taxes and wartime rationing helped displace porter as the dark ale of choice in the United Kingdom. Dry stout's modest alcohol content and easy drinkability make it popular for sipping during long evenings in the pub.

The roasted barley imparts a mild, dry roast aroma and flavor with hints of coffee. The beer has a firm hop bitterness that is also accented by the bitter acridness from roasted barley. Some versions may have a background sourness to add balance and complexity that reflects the historical practice of blending older beer soured by *Brettanomyces* yeast. The body is medium light to medium and reflects a fuller, smoother mouthfeel because of the body-building beta glucans found in raw barley. Dry stout is frequently served with nitrogen gas, which also adds to the impression of body and creamy smoothness. Dry stout is a very approachable and quaffable beer with much milder, balanced flavors than those of its bolder cousins in the stout family.

Examples: Guinness Draught (also canned), Murphy's Irish Stout, Beamish Irish Stout, O'Hara's Celtic Stout, Dorothy Goodbody's Wholesome Stout, Orkney Dragonhead Stout, Boulevard Dry Stout.

Sweet Stout

Sweet stout is made with the addition of lactose sugar derived from milk. Yeast cannot metabolize lactose (just like lactose-intolerant people), so it remains unfermented in the beer, where it adds mild sweetness and body. Sweet stout is often touted as a nutritious, healthful beer and even named milk or cream stout. Guinness capitalized on this theme and created several slogans: "Guinness is good for you", "My Goodness, My Guinness", and "Guinness for Strength". Milk stout was likely developed to fortify the beer and to enhance its healthful image of providing nourishment, energy, and curative powers from all kinds of ills. It was even held as ideal for nursing mothers and invalids, with a style of milk stout in Australia even acquiring the name invalid stout. The British government eventually prohibited the use of "milk" in the name, so the beers became known as sweet stout. Outside of Britain, milk stout, cream stout, and sweet stout are used interchangeably. Sweet stout typically has the mild, approachable, roast malt character of dry stout but with less bitterness to allow for a semisweet chocolate finish and fuller mouthfeel.

Examples: Mackeson XXX Stout, Watneys Cream Stout, Farson's Lacto Milk Stout, St. Peter's Cream Stout, Sheaf Stout.

Oatmeal Stout

Oatmeal stout is another example of stout, with the additional ingredient of oats to enhance the wholesome, nutritious image of the beer. For this reason, oats were often used in sweet stout. Oats are a difficult brewing ingredient because it is sticky (like in globs of oatmeal), is hard to lauter, causes haze, and can impart grainy astringency. For these reasons, oats are used in moderation (<5 to 10% of the grist). However, oats are high in oil and protein, which lend a smooth, silky mouthfeel that is characteristic of the style. Oatmeal stout often has a subdued roasted flavor, moderate bitterness, and smooth finish with a hint of sweetness.

Examples: Samuel Smith Oatmeal Stout, Young's Oatmeal Stout, McAuslan St-Ambroise, Maclay Oat Malt Stout.

	Bitterness (IBU)	Alcohol (% ABV)	Color (SRM)
Dry (Irish) stout	30–40	3.8–5.3	30+ (black)
Sweet stout	15–25	3.1–5.5	30+ (black)
Oatmeal stout	20–40	3.8–5.5	25+ (light black to black)

Imperial (Russian) Stout

Imperial (Russian) stout is another example of a strong export beer made with increased alcohol and hop levels to protect it during a long overseas voyage. The names "imperial" and "Russian" were given to this style because, in the late 1700s, a strong version of porter was exported to the imperial court of Russia. The Courage brewery produced an early example of this style, and the brewer still states on its label, "Originally brewed for Catherine II Empress of all the Russias". Imperial Russian stout is one of the most powerful and richest of all beer styles. It is dark brown to black, has a full body, and has a rich bouquet of roasted malt with coffee and chocolate flavors, fruity esters, bitterness, and spicy warming alcohols. Under the stress of high-alcoholic fermentations, the yeast produces an abundance of esters and higher alcohols with dark fruit flavors of raisin, plum, prune, current, and cherry. This beer can be cellared for years, where the slow process of oxidation softens the harshness of the dark malt phenols, mellows the hop intensity, transforms the simple ethanol into flavors of sherry and port and where the fruity bouquet grows by slow esterification of alcohols. The body is big, full, rich, and velvety with a warming finish.

Examples: Three Floyds Dark Lord, Bell's Expedition Stout, North Coast Old Rasputin Russian Imperial Stout, Stone Imperial Russian Stout, Samuel Smith's Imperial Stout, Scotch Irish Tsarina Katarina Imperial Stout, Thirsty Dog Siberian Night, Deschutes The Abyss, Great Divide Yeti, Southampton Imperial Russian Stout, Rogue Imperial Stout, Bear Republic Big Bear Black Stout, Great Lakes Blackout Stout, Avery The Czar, Founders Imperial Stout, Victory Storm King Imperial Stout, Brooklyn Black Chocolate Stout.

Foreign Extra Stout

Foreign extra stout is another example of an export stout credited to Arthur Guinness II that shares a common heritage with imperial stout and IPA. Noting the success of Burton brewers in selling IPA overseas, Guinness created foreign extra stout porter to prevent spoiling in route to the British colonies, especially those in tropical climates. The strength and character of foreign stout is likely similar to the strength and character of the strong porters that originally begat the "stout" designation. Today, Guinness exports an unfermented, hopped wort extract to various international breweries, especially in the tropics, where it is mixed with other local ingredients, such as sorghum in Nigeria. This beer is sometimes referred to as tropical stout, and the flavor and strength of the beer can vary from country to country. Foreign extra stout brewed in the tropics is often sweeter than the dryer extra stout exported to the United States.

Examples: Lion Stout (Sri Lanka), Dragon Stout (Jamaica), ABC Extra Stout (Singapore), Royal Extra Stout "The Lion Stout" (Trinidad), Jamaica Stout (Jamaica), Guinness Foreign Extra Stout (Ireland), Coopers Best Extra Stout (Australia).

American Stout

American breweries have embraced stout, and it is a common style found in many breweries. Americans of course supply their own interpretations of each style, especially through the use of American hops and the infusion of hop aromas. American versions may also be more malt driven, more bitter, and higher in alcohol content. Furthermore, liberal interpretations of style are more frequent in the United States since brewers may include coffee, chocolate, vanilla beans, and cherries in the beer or may age the beer in new oak or bourbon barrels.

Examples: Rogue Shakespeare Stout, Deschutes Obsidian Stout, Sierra Nevada Stout, North Coast Old No. 38 Stout, Bar Harbor Cadillac Mountain Stout, Avery Out of Bounds Stout, Lost Coast 8-Ball Stout, Mad River Steelhead Extra Stout.

	Bitterness (IBU)	Alcohol (% ABV)	Color (SRM)
Imperial (Russian) stout	50–80	7.0–12.0	25+ (light black to black)
Foreign extra stout	30–60	5.6–7.5	30+ (black)
American stout	35–70+	5.6–8.8	30+ (black)

Irish Red Ale

Irish beer is almost exclusively synonymous with one style, stout, which is produced by a small number of large international breweries in Ireland. International pale lagers also command a large part of the Irish market. Stout and lager have been so dominant that little is known of Irish beer styles before stout.

One notable example of an Irish ale style other than stout has been traced to the G. H. Lett Brewery, in County Wexford, which brewed a red ale until it closed in 1956. Years later, a member of the family, George Killian Lett, licensed the name to Pelforth in France and Coors in the United States, and each brewed a reddish beer named George Killian. Today, the style seems to exist largely for export under the name Irish red ale since the style has little following inside Ireland. Today, Murphy's, Beamish, and Smithwick's (Diageo-Guinness) brew Irish red styles along with a host of American brewers. In some versions of the style, the beers are even brewed as a lager.

Irish red ale is brewed with caramel malt, small amounts of roasted malt, or both, to create colors ranging from copper to deep reddish brown. The beers are medium bodied and malt driven with notes of caramel and toffee and, in some examples, hints of butter. Bitterness is modest with little or no hop aroma. The beers are usually thirst quenching and quaffable.

Examples: Three Floyds Brian Boru, Great Lakes Conway's Irish Ale (a bit strong at 6.5% ABV), Kilkenny Irish Beer, O'Hara's Irish Red, Smithwick's Irish Ale, Beamish Red, Caffrey's Irish Ale, Goose Island Kilgubbin Red Ale, Murphy's Irish Red (lager), Boulevard Irish Ale, Harpoon Hibernian.

	Bitterness (IBU)	Alcohol (% ABV)	Color (SRM)
Irish red ale	20–28	4.0–5.0	14–19 (copper to brown)

Scottish Ales

Scottish ales follow a progression of increasingly robust ales similar to the styles of English bitter but with an accent on malt instead of hops. Hops do not grow as well in the cold damp climate of Scotland as they do in the warmer south of England. Furthermore, high export duties imposed on English hops in earlier times by the British government discouraged their use in Scotland. The restricted access to hops caused brewing with herbs to hang on longer than it did in England. Heather was a popular botanical that is still used to make heather ale. However, barley grows well in Scotland, and it forms the signature character not only for Scotland's rich malty ales but also for its famous malt whiskeys. To accentuate their maltiness, Scottish ale brewers use high-temperature mashes to produce a dextrinous wort that creates the sweet backbone for many of their beers. Scotland's northern climate may also have influenced the practice of fermenting at low temperatures. While the Scots are traditionally ale brewers, the cooler fermentation and conditioning temperatures that extended the maturation times are analogous to the practices followed by German brewers for smooth-tasting bottom-fermenting lagers and top-fermenting *Alt* and *Kölsch*.

Color and malt flavor in Scottish ales are generally obtained by using small amounts (<2%) of dark-roasted barley malt or unsprouted (slack) barley rather than larger portions of lighter crystal, as used in English pale ale. The use of roasted malt may be responsible for the perception of hints of smoke in certain examples. While the peated malt used in

Scotch whiskey is not a traditional ingredient in Scottish ale, some brewers (especially Americans) have been drawn to include it as part of the grist. Oats are also a cold-weather grain common in Scotland that contributes to the full-bodied mouthfeel of some Scottish ales.

In tribute to earlier times, Scottish ales are still identified by an old taxation system based on beer strength and the old unit of currency called the shilling. Scottish light, heavy, and export are also referred to as 60-, 70-, and 80-shilling beers, respectively. (The symbol for shilling is "/-".) Stronger versions of ales from Scotland (Scotch ale or wee heavy), discussed later, may be rated from 90 to 160/-.

Scottish Light (60/-)

Scottish light (60/-) is light amber to light brown in color, with hints of roasted malt or caramel from traditionally long boils, a low level of bitterness, and virtually no hop aroma. Alcohol levels are low, making it an ideal session beer. It is usually served only from the cask in the United Kingdom and is hard to find outside of Scotland.

Examples: Belhaven 60/-, McEwan's 60/-, Maclay 60/- Light.

Scottish Heavy (70/-)

Scottish heavy (70/-) is the big brother of Scottish light but usually darker in color and higher in alcohol content.

Examples: Caledonian 70/- (Caledonian Amber Ale in the United States), Belhaven 70/-, Orkney Raven Ale, Maclay 70/-, Tennent's Special Ale, Broughton Greenmantle Ale.

Scottish Export (80/-)

Scottish export (80/-) implies "export" strength but still modest in bitterness and alcohol level relative to export stout and IPA. Export has a robust malt character with pronounced caramel notes and hints of roasted smokiness.

Examples: Orkney Dark Island, Caledonian 80/- Export Ale, Belhaven 80/- (Belhaven Scottish Ale in the United States), Southampton 80 Shilling, Broughton Exciseman's 80/-, Belhaven St. Andrews Ale, McEwan's Export, Inveralmond Lia Fail, Broughton Merlin's Ale, Arran Dark.

	Bitterness (IBU)	Alcohol (% ABV)	Color (SRM)
Scottish light	9–20	2.8–3.8	14–17 (copper to light brown)
Scottish heavy	12–20	3.5–4.5	14–19 (copper to brown)
Scottish export	15–25	4.0–5.0	14–19 (copper to brown)

Strong Ales

Alcohol is a by-product of fermentation that at high levels becomes toxic to yeast. Alcoholic stress on yeast changes the metabolic by-products of fermentation, which generally increases the amount of fruity esters and spicy fusel alcohols. Therefore, the range and depth of flavors in strong beers is not limited to just the impact of greater ethanol levels and larger portions of malt and hops but also of elevated fermentation flavors.

Before continuous sparging became the norm, strong beers were produced using the parti-gyle method of mashing, in which only the first runnings of wort with the highest extract levels were collected from the lauter tun. The extract was further concentrated during long boils to evaporate excess water. The long boils also caramelized the highly concentrated sugars that darkened the wort and enhanced the malty character of the crystal and dark malts. Strong ales typically have a full body and a sweet finish that is balanced by generous portions of bittering hops without overwhelming the malt-driven flavors. The alcoholic character is often pronounced and warming with vinous notes.

Strong ales are often aged for the increased development of esters, the mellowing of tannins, and the oxidation of alcohols to sherry and rumlike aldehydes. A vertical tasting comparing a series of vintages is a way to experience the cumulative flavor changes as a beer ages.

The definition of "strong" is expanding. While the upper limit of alcohol content was generally 8–10% ABV, new interest in creating stronger beers, especially in America, has been expanding the upper limits to 12 and 14% ABV, largely by employing alcohol-tolerant wine yeasts to finish fermentation. A handful of American brewers have even created beers (without distillation or dewatering) in excess of 20% ABV through various proprietary techniques. A second charge of yeast may be added at the end of fermentation to assist the original yeast exhausted from fermenting the high levels of sugar and stressed by alcohol. The second addition of yeast is better able to remain viable during the long maturation period. In the early twentieth century, barley wine brewers often roused inactive yeast by rolling the cask across the floor in a practice called "walking the cask".

While the term "strong ale" is used to describe a broad category of beers, use of this title by brewers in the United States is illegal because federal government rules prohibit the use of terminology that implies alcohol strength.

Scotch Ale

Scotch ale is the name for the strong ales of Scotland. Scotch ale must not to be confused with the lower-alcohol Scottish ale discussed earlier, which has an alcohol content of around 5% or lower. Scotch ales are sometimes referred to as wee heavy and are the Scottish counterpart to English barley wine and should not be confused with the lower-alcohol Scottish heavy. Like Scottish ales, Scotch ales have subdued bitterness and little hop aroma, so the emphasis is on the big, full-bodied, malty heart of the style. High levels of alcohol assist the hops in balancing the malty caramel sweetness. Fruity esters may not be as prevalent as they are in other strong beers because of Scotland's tradition of cool fermentation. Because of the common use of small portions of dark-roasted malt, some examples may exhibit an earthy or smoky character.

Examples: Traquair House Ale, Belhaven Wee Heavy, McEwan's Scotch Ale, Founders Dirty Bastard, MacAndrew's Scotch Ale, AleSmith Wee Heavy, Orkney Skull Splitter, Inveralmond Blackfriar, Broughton Old Jock, Gordon Highland Scotch Ale, Dragonmead Under the Kilt Wee Heavy.

English Old Ale

English old ale is a name that originally implied a long aging or maturation period to develop complexity, especially a sour character from the action of slow-working *Brettanomyces* yeast. The tart vinous flavors of these "old" or "stock" ales were then blended with younger beers to enhance their character and complexity. Old ale and stock ale are used interchangeably.

As advances in single-strain yeast culturing and sanitation were made and steel tanks replaced wooden casks, the *Brettanomyces* character of old ale was gradually eliminated, along with the practice of blending, as consumer tastes developed a preference for cleaner, fresh-tasting ales. Eventually, old ale came to simply denote a strong, well-conditioned ale, brewed as a high-gravity version of a brewer's existing bitter or mild brand or as a separate recipe formulated similar to barley wine. Today, old ales are rich and malty, are full of color, and have a sweet finish. Beers of this style often include the word "old" in their name, which is frequently taken from the name of a historical or fictional character in a manner that incorporates a bit of humor, such as Old Tom, Wobbly Bob, Old Hen, and Old Engine Oil. One brewery produces a particularly strong bottled old ale (12% ABV) named after the writer Thomas Hardy, which is vintage-dated, that the brewery suggests cellaring for a minimum of 5 years and up to 20! Aged examples develop sherry and portlike flavors. Old ales are frequently brewed as seasonal winter warmers and Christmas ales. Christmas ales may include spices, such as ginger, nutmeg, and cinnamon, in a fashion similar to mulled wine.

Examples: Gale Prize Old Ale, Thomas Hardy's Ale, Burton Bridge Olde Expensive Ale, Marston's Owd Rodger, Greene King Olde Suffolk, J.W. Lees Moonraker, Harviestoun Old Engine Oil, Fuller's Vintage Ale, Harveys Elizabethan Ale, Theakston Old Peculier (peculiar at 1.057 original gravity), Young's Winter Warmer, Sarah Hughes Dark Ruby Mild, Samuel Smith's Winter Welcome Ale, Fuller's 1845, Fuller's Old Winter Ale, Great Divide Hibernation Ale, Founders Curmudgeon, Cooperstown Pride of Milford Special Ale, Coniston Old Man Ale, Avery Old Jubilation.

English Barley Wine

English barley wine was traditionally an English brewery's strongest offering, which at one time was also referred to as "malt" wines. Brewers may have chosen the name because of the respect that consumers gave to vintners and the brewer's desire to produce a beer that could match wine not only in strength but also in quality and character. This dextrinous ale, which is pushed to the yeasts' limits of alcohol tolerance, is generally fruity with malty sweet notes of caramel, toffee, dark fruits, and molasses. Color may range from deep amber to copper and brown. The malt bill is usually a base of pale malt and modest amounts of crystal and little, if any, dark malts. Sugar and malt extracts may be used to boost wort gravity. Dark beer color is often the result of wort caramelization in the kettle since the flavor of roast is not traditional. Bitterness levels can be quite high, but the perception is muted by the balancing sweetness of the rich malt character. Some examples may be dry hopped. Aging mellows the bitterness and produces sherry and spicy rum flavors along with dark fruit and molasses notes. Barley wine is typically stronger than old ale and lighter in color than Scotch ale, but the line between these strong ales is often blurred. Barley wine in England often comes in small, 7-ounce (180-milliliter) "nib" bottles.

Examples: Burton Bridge Thomas Sykes Old Ale, J.W. Lees Vintage Harvest Ale, Robinson Old Tom, Fuller's Golden Pride, AleSmith Old Numbskull, Young's Old Nick (unusual at 7.2% ABV), Whitbread Gold Label, Dominion Millennium, North Coast Old Stock Ale (when aged), Weyerbacher Blithering Idiot.

American Barley Wine

American barley wine is typically maltier and more bitter and has more hop aroma from the more frequent use of dry hopping when compared with old ale and English barley wine. The citrus and cedar resin aromas of American hops also stand in contrast to the more herbal and earthy English varieties. The average alcohol level may also be higher in American examples. American barley wine tends to have more malt character, be less bitter, and have a richer body when compared with American double IPA. Barley wine sold in the United States must use the name "barley wine-style ale" so as to avoid any confusion that the product is beer and not wine.

Examples: Sierra Nevada Bigfoot, BridgePort Old Knucklehead, Great Divide Old Ruffian, Victory Old Horizontal, Rogue Old Crustacean, Avery Hog Heaven, Bell's Third Coast Old Ale, Anchor Old Foghorn, Three Floyds Behemoth, Stone Old Guardian, Hair of the Dog Doggie Claws, Lagunitas Olde GnarlyWine, Smuttynose Barleywine Style Ale, Flying Dog Horn Dog.

	Bitterness (IBU)	Alcohol (% ABV)	Color (SRM)
Scotch ale	25–35	6.5–8.4	17–24 (deep copper to dark brown)
English old ale	30–65	6.3–9.5	14–20 (copper to medium brown)
English barley wine	35–55	8.4–13.1	17–24 (reddish brown to dark brown)
American barley wine	50+	9.0–14.0	17–24 (reddish brown to dark brown)

Germany and Continental Europe

Germany is widely recognized as a country that loves beer and its brewing traditions. Lager beer has its roots in Germany, from where it grew into the world's most popular beer style. Even in the United States, with a thriving craft beer industry, approximately 90% of all beers sold are still pale lagers. However, Germans do not deserve all the credit. Brewers in other countries also played a part in the development of lager brewing, particularly Louis Pasteur from France, Anton Dreher from Austria, Emile Christian Hansen from Denmark, and of course, those in the city of Pilsen in the Czech Republic, where the pilsner beer style was born.

An understanding of the German-Continental brewing tradition would be incomplete without an understanding of the *Reinheitsgebot*, or German beer "Purity Law". Enacted in 1516 by the rulers of Bavaria, it limited beer to three ingredients: malted barley, hops, and water (yeast had not yet been discovered and became part of the law later). Today, it is regarded as the oldest surviving consumer protection law in the world because the basic tenant of the 1516 edict survives in the federal *Vorläufiges Biergesetz* ("Provisional Beer Law"):

> *Zur Bereitung von untergärigem Bier darf, ..., nur Gerstenmalz, Hopfen, Hefe und Wasser verwendet werden.* (For the preparation of bottom-fermenting beer, ..., only barley malt, hops, yeast, and water may be used.)

The Provisional Beer Law covers many other aspects of brewing by applying this basic tenant to modern methods of production and by recognizing exceptions, particularly for top-fermenting beer, that may use other malted grains, most notably wheat.

In 1985, the European Union ruled that Germany could not bar imported beers because they did not conform to German law. However, for German brewers selling inside Germany, the rules still apply if the brewer wants to call the product "beer" and place the coveted claim on the package: *Gebraut nach dem Reinheitsgebot* ("Brewed according to the Purity Law"). There are critics on both sides of the question asking if the restrictions should be repealed. Advocates claim that the rules have protected the quality of German beer from the use of adjuncts, colorants, and other questionable practices found in other countries. Critics claim that it is too restrictive and prevents German brewers from exploring new styles of beers, which American, British, and Belgian brewers are able to pursue. With a narrower range of ingredients and a Germanic sense of order that frequently defines by law or tradition how a beer is constructed, German beer styles are often easier to categorize than beers from other brewing traditions.

German beer is all about clarity of flavor and balance. Both ales and lagers are typically fermented at the low end of their temperature range to produce a clean fermentation character. German hops are noted for their delicate noble character and the fine bitterness they impart. Dry hopping is not a traditional technique, and the hop aroma imparted by late kettle hops is restrained, mild, and floral, without the grassy, pungent character of British and, especially, American ales. The balanced flavors of hops and yeast allow the malt in German beer to play a prominent role. Without adjuncts, German beers present a firm malt base even in light-bodied pilsners. In full-bodied beers, malt character is typically built by using lots of medium-colored, smooth-tasting, and caramel-toasty malt as opposed to the common English practice of using a small portion of dark crystal or roasted malt.

Continental Lager Beers

Sometime in the late Middle Ages, brewers in the area of southern Germany began practicing cool fermentation and cold maturation by using ice cut from lakes in the winter and stored in underground brewing cellars. Over time, this practice selected for yeast that could ferment at low temperatures, at which competing beer-spoilage microbes were largely inactive. Brewers in this area also turned to the exclusive use of hops for flavoring and preserving their beers. The combination of low temperatures and hops provided a stable, clean-tasting beer that would obtain improved clarity during periods of cold storage or "lagering". (*Lagern* means to "store" in German.) In the mid-nineteenth century, brewers outside Bavaria, e.g., Bohemia, Austria, and the United States, started adopting lager brewing methods. With the invention of refrigeration, lager brewing spread over a larger area to include countries where natural ice was not available. Today, lager brewing dominates beer production inside Germany and across the globe.

Vienna Lager

The first lagers were undoubtedly dark, brown beers owing to the primitive malting techniques of the late Middle Ages. In the 1830s, German Gabriel Sedlmayr II from Munich and Austrian Anton Dreher from Vienna toured breweries throughout Europe and, in particular, noted various types of brewing innovations (e.g., steam power, hydrometer), especially indirect-heated kilns in England that produced pale malt. In comparison to the brown malt of the day, a light-colored malt with a reddish hue was introduced by Dreher in Vienna and a somewhat deeper amber malt was introduced by Sedlmayr in Munich. Dreher's malt became known as Vienna malt and the red beer he introduced in 1841, Vienna lager. Ironically, the beer style seemingly vanished from Vienna during the twentieth century because of the overwhelming popularity of yet paler lagers. However, immigrants to Mexico took the style with them. Dos Equis and Negra Modelo are two examples of Vienna-inspired lagers brewed in Mexico that have a lighter body than the original examples owing to the use of adjuncts. Vienna lager is a bit of a revisionist style since there is no known continuously brewed example of the style from its place of birth. Nevertheless, American brewers have reconstructed style guidelines from evidence that could be pieced together from brewing history. The color of Vienna lager is reddish amber to light copper with a clean malt flavor and hints of caramel or toast. Hop bitterness is modest and aroma is generally mild or absent.

Examples: Negra Modelo (Mexico), Dos Equis (Mexico), Noche Buena (Mexico), Sam Adams Vienna Style (Massachusetts, United States), Capital Wisconsin Amber (Wisconsin, United States), Live Oak Big Bark Amber Lager (Texas, United States).

Märzen/Oktoberfest

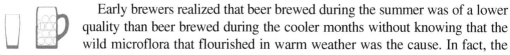

Early brewers realized that beer brewed during the summer was of a lower quality than beer brewed during the cooler months without knowing that the wild microflora that flourished in warm weather was the cause. In fact, the *Reinheitsgebot* of 1516 decreed that beer could only be brewed between St. Michael's Day (September 29) and St. George's Day (April 23), which was enforced in Bavaria until 1865. Because the last beers of the season were typically brewed around March, they were called *Märzen*, or "March" beer. The beer typically had a slightly higher alcohol content to preserve it over the summer. *Märzen* was the last beer consumed (i.e., in October) from the spring brewing season before the resumption of brewing in the fall produced fresh beer supplies.

On October 12, 1810, the prince of Bavaria was married in Munich. To honor the royal couple, the anniversary of the wedding continued to be celebrated annually, which eventually grew into the world's largest beer festival—Oktoberfest. Given the time of year, *Märzen* beer would have been the seasonal beer available at this time, although it was originally brewed in the style of the traditional dark brown Munich lager. In 1871, Gabriel Sedlmayr II of Spaten developed a new paler, amber lager based on Anton Dreher's Vienna lager and classified it as a *Märzen*. Spaten offered the beer at Oktoberfest in 1872, and the style was so popular that the new Oktoberfest *Märzen* became the traditional style served by Spaten and other brewers at Oktoberfest. Just as the festival beer transitioned from a dark lager to a amber lager in the late 1800s, the beer in the late 1900s morphed into a deep golden lager more in the export style but still brewed with an elevated alcohol level, traditionally at 13.5–14.0°Plato. Munich's brewers likely observed that the paler version was less satiating, a characteristic highly preferred by patrons consuming multiple liters during long hours of eating and merrymaking. The traditional amber Oktoberfest *Märzen* still exists but largely as an export beer consumed outside Munich. The golden version served at Oktoberfest is now known simply as *Festbier* ("festival beer") or *Wiesn* ("meadow") beer in reference to the field where Oktoberfest was held.

Oktoberfest *Märzen* is a smooth, malt-driven beer with a clean, toasted malt character and subtle hints of toasted caramel sweetness from a generous portion of Munich malt, Vienna malt, or both, often representing 50% or more of the grist. Small amounts of caramel malt may be included but never dark-roasted malts, since chocolate and coffee flavors are not appropriate. Decoction mashing is frequently used to further heighten the malt character. Hop bitterness is moderate with little if any hop aroma. The beer has a medium body with a clean, smooth, malty finish. While descended from Vienna lager, Oktoberfest *Märzen* is generally darker, maltier, and higher in alcohol content.

Examples: Paulaner Oktoberfest, Ayinger Oktober Fest-Märzen, Hacker-Pschorr Original Oktoberfest, Hofbräu Oktoberfest, Spaten Oktoberfest, Dry Dock Reines Märzen, Widmer Okto Festival Ale.

Munich *Dunkel*

Munich *Dunkel* or Munich "dark" is descended from the common brown lager that was brewed when the *Reinheitsgebot* was enacted. The primitive direct-heated kilns of the day left some kernels slightly charred and smoky, which created the dark brown color. After Gabriel Sedlmayr II introduced the indirect-heated kiln in the mid-1800s, the brown malt used to brew *Dunkel* took on a cleaner taste and a more-consistent color. This new amber malt became known as Munich malt. *Dunkel* remained the standard lager in Munich through the end of the nineteenth century, but the same kiln technology that refined the taste of amber Munich malt was also capable of producing pale malt, which steadily gained wider use in creating a pale *Helles* lager that eventually supplanted *Dunkel* as Bavaria's standard lager. *Dunkel* is still brewed but frequently by small traditional brewers or as a specialty or seasonal beer by larger producers. Because of *Dunkel*'s deep roots in lager brewing history, it represents a defensible starting point from which all lager beer styles descended.

The development of *Dunkel* in Munich is not surprising given Munich's very alkaline brewing water, which the slightly acidic dark malt helped counteract. It is also not surprising that the rise of pale Munich *Helles* coincided with the modern development of the concept of pH and of water-treatment methods. Today, Munich brewers producing pale lagers practice extensive methods to remove alkalinity from their water.

Munich *Dunkel*, or simply *Dunkel*, is a malt-accented beer that is deep amber to dark brown. The extensive use of dark Munich malt provides a firm base of rich toasty, caramel flavors that are often enhanced with the use of decoction mashing. Although roasted character is inappropriate, small amounts of roasted, often dehusked and debittered, malt (<1%) are sometimes used to deepen the color and provide hints of chocolate and coffee. Hop bitterness is moderate. *Dunkel* is medium to full-medium bodied with a clean lager finish and a slight malty sweetness.

Examples: Ayinger Altbairisch Dunkel, Hacker-Pschorr Münchner Dunkel (Alt Munich Dark), Paulaner Alt-Münchner Dunkel, Weltenburger Kloster Barock Dunkel, Ettaler Kloster Dunkel, Hofbräu Dunkel, Kaltenberg König Ludwig Dunkel. Brewers outside of Bavaria, such as Warsteiner, Beck's, or Heineken, often produce a dark lager that is usually dryer and less full bodied.

Schwarzbier

Schwarzbier is associated most with southern and southeastern Germany, particularly Franconia and Thuringia. *Schwarz* means "black" in German, and although this is Germany's darkest beer, it is not opaque black like many stouts. Munich malts and small amounts of roasted malt (<1%) produce the dark brown color.

Schwarzbier is dryer and more bitter than *Dunkel* and the malt flavors lean more toward coffee and chocolate and less to caramel. However, it is not roasty like porter. Dehusked and debittered roasted malts may be used to produce a mild, dry finish and deep color. In fact, the beer has been called *Schwarz Pils* to reflect its clean, bitter finish. *Schwarzbiers* are brewed in other countries besides Germany, e.g., *černý pivo* in the Czech Republic.

Examples: Köstritzer Schwarzbier (Germany), Kulmbacher Mönchshof Premium Schwarzbier (Germany), Sapporo Black Beer (Japan).

	Bitterness (IBU)	Alcohol (% ABV)	Color (SRM)
Vienna lager	22–30	4.8–5.4	6–14 (light amber to copper)
Märzen/Oktoberfest	18–25	5.0–5.9	5–17 (gold to reddish brown)
Munich *Dunkel*	15–25	4.8–5.3	17–22 (light brown to dark brown)
Schwarzbier	22–32	3.8–5.0	22–30+ (dark brown to black)

Pilsner

Historians link the ancestry of the world's most successful beer style, pale lager, to Pilsen in the Czech Republic, where the serendipitous meeting of pale malt, noble hops, soft water, and lager yeast created a new lager style—pilsner.

In 1841, Pilsen city fathers, displeased with the poor quality of the local beer, hired Bavarian brewmaster Joseph Groll to brew a pale lager beer made in the same fashion as Anton Dreher's Vienna lager, only paler. The local Moravian malt was of high quality, and the especially soft water helped minimize color because of its low alkalinity. The soft water also allowed a high hopping rate, yet the bitterness remained delicate and refined. The local Saaz hops with their peppery noble aromas were perfectly suited to flavor this elegant beer brewed with clean fermenting lager yeast that Groll brought from Bavaria. The style grew rapidly in popularity and was copied by many brewers in continental Europe, the United States, and around the world. In reference to its birth place, the beer became known as pilsner, and the beer from the original brewery in Pilsen was named *Pilsner Urquell*, which in German, the language of the then-ruling Austrian monarchy, means "original source" (*Ur* = original, *Quell* = source). Germans consider pilsner to be an appellation assignable only to the original city, and they use the abbreviated name *Pils* to refer to German beers of this style.

Pilsner is clean tasting with an assertive, but delicate, hop-driven noble bitterness that is never grassy or rough. Floral noble hops from late kettle hopping provide a mild but pleasing floral aroma. The pale pilsner malt provides a clean background, medium body, and a well-attenuated finish, the dryness of which is accentuated by the bitterness.

Bohemian Pilsner

Bohemian or Czech pilsner may have a slightly deeper golden color and maltiness in those examples that have a slight degree of caramelization from multiple decoctions.

Examples of Bohemian Pilsner: Pilsner Urquell, Budweiser Budvar (labeled Czechvar in the United States), Czech Rebel Beer, Staropramen, Gambrinus Pilsner.

German *Pils*

German *Pils* is a style more associated with northern Germany than with Bavaria. Northern German *Pils* tends to be very dry, clean, pale, and bitter. While traditional brewers may use a decoction mash, it is usually a single decoction that does not add much color or malt flavors to the beer. In some examples, the brewer may even mill the malt and remove the husks before mashing to avoid extraction of harsh astringency from the husks. Soft water is beneficial in brewing *Pils* to reduce color, lower extraction of husk astringency, and allow for a mellow bitterness.

Examples of German *Pils*: Bitburger Premium Beer, Warsteiner Premium Verum, König Pilsener, Jever Pilsener, Holsten Pils, Dinkel Acker CD-Pils.

Dortmunder Export

Dortmunder export is named after Dortmund, Germany. The term "export" indicates a beer that is brewed with a slightly higher alcohol content to improve stability for beers that are "exported" and require a longer shelf life and durability to harsh conditions. *Dortmunder* export is a golden lager similar to German *Pils*, but it is higher in alcohol, with a firmer malt body and finish and, typically, with less bitterness and hop aroma. Especially in Bavaria, the export style refers to a maltier, higher-alcohol version of the brewer's *Helles*. In fact, the strong, malty pale lagers served at the Oktoberfest may be classified as an export-style lager or export *Helles*.

Examples: DAB Export (Dortmund), Dortmunder Union Export (Dortmund), Dortmunder Kronen (Dortmund), Ayinger Jahrhundert Bier (Bavaria), Augustiner Edelstoff (Bavaria), Great Lakes Dortmunder Gold (United States).

Munich *Helles*

The Spaten brewery is credited with originating this pale golden lager in 1894 at a time when Munich's most common beer was still *Dunkel*. Eventually, *Helles* (meaning "pale or bright") overtook *Dunkel* in the twentieth century as Munich's most popular lager beer. It is brewed with pilsner malt for a pale, bright color and clean malt-driven flavor. Small amounts of light-colored caramel malt may be included to enhance the body and emphasize maltiness. *Helles* is moderately bitter and usually has little or no hop aroma. In fact, the restrained bitterness level, which is lower than that of pilsner, may have resulted from the highly alkaline water in Munich, which contributes to a coarse bitterness in highly hopped beers. Even today, there seems to be a preference for more highly hopped beers in northern Germany than in Bavaria. Unfiltered examples of *Helles* are called *Kellerbier* ("cellar beer") or *Naturtrüb* ("naturally turbid").

Examples: Weihenstephaner Original, Hacker-Pschorr Münchner Gold, Mahr's Bräu Hell, Paulaner Original Münchner, Spaten Premium (München), Bürgerbräu Wolnzacher Hell Naturtrüb, Augustiner-Bräu Edelstoff.

International Pale Lagers

Pale lagers are the most widely copied and interpreted beer styles in the world. They may range in flavor from the traditional pilsner to *Helles* to versions of much lower bitterness and body, such as the adjunct lagers common in North and South America. These beers typically have a light to medium body, have drinkability, and are refreshing.

Examples: Kingfisher (India), Tsingtao (China), San Miguel (Philippines), Sapporo (Japan), Harp (Ireland [Guinness]), Stella Artois (Belgium), Kronenbourg (France), Peroni (Italy), Heineken (Holland).

	Bitterness (IBU)	Alcohol (% ABV)	Color (SRM)
Bohemian pilsner	30–45	4.0–5.5	3–6 (light yellow to light gold)
German *Pils*	25–40	4.5–5.3	3–4 (light yellow)
Dortmunder export	22–32	5.0–6.0	3–6 (light yellow to light gold)
Munich *Helles*	16–25	4.8–5.3	4–6 (yellow to light gold)
International pale lagers[a]	12–25	4.5–5.2	3–4 (light yellow)

[a] No specifications given by the North American Brewers Association (NABA).

Rauchbier

Rauchbier

Rauchbier means "smoked beer" in German. This style is most frequently associated with the city of Bamberg in the northern Bavarian region of Franconia, where a number of small breweries still use a portion of smoked malt, traditionally from beechwood. *Märzen* is frequently the beer style used to make *Rauchbier*, but there are also examples of *Helles* or *Hefeweizen Rauchbier*. The intensity of smoke flavor can be intense, almost baconlike, or very mild and subtle. The smoked beer retains the identity of the base beer style, which is given another dimension of smoke flavor.

Examples: Aecht Schlenkerla Rauchbier Märzen, Kaiserdom Rauchbier, Eisenbahn Rauchbier, Victory Scarlet Fire Rauchbier, Spezial Rauchbier Märzen, Saranac Rauchbier.

Steinbier

Before metal kettles were available for wort boiling over fire, brewers would sometimes create a boil by dropping super-hot stones into the wort. The stones caused considerable caramelization of the wort and produced hints of smoke flavor. After boiling, the caramel sugar-coated stones could be placed in the fermenter to provide additional sugar for the yeast and to add additional flavor to the beer. Only a small number of breweries still produce *Steinbier* or "stone beer" in this way in order to capture the unique flavors produced by this unusual wort boiling method.

Example: Rauchenfelser Steinbier.

Style Variations

Any beer can be brewed with smoked or even peated whiskey malt to create a variation on any style. Beers using dark-roasted malts, such as porter and stout, provide some of the most common examples of smoked-beer styles.

Examples: Alaskan Smoked Porter, Stone Smoked Porter, Bell's Smoked Stout.

Bock Beers

Bock beer is a style that was born in the northern German town of Einbeck and grew in popularity and prominence in Bavaria. Einbeck was a member of the Hanseatic League, a federation of city states that obtained semiautonomous status from their feudal princes, including the right to brew beer. The Hanseatic cities formed this league for self-defense and to protect trade, including the export of beer, the quality of which was closely protected by brewers' guilds. Einbeck was especially renowned for its top-fermenting beer made with barley and wheat that was exported throughout Germany, including Bavaria. Recognizing the advanced state of brewing in Einbeck compared with that of Munich, the Bavarian royal family brought brewmaster Elias Pichler from Einbeck to Munich to improve the quality of beer produced by their court brewery. In 1612, Pichler released his first version of Einbecker beer at the *Hofbräuhaus* (court brewery). The Bavarian version, which was brewed as a lager and produced with only barley malt, was so successful that it required several expansions of the brewery.

There are several explanations for the origin of the name "bock". Perhaps the most widely accepted is a derivation of the Bavarian pronunciation for an *Einbecker Bier*, *Ainpöckisch Bier*, shortened to *Pöckisch Bier* and finally *Bock Bier*. Bock also happens to be the German name for billy goat, so labels often contain the image of a goat.

Bock

Bock is a deep copper to brown beer made primarily from Munich malt that emphasizes smooth, round, toasty caramel malt flavors with mild sweetness. Decoction mashing is a traditional practice to enhance the color and malt flavor. With a starting original extract content of 16–18°Plato, bock often undergoes an extended lagering period to properly attenuate and produce mature smooth fermentation flavors. Nevertheless, the higher extract content may produce a slightly more estery and aromatic beer than the lower-gravity *Pils* and *Märzen* beers. Hop bitterness is substantial enough to balance the rich, full, malt body, but it is not dominating. Clean maltiness is the primary flavor impact of bock. Hop aroma is not characteristic of the style. Bock is often brewed as a special seasonal style, especially in the winter.

Examples: Einbecker Ur-Bock Dunkel, Aass Bock, Sandlot Brewery Bock.

Maibock/Heller Bock

Maibock/Heller Bock is the youngest member of the bock family owing to the modern development of pale malt used to create a lighter color than that of traditional dark bocks. The paler *Maibock* ("May bock") helps provide a transition from the darker bocks of the winter and early spring to the lighter *Helles* for the beer-garden season of summer. The paler style also capitalized on the growing popularity of pale lager by providing a pale, strong lager. *Maibock/Heller Bock* is brewed to the same original gravity as traditional bock but with a large portion of pale malt and smaller amounts of amber Vienna or Munich malts if a deeper color is desired. *Maibock/Heller Bock* may be slightly more bitter than traditional bocks.

Examples: Einbecker Mai-Ur-Bock, Hofbräu Maibock, Ayinger Maibock, Mahr's Bock, Hacker-Pschorr Hubertus Bock.

Doppelbock

Doppelbock literally means "double bock" but does not signify alcohol strength double that of regular bock. In Germany, a traditional bock has an original extract of 16–18°Plato. *Doppelbock* has an extract content in excess of 18°Plato.

The origins of the style are traced back to monks that arrived in Bavaria around 1630 and were followers of St. Francis of Paula, Italy. The Paulaner monks were dispatched to Bavaria during the time of the Counter Reformation to renew the church and ensure that Bavarians remained within the fold of the Catholic church. (Bavaria remains largely

Catholic, owing to the historical influence of the Catholic church in this area. In fact, the German name for Munich is *München*, meaning "city of monks".) Like other monasteries at this time, the monks brewed their own beer and led a devout life, including fasting. The 46 days of Lent preceding Easter was a particularly important season in the church year for reflection and fasting. While solid food was restricted, liquids were not, and the monks brewed a particularly strong nutritious beer to sustain them during this long period of fasting. They named the strong beer *Salvator*, meaning "savior" in Latin. In 1780, the elector duke granted the monks the right to sell their highly renowned *Doppelbock*. However, Napoleon confiscated much of the church's property in 1799, including the Paulaners' brewery (as he did with the Trappist monks of northern France). Eventually, the brewery became a secular concern that still exists; it retained the name Paulaner and continues to brew *Salvator Doppelbock*.

Doppelbock remains a popular seasonal beer released in late winter for Lent (also termed *Starkbierzeit* or "strong beer season"). The Paulaner brewery still holds a ceremonial tapping of the first *Salvator* keg on March 19, St. Joseph's Day. By the late 1800s, many other Munich breweries were releasing their own versions of *Doppelbock* with names ending in "ator" in homage to the original example.

Doppelbock is a rich, dark, malty brew with a constitution similar to that of a standard bock but with higher levels of alcohol, fuller body, and overall more-intense malt- and alcohol-based flavors. These brews are traditionally double decocted to increase the color and malty caramel flavors. They often undergo long, cold maturation periods to allow full attenuation and mellowing of the flavors. The high-gravity wort produces increased levels of fruity esters and spicy alcohols, but *Doppelbock* is still a relatively clean-tasting beer, as compared with barley wine, because of the cold-fermenting lager yeast. In comparison to strong ales, the absence of noncompeting yeast flavors allows the malt character of this beer to take center stage. The absence of alcohol-heightening but body-lightening sugar or other adjuncts forbidden by the *Reinheitsgebot* provides *Doppelbock* with a rich malt character.

Examples: Paulaner Salvator, Spaten Optimator, Ayinger Celebrator, Weihenstephaner Korbinian, Augustiner Maximator, Löwenbräu Triumphator, Tucher Bajuvator, Bell's Consecrator, Sam Adams Double Bock.

Eisbock

The origin of *Eisbock* is frequently attributed to the Franconian city of Kulmbach in northern Bavaria. Folklore holds that, when a barrel of bock was unintentionally allowed to freeze, brewers discovered that only the water froze but the alcohol did not, thus concentrating the alcohol content and flavors. Because the beer was frozen, it became known as *Eisbock*, meaning "ice bock". When the brewer freezes a bock (or more typically a *Doppelbock*), the ice floats to the top of the tank. The dewatered, high-alcohol beer is then drained from below, leaving the ice behind. The beer takes on a distinctively alcoholic character in mouthfeel and aroma from the concentrated levels of esters and fusel alcohols that impart dark fruit flavors, such as prune and raisin. The caramel malt flavors are also concentrated, which creates a full body and rich semisweet finish. Freezing reduces the solubility of proteins and harsh polyphenols, which are more readily removed during filtration, producing a smoother-tasting beer.

German *Eisbock* is not to be confused with North American ice beer, which is usually a version of the brewery's pale lager. In North America, the freezing is not used to concentrate the alcohol but rather to enhance the removal of harsh flavors to produce a milder beer. In fact, the removal of water by freezing is considered a form of distillation in the United States, and *Eisbock* production requires a distiller's license. Therefore, North American ice beers are frozen, thawed, and filtered or they are diluted with water after separation from the ice to return the beer to its original alcohol content.

Examples: Kulmbacher Reichelbräu Eisbock, Eggenberg Urbock Dunkel Eisbock, Niagara Eisbock.

	Bitterness (IBU)	Alcohol (% ABV)	Color (SRM)
Bock	20–30	6.3–7.2	10–20 (light copper to brown)
Maibock/Heller Bock	20–35	6.3–7.4	2–7 (straw to light amber)
Doppelbock	18–30	6.0–9.0	12–25 (dark amber to dark brown)
Eisbock	26–35	9–14.0	17–25 (deep copper to dark brown)

German Ales

Germans do not have a word per se for "ale" and designate the two major classifications of beer as top fermenting (*obergärig*) for ales and bottom fermenting (*untergärig*) for lagers. While bottom-fermenting lager beers are by far the most popular, with *Pils* alone accounting for 60% of the German beer market, top-fermenting beers are still dominant in several areas. In particular, *Weizen* in Bavaria, *Kölsch* in Cologne, and *Alt* in Düsseldorf hold the largest market shares in their respective areas. The fourth major top-fermenting style is *Berliner Weisse*, which is actually a mixed fermentation of top-fermenting yeast and acid-producing *Lactobacillus* bacteria. Unlike lager beer that can only be brewed with malted barley, any malted grain is permitted under German law in producing top-fermenting beers. While wheat is by far the most common, specialty beers may include rye (*Roggenbier*) or an heirloom grain related to wheat—emmer (*Emmerbier*) or spelt (*Dinkelbier*). While Bavarian wheat beers retained distinctly estery and phenolic yeast strains that are typically fermented at high British and Belgian ale temperatures, the *Kölsch* and *Alt* styles gravitated to lower lagerlike fermentation temperatures and conditioning to produce a clean, mellow character.

Bavarian *Weizen* (Bavarian Wheat Beer)

When the *Reinheitsgebot* became law in Bavaria in 1516, it allowed only barley malt in brewing bottom-fermenting lagers; however, the use of malted wheat in top-fermenting ales continued. At the time of its enactment, the *Reinheitsgebot* served other purposes besides setting quality standards for brewers. It also codified beer prices and taxation, and some historians believe that the exclusion of malted wheat was not because it was an inferior ingredient but to employ it principally for breadmaking to avert hunger. In fact, the Degenberger family had been brewing wheat beer in Bavaria under royal authority since the late 1400s, and they refused to give up this feudal right after 1516. In 1602, when the last male Degenberger died without an heir, the right to brew wheat beer reverted back to the ruling Wittelsbacher family, who did not stop production but took full advantage of their profitable monopoly by opening a series of royal wheat beer breweries throughout Bavaria, including a *Weisses Bräuhaus* on the current location of the *Hofbräuhaus* in Munich.

However, wheat beer lost favor to lager beers by the mid-1800s, and in 1856, the lease on the *Weisses Bräuhaus* became available. Due to falling demand, the royal family was willing to transfer control of the wheat beer brewery to George Schneider. However, in 1872, the royal family wanted to regain control of the old *Weisses Bräuhaus* to expand their more-profitable brown lager brewery next door. Schneider agreed to return the brewery but under the condition that wheat beer brewing would become the right of any commercial brewer.

Commercial brewing of wheat beer continued after 1872 but production declined, falling to only 100,000 hectoliters in 1951, or a mere 1% of beer sales in Bavaria. Wheat beer appeared close to extinction, but the tide turned and consumers returned to the hazy, unfiltered, bottle-conditioned wheat beer that harkened back to more-traditional brewing techniques. Slowly the popularity of wheat beer grew until it roared back in the 1980s, eventually increasing to one-third of the Bavarian beer market after the turn of the twenty-first century.

Unfiltered wheat beer is turbid from the high level of wheat protein that binds with tannins to form haze. Another source of turbidity is the yeast necessary for the secondary fermentation in bottle conditioning. Wheat beer contains significantly more carbonation than lagers. Protein is foam positive, so when the abundant wheat protein combines with generous carbonation, the result is a thick, long-lasting rocky head.

Bavarian wheat beers are unique in Germany in that their signature yeast strain produces large amounts of fruity esters, spicy phenols, and aromatic alcohols. The flavor impression, especially in pale wheat beers, is dominated by these fermentation by-products. Wheat beer is known for an easily identifiable ester with an aroma of bananas. Another important aroma is the phenolic compound that resembles clove. Other common phenolic flavors are vanilla, nutmeg, and smoke. Hop bitterness and aroma are purposely kept low to avoid competition with these desirable yeast-derived flavors. The resuspended yeast in unfiltered varieties produces a full smoothness that intensifies the bread-like character of the malt. In Germany, wheat beer must contain at least 50% wheat malt, with some examples containing as much as 70–75%. Wheat malt contains no husk, and since malt husks create the filter bed for lautering, the use of wheat malt in percentages greater than 70–75% is impractical.

Hefeweizen

Hefe in German means "yeast" and *Weizen* means "wheat". The combination indicates that the wheat beer has undergone a secondary fermentation in the bottle (*Flaschengärung*) and contains live yeast inside (*mit Hefe*). *Hefeweizen* is also referred to as simply *Weizen* or *Weissbier*. *Weiss* in German means "white", so *Weissbier* means literally "white beer". While *Hefeweizen* is far from white, this term may go back to a time when the common beer in Bavaria was a brown lager that made the paler wheat beers look white in comparison. Also, simply the closeness in sound of *Weizen* und *Weiss* may have brought about the interchangeable usage.

Hefeweizen is the most popular style of Bavarian wheat beer. The beer is spritzy, effervescent, well attenuated, and low in bitterness, which makes it easy drinking, thirst quenching, and refreshing. For these reasons, it is a popular summer drink. But *Hefeweizen* is by no means a session beer to be enjoyed only in warm weather. This is a nutritious beer, often weighing in at 13°Plato, that still fortifies laborers on their midmorning break in Bavaria. It is also the beer that accompanies a traditional Bavarian breakfast of *Weisswurst und Brez'n* ("white sausage" and a Bavarian "pretzel").

Protein and yeast form a prominent turbid haze. Color ranges from yellow to gold, with some examples having even a darker reddish hue. *Weissbier* is well attenuated yet is not thin bodied due to the resuspended yeast and protein that build a soft mouthfeel and breadlike maltiness. High carbonation produces a spritzy effervescence and creamy head. Hop bitterness is low, so the fermentation-driven esters and phenols take center stage. Phenols contribute flavors of clove, nutmeg, smoke, and vanilla. The dominant ester provides an aroma of banana, bubble gum, or candy circus peanuts. The yeast sediment is typically roused when pouring.

Examples: Weihenstephaner Hefe Weissbier, Schneider Weisse Weizen Hell, Paulaner Hefe-Weizen, Hacker-Pschorr Weisse, Plank Bavarian Hefeweizen, Ayinger Bräu-Weisse, Dry Dock U-Boat Hefeweizen.

Kristall Weizen

Kristall Weizen is a clear, nonturbid, filtered version of *Hefeweizen*. It lacks the full mouthfeel and bready malt character of *Hefeweizen* because yeast and insoluble protein particles have been filtered out. In all other characteristics, the beer is similar to *Hefeweizen*.

Examples: Weihenstephaner Kristall Weissbier, Franziskaner Weissbier (Kristallklar), Tucher Kristall Weizen, Erdinger Weissbier Kristallklar.

Dunkelweizen

Dunkelweizen is brewed and fermented in a fashion similar to that of *Hefeweizen* but with the addition of amber Munich and caramel malts that produce a deep copper to brown color. Its flavor includes the same characteristic banana esters and clove, nutmeg, smoke, and vanilla phenols as does pale *Hefeweizen*, but these flavors are experienced differently because of the caramel and cocoa flavors from the darker specialty malts. The beer is turbid, bottle conditioned, highly carbonated, and served in the same manner as *Hefeweizen*.

Examples: Weihenstephaner Hefeweissbier Dunkel, Ayinger Ur-Weisse, Franziskaner Dunkel Hefe-Weisse, Schneider Weisse Original, Hacker-Pschorr Weisse Dark, Tucher Dunkles Hefe Weizen, Edelweiss Weissbier Dunkel, Erdinger Weissbier Dunkel, Kapuziner Weissbier Schwarz.

Weizenbock

Weizenbock or "wheat bock" is wheat beer's version of the bock style borrowed from the lager family. It is often a seasonal beer, appearing at Christmas or during Lent. The Schneider brewery's Aventinus *Weizenbock* (18.5°Plato) first produced in 1907 is credited as the first wheat beer to be marketed as a *Weizenbock*. Although pale versions exist (e.g., Weihenstephaner Vitus), *Weizenbock* is typically dark copper to brown and similar to *Dunkelweizen* in design but with a higher original gravity, which creates an elevated level of alcohol and a caramel malty sweetness. The higher starting gravity can also cause a higher level of fruity esters and fusel alcohols that may express themselves as rum or brandylike flavor notes. *Weizenbock* is unfiltered and turbid from protein haze and yeast. The expected yeast flavors of banana, nutmeg, smoke, and vanilla remain along with caramel and cocoa flavors from the dark specialty malts. Pale versions also have residual sweetness but with a rich bready maltiness instead of caramel.

Examples: Schneider Aventinus, Schneider Aventinus Weizen Eisbock, Plank Bavarian Dunkler Weizenbock, Plank Bavarian Heller Weizenbock, Erdinger Pikantus.

	Bitterness (IBU)	Alcohol (% ABV)	Color (SRM)
Hefeweizen	10–20	4.9–5.5	3–6 (yellow to gold)
Kristall Weizen	10–16	4.9–5.5	3–6 (yellow to gold)
Dunkelweizen	10–16	4.8–5.4	17–26 (light brown to dark brown)
Weizenbock	10–18	6.9–9.4	17–26 (light brown to dark brown)

Rye Beer

Bavarian rye beer, or *Roggenbier*, is brewed in the same manner as is *Weizen* (hazy, unfiltered, highly carbonated), using the same estery-phenolic yeast strains but substituting rye malt for the wheat malt. The color is usually a hazy dark reddish orange or reddish copper. Rye, like wheat, is huskless, high in protein, and mostly used in breadmaking rather than in brewing. Rye malt has a more-assertive flavor, sometimes described as spicy, compared with that of wheat malt. Rye is not grown specifically as a malting variety, so commercial examples of rye beer are not common, and rye is still often associated with artisanal or indigenous styles, such as *Kvass*, a Russian rye beer. American versions of rye beer may follow a variety of styles using various yeast strains, hops, and malted or unmalted rye.

German Examples: Paulaner Roggen (formerly Thurn und Taxis, no longer imported into the United States), Bürgerbräu Wolnzacher Roggenbier.

American Examples: Founders Red's Rye, Redhook Sunrye, Real Ale Full Moon Pale Rye Ale.

	Bitterness (IBU)	Alcohol (% ABV)	Color (SRM)
Bavarian *Roggenbier*[a]	10–20	4.5–6.0	17–22 (light brown to brown)
American rye beer	10–35	4.9–5.5	3–7 (straw to light amber)

[a] Beer Judge Certification Program (BJCP) style guidelines.

Other German Ales

Germany is widely known for its lagers and wheat ales, but several other important ale styles are produced in Germany. *Kölsch* from the city of Cologne (*Köln*), and *Alt* from the city of Düsseldorf are two top-fermenting beers from two northern cities that elected to hold onto the old tradition of brewing ales, albeit employing cooler fermentation and cellaring conditions then do the English and Belgians. While these two cities share a close geographical proximity and cling proudly to the old tradition of brewing ales, the two styles are distinctively different and patriotically championed within their respective cities.

Kölsch

Cologne is an ancient Roman city that grew into a major mercantile center as part of the Hanseatic League of free cities in the Middle Ages. Since a free city was granted considerable independence from the feudal laws of the time,

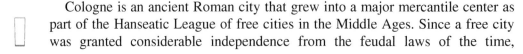

Cologne thrived along with its sister cities in the league as centers of commerce, including the brewing and exporting of beer. Free enterprise and market competition helped brewers in Cologne and other northern cities surpass their southern German neighbors in the quality of their beer (see Bock above). In fact, to retain its brewing identity, the city of Cologne actually forbade the brewing of bottom-fermenting beer in 1603 in response to the *Reinheitsgebot*, which established the dominance of bottom-fermenting beer in Bavaria. Almost 350 years later, Cologne brewers would again establish by law their unique identity as top-fermenting beer brewers with the *Kölsch Konvention*.

The spread of pale lager brewing also reached Cologne in the nineteenth century. While lager beer grew in popularity, the brewers of top-fermenting beer did not totally abandon their traditional brewing but rather modified it to create a new type of beer. Probably in recognition of the popularity of the clean, refreshing, bitter *Pils*, certain top-fermenting beer producers began using pilsner malt, fermenting at the lowest temperature limits (e.g., 60°F/16°C) to produce a less fruity taste and finishing the beer with a long, cold maturation period. Essentially, Cologne began producing *Pils* but with top-fermenting yeast, which they named *Kölsch*, after the city where it was brewed. *Kölsch* is also the name of the local Low German dialect, making it the only language that can be both spoken and enjoyed!

Nevertheless, *Pils* became the dominant beer style in Cologne after World War II. In 1948, an association of local breweries created a formal agreement called the *Kölsch Konvention* to preserve their local beer style and protect it from outside imitators and even against local producers that switched to bottom-fermenting yeast. The main tenant of the agreement states,

> "The designation '*Kölsch*' may only be used for pale, highly attenuated, hop-emphasized, top-fermented '*Vollbier*' (i.e., 11–14% extract) that is produced according to the *Reinheitsgebot* within the *Kölsch* area of origination."

Their efforts proved highly successful since *Kölsch* overtook *Pils* in popularity in Cologne, and in 1986, the German government adopted the *Kölsch Konvention* as federal law, giving legal status to the *Kölsch* name. This meant that only the two dozen or so member breweries in and around Cologne could call their beer *Kölsch*, thus creating an *Appellation d'Origine Contrôlée*. In 1997, the European Union also recognized this same appellation. Therefore, in the European Union, only sparkling wine from the Champagne region of France can be called champagne and only pale, top-fermenting beer brewed in Cologne can be called *Kölsch*.

Kölsch is a very pale, refreshing beer with distinct noble hop bitterness. The beer resembles *Pils* in many ways but may have a hint of fruitiness to indicate that it is still an ale. Because it is top fermented, other malts besides barley are permissible ingredients, and on occasion, some brewers may include up to approximately 15% pale wheat malt in the grist. Authentic German examples are not widely available in the United States, but craft brewers frequently offer the style for their customers who prefer light golden lagers. Although not legally required to recognize the *Kölsch* appellation in the United States, respectful brewers label these beers "*Kölsch*-style" beer to indicate it was not brewed in Cologne.

Examples: Reissdorf Kölsch, Gaffel Kölsch, Früh Kölsch, Küppers Kölsch, Sünner Kölsch.

Alt

Alt in German means "old" in reference to the older tradition of brewing with top-fermenting yeast. The city most associated with *Altbier* is Düsseldorf in northern Germany, a mere 45 kilometers north of Cologne. Like *Kölsch*, *Alt* brewers use low fermentation temperatures and long, cold-conditioning times to mellow their brews, but unlike their brothers in Cologne, they did not embrace the new pale malt but instead retained the traditional copper color through the use of Munich and caramel malts. A small portion of wheat malt may also make up part of the grist.

Both Cologne and Düsseldorf have lively pub cultures that include serving *Kölsch* and *Alt* in a narrow, straight-side glass called a *Stange* ("pole"). *Kölsch* glasses are a mere 20 centiliters (~6.75 ounces), which the waiter brings to the table in a special tray carried by a handle. If the waiter sees an empty glass, he simply replaces it with a full one until the patron says stop. The old section of Düsseldorf is known as the *Altstadt* or "old city", which hosts a dense number of pubs in the radius of a few blocks. *Alt* is served in similar fashion, but the *Düsseldorfer Stange* is a bit larger than the *Kölsch Stange*.

Although the cities are close neighbors that share a passion for preserving an old tradition of brewing, they are quite protective of their individual interpretations of ale. Cologne is proud of the clean, refreshing character of their pale *Kölsch* with its subtle nuances, while Düsseldorf views *Kölsch* as just an imitator of the ubiquitous *Pils*, with only the amber *Alt* and its assertive bitterness representing a true example of the old brewing traditions.

Alt is copper to brown with rich, toasted caramel malt flavor from the use of Munich malt. It has a firm bitterness but with little or no hop aroma. The body is medium in mouthfeel with a clean, well-attenuated finish and minimal fruity esters that may be found in other ales. While similar to English pale ale in color and bitterness, it lacks the assertive hop aroma and fermentation esters found in pale ale.

Examples: Diebels Alt, Schlösser Alt, Frankenheim Alt, Uerige Alt, Füchschen Alt, Schumacher Alt, Original Schlüssel, Dry Dock Bismarck Alt.

	Bitterness (IBU)	Alcohol (% ABV)	Color (SRM)
Kölsch	20–32	4.8–5.3	3–5 (straw to light gold)
Alt	25–45	4.5–5.0	14–20 (copper to brown)

Berliner Weisse

Berliner Weisse is Germany's version of sour ale, but the fermentation of *Berliner Weisse* is not "wild" as found with some Belgian interpretations. Rather, *Berliner Weisse* uses a mixed fermentation of top-fermenting yeast to produce alcohol and a separately propagated culture of *Lactobacillus delbrueckii* to create a clean, controlled lactic sourness. *Berliner Weisse* is named in part because of the pale wheat malt that makes up to 50–70% of the grist and the remainder of pilsner malt, which lend the pale color and white foamy head. *Weiss* means "white" and the naming of *Berliner Weisse* is connected to Bavarian *Hefeweizen* (see *Hefeweizen* above). A very low level of bittering hops is used because the bacteriostatic effect of the hop alpha acids would suppress the work of the *Lactobacillus* bacteria. In fact, in traditional brewing practices, the hops are added to a decocted mash to reduce the contribution of the alpha acids and the wort was not boiled but only heated to near boiling.

Berliner Weisse is pale, unfiltered, unpasteurized, bottle conditioned, highly carbonated, low in alcohol, dry, tart, and fruity. The beer can be kept for years for further character development. Napoleon's forces named it the "Champagne of the North" because it was dry, pale, tart, and effervescent like the sparkling wine from their homeland. It is particularly appreciated as a summer refresher and almost always enjoyed with a straw from a shallow, wide-mouthed goblet with sweet syrup added before serving to balance the tartness. The most popular syrups are red raspberry (*Himbeersirup*) and green woodruff (*Waldmeistersirup*), a sweet vanilla-tasting herb historically found in gruit. In this sense, *Berliner Weisse* is similar to modern sweet fruit lambics but without much of the rustic character from barrel aging and spontaneous fermentation. The *Berliner Weisse* name is also recognized as an appellation in Germany, and any beer not brewed in Berlin must use the name "*Berliner*-style" *Weisse*.

Examples: Schultheiss Berliner Weisse, Berliner Kindl Weisse, Weihenstephaner 1809 Berliner-Style Weisse.

	Bitterness (IBU)	Alcohol (% ABV)	Color (SRM)
Berliner Weisse	5–15	2.5–4.0	3–8 (light yellow to deep gold)

North America

Previous sections reviewing the development of beer styles of Belgium and France; Britain, Scotland, and Ireland; and Germany and continental Europe identified the interconnected web of climate, agriculture, politics, economics, and culture that influenced the development of beer in these areas. While factors specific to each region guided the evolution of beer, these brewing cultures did not exist in isolation and brewing techniques and technology were often exchanged across borders. Because North America is a region settled by immigrants, the brewing traditions that the various ethnic groups brought with them formed the foundation for brewing in the New World. The United States was originally a British colony, and the beers enjoyed by the colonists reflected the influence of British traditions. In the mid-nineteenth century, a massive wave of German-speaking immigrants arrived. They brought with them the taste for lager beer and the knowledge to brew it. This was also an era of giant leaps in brewing innovation, including microbiology, malting, and refrigeration, that made the brewing and marketing of lager beer possible. These converging events made lager the dominant beer style in the United States by the time of Prohibition; these developments were mirrored in Canada and Mexico as well. Any ale brewing traditions that remained were largely destroyed by Prohibition.

This is not to say that local influences did not mold North American beers to a slightly different form than the model found in the mother country. The substitution of North America's native grain, corn (maize), for barley is one of the most influential examples. The fact that North America has always looked to Europe for its brewing inspirations explains why North American brewers, especially those in the United States, proudly copy beer styles from other brewing countries. Large domestic lager brewers have frequently referred to the authentic "German" quality of their beers. The craft beer movement has also triggered a keen interest in rediscovering forgotten styles from other countries. Resurrection in the United States of once popular styles has even awakened new interest in these styles in their land of origin, such as India pale ale and porter in the United Kingdom. The commercial success of American brewers offering a variety of international styles is also drawing the attention of international brewers, who are now experimenting with styles from outside their geographic borders.

While American brewers may have drawn inspiration from other brewing traditions, they have also made large contributions in expanding the limits of traditional styles and thereby adding unique examples to the list of beer styles. Examples include specialty Belgian-style ales, American versions of pale ale, India pale ale, brown ale, stout, and barley wine. The descriptions of the North American beer styles previously described and those that follow display the connection to their European heritage but also highlight the American love of innovation and nonconformity.

North American Lagers

To see the influence of German immigration on North American lager beers, one need only look at the names of major current and past breweries: Anheuser-Busch, Miller, Coors, Pabst, Schlitz, Blatz, Bohemia, and Yuengling. The principle difference in North American lagers was the widespread use of corn in the grist. Corn is a native grain that grew well, was affordable, and was readily available. However, it also worked well with the six-row barley grown in North America, which had higher protein levels and more husk than the traditional two-row European varieties. Brewers used corn grits to dilute the malt protein and the excess barley husks; the filterability of the mash was maintained when using the huskless corn. The corn (and rice) also reduced the color of the beer and lightened the body, which over time became attributes that consumers of North American lagers highly prized. For descriptions of related styles, including malt liquor, ice beer, and low-carbohydrate beer, see Chapter 2.

American Standard Lager

American standard lager is based on Old World pilsners with approximately 5% ABV, but it is brewed with a lighter color and body and a much lower level of bitterness and very little or no hop aroma. Evidence exists that pre-Prohibition examples may have more closely reflected the character of their European cousins but became lighter in character to reflect changing consumer tastes. These beers are typically light to medium bodied with a clean, crisp malt character that may in some examples present hints of sweetness or graininess and slight notes of fruity esters. American standard lagers are well carbonated and, when enjoyed at the customary low temperature, may end with a dry finish from the dissolved carbon dioxide in spite of the low level of bitterness. These beers are brewed to be light and refreshing.

Examples: Budweiser, Miller High Life, Coors Banquet, Pabst, Schlitz, Busch.

American Light Lager

American light lager was developed in North America initially as a diet beer and is typically a version of the breweries' American standard lager but with lower calories, alcohol by volume, body, bitterness, and malt character.

Examples: Bud Light, Miller Lite, Coors Light, Keystone Light, Busch Light.

	Bitterness (IBU)	Alcohol (% ABV)	Color (SRM)
American standard lager	7–15	4.0–5.0	2–4 (light yellow to yellow)
American light lager	5–15	3.5–4.4	2–3 (light yellow to yellow)

North American Ales

America has a history of brewing ales that goes back to early colonial times; however, the strong demand for lager beer forced many ale brewers to convert to lager and others to close with the start of Prohibition in 1920. With the end of the great American experiment, the number of ale breweries to reopen in 1933 was even smaller. Continued pressure from the popularity of lager beer and consolidation in the brewing industry caused the number of small ale and lager breweries to contract. By the latter half of the twentieth century, only a few styles of ale were brewed and only a few with truly American origins, most notably steam beer (California common) and cream ale.

California Common

California common was born in California in the late nineteenth century more out of necessity than by design. Brewers of lager beer had no access to ice on the temperate West Coast to ferment and condition their beer properly. So, they simply pitched lager yeast at ambient temperatures more compatible with ale fermentation. To mitigate the lack of refrigeration, brewers employed shallow-pan fermenters that helped dissipate the heat of fermentation. The beer fermented rapidly and was often racked into barrels before the beer fully attenuated. The remaining extract fermented in the cask, creating an uncommonly high level of carbon dioxide pressure. When the cask was tapped, the violent escape of carbon dioxide was said to resemble steam, and the beer became known as steam beer (at least this is one plausible origin of the name, but others also exist). By the 1960s, only one steam beer brewery was left—Anchor Brewing Company in San Francisco. When it was near closure in 1965, Fritz Maytag bought ownership in the brewery and was successful in saving it. In 1981, Anchor Brewing Company trademarked the name Steam Beer when competitors began copying the style and name. Other beers of this style are now called California common.

California common is an amber-colored, medium-bodied beer with low to medium fruity esters, toasty and caramel malt flavors, and medium to firm hop bitterness and flavor. It is stylistically similar to an American pale ale but lacks the citrus hop character because of the use of European hop varieties, such as Northern Brewer, as opposed to resinous and citrus American hops, such as Cascade.

Examples: Anchor Steam Beer, Southampton Steam Beer, Flying Dog Old Scratch Amber Lager.

Cream Ale

Cream ale was developed by brewers who wanted a light, pale, refreshing ale that could satisfy the taste of the increasing number of lager beer drinkers. At one time, it was also referred to as sparkling ale. In fact, cream ale is brewed in much the same way as an American standard lager with pale malt, adjuncts, low bitterness, and a refreshing finish, except with a clean-tasting, top-fermenting yeast. The similarities between cream ale and American standard lager are evidenced by the fact that some brewers use lager yeast in their version of the style.

Examples: Genesee Cream Ale, Hudepohl-Schoenling Little Kings Cream Ale, Anderson Valley Summer Solstice Cerveza Crema, Sleeman Cream Ale, New Glarus Spotted Cow, Wisconsin Brewing Whitetail Cream Ale, Pelican Kiwanda Cream Ale.

American *Hefeweizen*

American *Hefeweizen* is usually a pale beer with a mild malt flavor from pale barley malt and malted or unmalted wheat. It has modest bitterness and little or no hop aroma. It is unfiltered to cast a pale haze. Many examples are also bottled conditioned, in which case the brewer may call it a *Hefeweizen* in reference to Bavarian *Hefeweizen* of similar appearance. However, the American versions are fermented with English-style ale yeast, which lacks the distinct banana and clove flavors of the Bavarian version. American wheat beer is a newer style created by craft brewers who wanted an easy-drinking offering in their line of beers or were looking for a style of *Hefeweizen* that could be fermented without adding a second yeast strain to their standard house ale yeast. American wheat beer may also include spices, such as in Belgian *wit*, or become the base for beers with added fruit. These beers are often served with a slice of lemon, perhaps to mimic the citrus flavors in Belgian *wit* or the fruity esters of Bavarian *Hefeweizen*.

Examples: Boulevard Unfiltered Wheat Beer, Harpoon UFO Hefeweizen, Pyramid Hefeweizen, Widmer Hefeweizen, Goose Island 312 Urban Wheat Ale, Sierra Nevada Unfiltered Wheat Beer, Anchor Summer Beer.

	Bitterness (IBU)	Alcohol (% ABV)	Color (SRM)
California common	35–45	4.0–5.4	12–18 (reddish amber to medium brown)
Cream ale	7–22	4.2–5.6	2–7 (light yellow to deep gold)
American *Hefeweizen*	10–35	3.8–5.6	3–14 (yellow to copper)

Other American Styles

The following American styles are described in previous sections of this chapter.
- American India pale ale
- Double/imperial India pale ale
- American brown ale
- American stout
- American barley wine

Acknowledgment

The drawings of the glassware appropriate for each style of beer are courtesy of Rastal GmbH & Co. KG.

Chapter 4:
Beer Freshness

Bill White

Brewers go to great lengths to brew beer with consistent flavor and quality from batch to batch. Furthermore, the brewing industry has for centuries researched and tested new methods and technologies to improve quality, maintain consistency, and protect freshness. Within the last 150 years, brewers have extended the shelf life of packaged beer to limits unimaginable to their predecessors. Although its freshness limits have been extended, beer is still a perishable food product that is meant to be consumed soon after leaving the brewery. Except for certain high-alcohol beers that are similar to wine in character, the quality of beer progressively deteriorates after it leaves the brewery. The farther it travels, the more it is handled, and the longer the time until it is consumed, the greater the risk to freshness and quality. The brewer can only do so much to protect beer freshness. Ultimately, it is the responsibility of the distributor, truck driver, retailer, tavern owner, and server to maintain the quality of the beer until it is served to the consumer.

Because beer is affordable, widely available, and consistent in its flavor and quality, many consumers wrongly assume that it must be produced with highly processed ingredients and preservatives like many other modern foods and beverages. To the contrary, it is very rare for beer to contain any added preservatives. The brewer's diligence in maintaining highly sanitary conditions in the brewery preserves the flavor of beer, although some brewers may also use pasteurization or sterile filtration to extend the beer's shelf life. Wine in its modern form could not exist without the extensive use of added sulfites to prevent the oxidative browning of the fruit and the actions of wild yeast and bacteria that could sour wine. Because some consumers are allergic to sulfites, both beer and wine labels must indicate whether the level of sulfites added and naturally occurring exceeds 10 parts per million (ppm). However, the content of naturally occurring sulfites in beer is beneath this threshold. Brewers do not need sulfites to control microbiological flora, because unlike wine must, brewer's wort is sanitized by boiling.

Chapter 1 documents the consolidation of breweries in the United States during the late nineteenth and twentieth centuries. The result was the sale of only a few brands of beer by a small number of national breweries. Although consumers had a limited choice of brands, the small number of brands helped ensure rapid turnover of the product, which meant fresh beer was usually available on tap or in the store. During the 1980s, the number of import brands increased and microbreweries started producing a wider selection of specialty beers. Soon retailers who previously carried five or six brands carried dozens, which meant the beer turned over at a slower rate, with some beers being stored beyond their freshness limits.

This chapter outlines the conditions and retail practices that put beer freshness at risk and provides methods for wholesalers and retailers to deliver the freshest beer possible to consumers.

Beer Is Food!

The most important principle of beer freshness is the realization that beer is a food. Outside influences that accelerate the deterioration of freshness in most foods, such as storage time, temperature, exposure to oxygen, exposure to light, and rough handling, have the same deleterious effects on beer. Therefore, what's good for food freshness is usually good for beer freshness.

A good mnemonic device for the proper handling of beer is the "Four Ts".

- Time
- Temperature
- Turbulence
- Twilight

For the wholesaler, retailer, and consumer, diminished freshness is primarily caused by oxidation, which results in stale flavors, or by microbial contamination from wild yeast or other microbes, which produces off-flavors. Limiting beer's exposure to time, temperature, turbulence, and light slows the freshness-robbing effects of oxygen and spoilage microbes.

Shelf life is defined as the average number of days at 70°F (21°C) that a beer retains an acceptable flavor profile. Brewers determine shelf life for each of their beers by taste analysis. To perform a shelf life taste, analysis brewers collect several cans or bottles of a beer that were filled on the same date. These samples are then stored at 70°F (21°C). At progressive time intervals, a sample from the stored beer is taste evaluated against a fresh sample of the same beer in a similar package. Once the stored beer's taste is judged to be out of character, the length of time taken to get there is established as the beer's shelf life. For example, a tasting panel may taste a different bottle at weekly intervals until one of the bottles tastes stale (out of character). This process is completed several times, and the average number of days from the packaging date to when the flavor change is detected becomes the shelf life.

Time

For the vast majority of beer, its flavor is at its peak when it leaves the brewery and only deteriorates from that point forward. The less time beer spends in transit and storage, the less time oxygen and microbes have to deteriorate the freshness of beer. Brewers go to great lengths to protect beer from oxygen absorption and the introduction of unwanted microbes during all parts of the brewing process, including packaging. It is also important that oxygen intrusion into the sealed package (i.e., bottle, can, or keg) be controlled. But, no matter how diligent they are, even a few parts per million of oxygen picked up when filling eventually causes staling. As flavors in beer oxidize, they may first lose flavor intensity and vibrancy, then become dull, and finally taste and smell like cardboard. This is especially true for beers of normal or moderate alcohol content.

There are exceptions to every rule, and some beer drinkers, like wine drinkers, appreciate the effects of controlled oxidation in beer. Bold tannic wines are often decanted and allowed to sit exposed to the air before serving so they can "breath". The oxygen they absorb is actually softening the astringent tannins to make them more palatable. This same effect occurs in barrel aging and when bottles of wine are cellared, since both containers have some oxygen entrained in them during the filling process. Bold tannic beers, especially those made from dark-roasted malts, may also soften from extended aging in the bottle. Oxidation also changes alcohols into aldehydes, which impart the signature flavor in intentionally oxidized wines, such as sherry or port. Strong barley wines, imperial stouts, and Belgian ales are sometimes cellared for years to allow the slow, controlled oxidation and maturation that produce these desired flavors. Barley wine is often a specialty beer produced once each year, and brewers may provide a date or vintage on the bottle for those consumers who annually buy their barley wines and cellar them. A popular way to drink these cellared beers is in a vertical tasting, in which different years or vintages of the same brand are consumed side by side to experience the flavor changes produced by aging.

Sizing the Beer Inventory and Number of Brands to the Level of Sales

Retailers should not stock more beer than they can sell within the limits of each beer's freshness expiration date. Stocking large inventories may reduce ordering costs and displaying beer on fully stocked shelves may present an appealing image to the consumer, but if the inventory is too large to turn over within each beer's freshness limit, the consumer receives damaged beer. If retailers choose marketing impact over freshness and chooses to sell stale beer from overstocked shelves rather than dump it, they may save the short-term cost of dumping stale beer, but they run the long-term risk of losing repeat customers who reject the stale beer.

First In First Out (FIFO)

FIFO means that the first beer received is the first beer shipped or sold. This principle applies in the warehouse, on the retail shelf, and at the on-premise establishment. It is best to rotate stock upon arrival. If there isn't time to rotate stock when a new shipment arrives, there is even less time later on. Furthermore, if the oldest stock is the easiest to get at, it goes a long way toward ensuring that the oldest stock is the first to go. Shelves that can be stocked from the back with the oldest product pushed to the front work well. Otherwise, for front-loading shelves, stockers must remove the existing product and place the new product to the rear.

The FIFO principle is also important in designing displays. If the display is a tall pyramid with a base six to seven cases deep, it is difficult to get at the older stock in the bottom middle. Likewise, beer placed under displays of promotional material is equally less likely to be rotated because of a reluctance to disturb the elaborate display above. Remember, even the best point-of-sale displays are for naught if the poor quality of the beer prevents repeat sales.

Beer Dating

Generally, all bottles, cans, kegs, and cartons are date coded. Breweries and their representatives use these codes to ensure that fresh beer is maintained in the market.

These codes should be checked on a regular basis to verify freshness and facilitate stock rotation. If the beer is not fresh, the distributor should be consulted regarding how to handle the situation. Code dates should be checked when the beer is received. If the beer is delivered outside of the acceptable code date, then the delivery should be refused.

Beer dating is coded in a variety of methods. Labels on bottles may be notched or etched by laser. Inkjet coders are generally used to date bottles, cans, crowns, cartons, and kegs. Coding can take the form of a best-before date or a packaging date. Retailers must know the breweries' recommended shelf life and how to read the codes, which are not always easy to decipher. Different brands and styles may have different recommended shelf lives, which may vary from a few weeks to several years, depending on the style, package, or storage conditions. If the method of date coding is not decipherable, the retailer should contact the supplier or brewery. If the retailer cannot obtain the recommended shelf life from the supplier or brewer, a maximum shelf life of 120 days after packaging is a good rule of thumb.

Examples of Beer Codes in the Industry

The easiest code to understand is a best-before, use-by, or expiry date, which clearly states the day, month, and year by which the brewery recommends the beer should be consumed. The disadvantage to this method is the inability to discern the age of the beer and whether the expiration date is reasonable. Other common codes may indicate the packaging date, also known as the born-on date (Fig. 4.1). Some codes are intended only for internal use at the brewery to monitor inventory, facilitate stock rotation, or trace and recall defective product (Fig. 4.2).

Figure 4.1. Many breweries use a simple-to-read calendar packaging date. (Courtesy K. Ockert)

Figure 4.2. Some breweries use more complicated packaging markings that provide a coded packaging date, location, machine number, etc. (Courtesy K. Ockert)

The following are examples of date coding methods.

Best-Before or Expiry Date

These codes are generally presented in a straightforward format, showing either the month and year or the day, month, and year. The code may consist of numbers only or show the month in letters followed by numerals for the day and year. The following are examples of codes for an expiry date of November 14, 2010.

- 11/10 or 1110
- 14/11/10 (Europeans may also use the format dd-mm-yy)
- Nov 14/10

Born-On or Packaging Date

Born-on dating describes the filling date of the bottle, can, or keg. For small breweries, the date may simply show the day, month, and year. For larger breweries, especially ones with more than one production facility, it is common to show the day, month, year, plant, line, and time of packaging. This allows traceability of a package back to a particular tank or brew number. While this level of detail is helpful to the brewery management, the complex formats can make interpretation by the retailer difficult. Furthermore, packaging dates give no indication of the suggested shelf life of the beer.

- m-dd-yy-st—This code states the month, day, year, and state where the beer was packaged. The month is represented by a letter. The letter is assigned in alphabetical order and corresponds to the number of the month, 1–12. Therefore, A = January, B = February, C = March, etc., and ending with M for December. The letter "I" is not used to avoid confusion with the number "1". The day and year are represented with two digits each and the state is represented by its U.S. Post Office abbreviation. The code M0706DE represents December 7, 2006, Delaware.
- m-dd-y-city-line hh:mm—This code is similar to the first one, but it contains more information and the year is designated with one digit, not two. The first letter relates to the month, as described above. The next two digits indicate the day of the month. The next number represents the last digit of the year. The information after the date is not important to the retailer for freshness dating but is useful to the brewer for internal purposes, as noted above. The letter following the year indicates the brewery, usually by the first letter of the state or city where it is located. The next number might indicate the bottling line, and the final four numbers show the time, in hours and minutes, that the package was coded on its way to the filling machine. Putting it all together, K146M2 11:42 might mean that the beer was bottled on October 14, 2006 in Montreal on line 2 at 11:42 am. Sometimes, the time of day can be coded as a single letter indicating the 24 hours in a day with the first 24 letters of the alphabet but not using "I" and "O", since they can be mistaken for the numbers "1" and "0".
- Lot-ddd-y—This is the Julian code commonly used in Europe, which indicates the day of the year and the year the beer was produced on. The "L" simply means that this particular number is a lot number. The first three numbers are the day of the year. In other words, January 1 equals 001 and December 31 equals 365. The code L2049 would mean July 23, 2009. In a leap year with an extra day in February, the date would be July 22. Extra letters or numbers can also be added to indicate the line of production or plant, etc.

Some breweries double code, using both a best-before and a packaging date code on the same package. A keg, for example, may have the best-before date code printed on the top of the keg, while the packaging details are printed on the bottom.

Temperature

Heat punishes beer by accelerating the loss of freshness caused by oxidation and microbial contamination, if there is any. Each packaged beer has a different rate of oxidation based on several factors, especially the amount of air uptake when filled. Tests conducted on a typical American standard lager showed virtually no oxidative aging when stored at 32°F (0°C). After 112 days at 68°F (20°C), the beer exceeded its acceptable oxidation limit. However, in just 10 days at 104°F (40°C), the beer reached the same oxidation level as it did after 112 days at 68°F (20°C) (Fig. 4.3). For this reason, if beer is shipped in unrefrigerated railcars or trucks during the summer, the freshness of the beer may be more extensively oxidized than the same beer shipped during the winter. Spoilage microbes also multiply more rapidly in high temperatures than in low temperatures. Beer, like other foods, remains fresh longer in the refrigerator than on the pantry shelf. Increasing the amount of heat or increasing the time of exposure increases the rate of freshness deterioration.

For brewers who pasteurize their beer, the balance between oxidative staling and microbial stability is always a compromise. The longer the bottle or can is heated and the higher the heat, the more effective pasteurization is at killing microbes in the beer. However, too much time and heat magnify the effects of staling oxidation. When us-

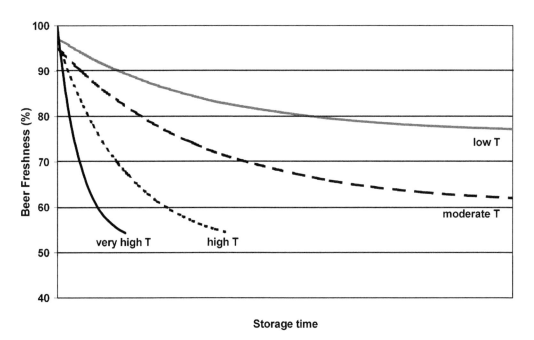

Figure 4.3. Beer freshness decreases very rapidly in warmer storage conditions than in cooler storage conditions. Shelf life is determined at a moderate storage temperature, i.e., 70°F (21°C). T = temperature. (Reprinted from Huige, 2004)

ing pasteurization, brewers must balance the need to protect beer from microbial spoilage with the goal to deliver fresh-tasting beer to consumers. Because exported beer may spend a longer time in transit and experience more severe environmental conditions along the way than a beer shipped and enjoyed locally, beer brewed for export or distant shipment tends to be more frequently and highly pasteurized than local beer.

The freshness and stability of beer is best preserved by shipping and storing beer as cold as possible. Distributors concerned about freshness store, transport, and deliver their beer refrigerated. When a retailer receives a shipment, it is best to place the beer directly in the cooler. Beer displayed inside a cooler stays fresher longer than beer stocked on the floor. For this reason, the amount of beer displayed outside the cooler should be kept at a minimum and restocked frequently.

Some consumers may ask for room-temperature beer because they cannot store it immediately in a refrigerator at home. There is a common belief that beer is damaged by letting it warm up, but this is a false assumption. Haze particles in beer are less soluble at low temperatures. This haze, known as chill haze, can occur when the beer is chilled and disappear when it warms; however, repeated cycling of the temperature can eventually cause the chill haze to become permanent. The haze affects appearance but not flavor. Beer oxidation is accumulative (Huige, 2004, p. 14). This means that beer stored for 1 month at 32°F (0°C) followed by 1 month at 68°F (20°C) incurs the same amount of oxidation as when stored at 68°F (20°C) for 1 month followed by 1 month at 32°F (0°C). It is always best to keep beer as cold as possible (without freezing) for as long as possible, even if it goes through several cycles of cooling and warming (Fig. 4.4).

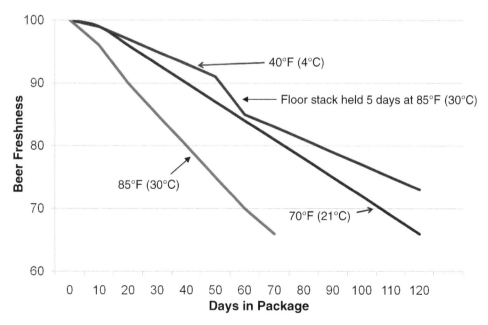

Figure 4.4. Temperature cycling between warm conditions and refrigerated conditions affects shelf life adversely only during the warm storage period. Beer kept in floor stacks should be re-refrigerated to help extend its shelf life. (Courtesy S. Presley)

Turbulence

Agitation also accelerates the staling effects of oxygen. Therefore, a case of warm beer in the trunk of a car going down a bumpy road on a hot summer afternoon is getting a double dose of accelerated oxidation from the turbulence and temperature.

Turbulence can also cause physical damage to the bottle, can, or keg, resulting in loss of carbonation, air intrusion, or biological contamination. For this reason, the physical integrity of each shipment should be verified before acceptance. Check for off-odors, carton damage, and evidence of abuse, leakage, or breakage. Inspect the date codes to ensure that the beer is fresh and the waybill to ensure that the contents are the same as what was ordered.

Anyone who has opened a warm can of beer knows that it foams excessively. For this reason, newly delivered kegs should be placed in the cooler for 24 hours before being tapped to make sure that they cool to the correct serving temperature and the contents have had time to settle down after bumping along on a truck and handcart.

Twilight

Light is damaging to beer because it produces a photochemical reaction that creates a skunky aroma in beer. Ultraviolet light from natural sunlight or fluorescent bulbs contains a specific wavelength that alters hop alpha acids and releases free radicals that react with the sulfur compounds in beer to produce a skunky aroma, which is also referred to in the brewing industry as light struck.

Beer in cans and kegs is completely protected from becoming light struck, but once poured into a clear glass, sunlight can produce this skunky aroma in a matter of minutes. Artificial lighting is of insufficient intensity to produce the light-struck character in the time it takes to drink a beer in a pub, but prolonged exposure to fluorescent light on a retail shelf or display case can produce a change. Moreover, beer poured into a glass in an outdoor beer garden is almost immediately at risk of going skunky. For this reason, the majority of beer packaged in bottles is done in brown glass, because it helps shield the beer from ultraviolet light. However, brown glass is not a perfect filter, and beer can become light struck given enough exposure time. Green bottles provide some protection, but far less than brown, with clear glass providing no protection. Because European brewers frequently package their premium brands (especially pilsners) in green bottles, care must be taken to store them in a dark place to prevent the beer from becoming light struck. For this reason, some brewers bottling in clear glass may use a specially modified hop product that does not become light struck. Some clear glass bottles may also have ultraviolet screening. Because retailers and consumers cannot know which clear bottles have been protected by either method, it is always advisable to store all bottled beer in the dark.

One can easily experience the light-struck effect by pouring a beer from any container into a glass and placing it in the sun and then comparing the light-exposed beer to one that has been kept in the dark. For this test to be successful, the beer being tested must not have been light struck during transport or storage prior to purchase. For beer in clear or green bottles especially, the beer must not be taken from lighted display cases, but should ideally be taken from unopened cardboard cartons that completely exclude light.

Tips to Avoid Light-Struck Beer
- Avoid light completely
  - Do not unpack bottles from their cardboard cases until they are ready to be consumed or displayed.
  - Never expose green or clear bottles to light, whether on storeroom shelves or in lighted coolers. It is best to act as if any direct exposure to ultraviolet light is too much for green and clear bottles. Brown bottles offer enough protection to allow short exposure to artificial ultraviolet light, but their exposure limits are never precisely known, so caution is always the best rule.
- When total avoidance is not possible
  - Purchase protective sleeves for florescent bulbs that partially filter the specific wavelength that produces skunky beer.
  - Place cans and brown bottles closest to the light and clear and green bottles farthest away.
  - Turn off all unnecessary lights.

Draft Beer Freshness

Draft beer is typically not pasteurized but is kept cold from the time it is filled and tapped. Therefore, it offers the customer an opportunity for a particularly fresh glass of beer, if the challenges of serving draft beer are met by the tavern owner. The challenges include the following.

- Kegs should be stored cold and tapped within 30–60 days.
- Once tapped, the keg should ideally be emptied within 5 days.
- The ideal gas pressure must be applied to the keg to maintain proper carbonation.
- The entire system of faucets and tubing should be cleaned every 2 weeks to avoid off-flavors from microbial contamination.
- The vinyl tubing must be replaced periodically.
- Draft lines must be kept cold from keg to faucet.
- The draft system must be properly balanced to deliver beer to the faucet at an acceptable flow rate without wasting beer through excessive foaming.
- Air should never be used as a counterpressure gas to dispense beer (only carbon dioxide or a carbon dioxide–nitrogen blend), unless the keg or cask will be emptied within a few hours before the contact with the air can cause staling or loss of carbonation.

Miscellaneous Freshness Issues

Marketing vs. Quality

The desire to present beer in a store or restaurant in an attractive, visible, and well-lighted setting is understandable to entice the consumer to buy the beer. However, beer should be displayed in the most effective manner to both protect freshness and promote sales. Few retailers promote the freshness of their product to consumers, but quality and freshness can also be selling points. Properly informed consumers will realize the importance of freshness over glitzy displays that expose the beer to heat, light, and excessively slow turnover rates.

Selection vs. Quality

Consumers appreciate variety. However, holding more beer in inventory than can be sold within the freshness limits of the beer is an ineffective way to build a reputation as a seller of quality beer.

Bar Code Scanning

Retail stores should use a handheld bar code scanner rather than a fixed scanner in the checkout counter. Laying bottle-conditioned beers flat to read the bar code on the label may disturb the yeast sediment. A handheld scanner allows the bottle to be held upright when the bar code is read.

Packing Bottles

Bottles should be placed upright in a sack or box for the consumer. This especially applies to bottle-conditioned beers, which must be kept upright to leave the lees undisturbed.

Storing Bottle-Conditioned Beer

Bottle-conditioned beer should be stored upright to keep the sediment settled at the bottom of the bottle. This is especially true for bottles with metal caps and for all bottles during the final cooling before serving. However, just like wine bottles, bottle-conditioned beers sealed with a cork should be stored on their sides if they are going to be stored for extended periods. Storing the bottles on their sides will keep the cork moist and fully expanded to maintain a tight seal for years. For transport and in a retail setting, it is acceptable to handle and present the bottles standing upright.

Providing Beer Style Descriptions

A reference guide should be available in the retail establishment for consumers to read so they can understand the flavor characteristics of a particular beer style. Furthermore, beer should be displayed in menus and on store shelves according to style. Arranging beer by color (dark vs. pale) provides little information to the consumer. Use of nonspecific prejudicial descriptors, such as heavy and strong, should be avoided.

Handling Beer Complaints

Complaints by the consumer should always be taken seriously. Too often, servers simply replace the beer with another brand to appease the consumer without ever checking to see if the consumer has a valid complaint. A qualified person should check the aroma in the returned glass and try a new sample, especially if the beer is on tap. If a problem exists, it should be corrected and the consumer's complaint validated. The consumer will appreciate a new fresh beer, but confirmation that their concern was acted upon will build trust in the proprietor's commitment to quality.

Daily Tasting Draft Beer

Tasting draft beers daily is an effective means to ensure quality beer, especially in establishments with a large number of taps. Involving bartenders and servers in this daily monitoring is a good way to develop sensory identification skills and style familiarity.

Selected Reference

Huige, N. J. 2004. Chemical engineering for quality brewing. Technical Quarterly Master Brewers Association of the Americas 41:9-17.

Chapter 5:
Serving Beer

Bill White

Drinking glasses are a relatively modern invention that came into wide use during the nineteenth century when industrial advancements allowed for low-cost production of glass containers. Prior to this time, beer was commonly enjoyed from ceramic or metal vessels. Color, clarity, and the foam collar were of little concern because the beer inside was not visible. When glass came into wide use, the clarity of the beer became an important visual quality for beer drinkers, which lead to the widespread practice of filtration. With the improvement of draft equipment, glassware also fully exposed effervescence and the enticing foam head, especially in the popular new spritzy lagers. In addition to displaying the visual quality of the beer it contains, glassware is also important in accentuating the aromatic character of beer in the same manner that it serves wine.

Reasons to Use a Glass

Glassware for beer is much maligned, abused, and misunderstood. Comments such as "Does a glass make any difference?" or "It's just a marketing tool" are frequently made by the uninformed. Bartenders prefer not to wash glassware since it is time consuming and takes care to perform properly. Some believe that their tips increase when they can serve more drinks by simply handing an opened bottle across the bar. Impatient customers do not like to wait the time it takes for their beer to be poured into a glass. Some even feel cheated when the glass has a collar of foam on it. However, beer tastes better from a glass, and bartenders and servers need to understand the reasons for this so that they can knowledgeably inform customers of the benefits of consuming/enjoying their beer in glassware. When customers realize how a beer's taste improves when it is properly served from a glass, they will also come to understand that the whole beer-drinking experience is transformed from the mundane to the special because of it.

Various factors are important in selecting the appropriate style and shape of beer glassware, including the following.
- Aroma
- Carbonation
- Size

Aroma

When beer is poured into a glass, the escaping carbon dioxide releases aromas that enter the nose, where the full impact of fruity esters, warm alcohols, flowery hop compounds, and toasty malts can be experienced. If enjoyed from a bottle, many of these aromas never reach the olfactory senses, which diminishes the intensity of the drinking experience. The headspace in the glass also allows the continuous release and containment of aromas throughout the drinking experience.

Carbonation

The effervescence and foaming ability of beer create unique demands on glassware and pouring techniques. Soft drinks and sparkling wine are also carbonated, but the foam quickly collapses because they do not have the building blocks for stable bubbles. Hops, and especially malt proteins, provide the binding agents that form the elastic film or "skin" of bubbles that trap escaping carbon dioxide at the surface. Because styles have different amounts of carbonation and foam-creating properties, style-specific glassware was developed to allow for the building of the proper level of foam.

With the release of carbonation, the mouthfeel and flavor of beer also change. As carbon dioxide comes out of suspension, beer loses its sharp carbonic bite, which softens its mouthfeel, resulting in a transition to a smoother yet still lively drinking experience. The consumer also consumes less gas and feels less bloated. The amount of carbonation is a personal preference, and the best way to control and enjoy carbonation is through pouring beer into a glass.

Size

To allow for the proper foam collar, the glass must by larger than the volume of beer poured. For most beer styles, this excess capacity is about 25%. For example, a 12-ounce beer would require a 16-ounce glass. The excess volume needed may vary with style—more volume for highly carbonated beer, and less headspace for lower carbonated styles. Glasses in Europe often have a horizontal line on the side indicating the proper fill level that provides for the correct collar of foam above. The line settles any questions about how much beer is in the glass or if the customer is getting a short fill.

Ideally, the whole content of the bottle should fit in the glass. This is particularly true for bottle-conditioned beers, such as Bavarian *Weizen*, in which the resuspended lees are swirled and poured into the glass, accentuating its cloudy appearance. If the glass is too small, the final content of the bottle, which contains the yeast, cannot be added to the glass. The result is inconsistent character, resulting in no yeast in the first sips from the glass and excessive turbidity after the final bottle volume is added. An exception is the straight-sided, 6-ounce glass that is used in some American bars to serve a 12-ounce bottled lager beer. This small glass allows for three separate 4-ounce pours plus foam. In this way, the beer can stay cold in the bottle until completely consumed. Traditional pint glasses in British pubs are imperial pints, measuring 20 ounces (568 milliliters). If these glasses are paired with a normal 16-ounce pint of canned beer, the glass will be underfilled and the visual effect of the beer diminished. Belgians sometime pour into oversized glasses that leave empty headspace to collect aromas in a fashion similar to how wine is poured.

Other Considerations

Glassware can also affect serving temperature. For beer enjoyed in a beer garden on a warm afternoon, a thick, well-insulated mug may help maintain beer temperature. Sturdy glassware is also important for the rough handling that occurs with exuberant toasting at celebrations such as Oktoberfest. Stemmed glassware or thick solid bases allow area to grip the glass without warming the contents. On the other hand, thin, round-bottom snifters or goblets allow the glass to be cupped in the hand to warm an overly chilled beer.

Glasses Are Made for Beer—Not Beer for Glasses

There will be times when the host at a tailgate, picnic, or sporting event will offer beer in a bottle, can, or plastic cup. Please drink it. Beer drinkers should not expect a mountain-top experience each time they have a beer. Beer tastes good and is a great thirst quencher, regardless of the container it is served in. Beer is unique among alcoholic drinks in that it is actually thirst quenching. Beer drinking is also a social experience. The expectation that beer should always be served in a glass should be overlooked when a friend offers it in only a can or bottle. Furthermore, there is a practical advantage to drinking beer from a brown bottle or can when in direct sunlight. Clear plastic or glass containers do not protect beer from the harmful rays of the sun, which can quickly turn the beer's flavor skunky. Likewise, it is perfectly acceptable to use plastic cups when circumstances make toting or using fine glassware impractical. In fact, there are many examples of clear acrylic and polycarbonate "glasses" for use when a normal glass is not practical. However, if a bartender slides a bottle across the bar without a glass, ask for one. If the bartender returns with a frozen one, ask for a nonfrozen one or have the frozen glass rinsed with cold water to remove the ice and slightly warm it. This action will remove potential off-flavors in the ice and prevent the beer itself from freezing and excessively foaming upon contact with the frozen glass. If there are no other beer glasses, ask for a 16-ounce highball glass or a large, red wine glass. The bartender should have some glass that will be suitable for beer. All that is needed is to ask courteously.

"Beer Clean" or "Beer Ready" Glassware

Most important, glasses must be dirt and germ free for obvious health reasons. Second, dried lipstick or oily fingerprints are completely unappealing to the consumer. Finally, fat, oil, petroleum-based detergents, and improperly rinsed sanitizers cause beer foam to collapse. When a beer glass is spotless, sanitary, and taint free, it is called "beer clean" or "beer ready". The following are industry-accepted procedures for cleaning, drying, and storing beer clean glasses.

Cleaning
Automatic Washer
Automatic washers should be dedicated strictly for glasses to avoid contamination by grease and oil from dishes and utensils. Washers may not remove lipstick and other difficult grime, so inspection and follow-up hand brushing and sanitizing may be necessary. Owners should request from vendors detergents specifically for glassware that are free of foam-destroying residues. Manufacturer-recommended dosages and water temperatures should be followed. Common washing temperatures of 130–140°F (54–60°C) require a sanitizer rinse. Rinses at or above 180°F (82°C) do not usually require application of a sanitizer. Check with your local health department for regulations specific to your area.

Figure 5.1. The three-sink method of cleaning glassware. **1,** Clean sinks. **2,** Prepare sinks. **3,** Wash glassware. **4,** Rinse and sanitize glassware. **5,** Air dry glassware. (Courtesy Diversey, Inc.)

Three-Sink Method

For hand washing, the three-sink method is commonly used and requires the installation of a dedicated stainless steel sink with three separate compartments. The first sink contains brushes and detergents and is where cleaning takes place. This is followed by rinsing in clean water in the second sink and submersing the clean glasses in the third sink filled with sanitizer (Fig. 5.1).

- Sink One—Clean: The first sink contains brushes standing in hot water and detergent. The number of brushes may be a pair or a set of three, and the brushes may be motorized or stationary. The contents of the dirty glass should be dumped, but not in the first sink so as to overload it with dirt. The person washing the glass must work its entire surface over the brushes, including the rim, interior, exterior, and bottom, until all the dirt is removed. Careful monitoring of the suds level and soil load is critical to the operation. As the level of suds diminishes because of soil loading, the effectiveness of the cleaning stage can be compromised. When such a condition is observed, the water and detergent must be replenished. Enough detergent must be dosed for effective cleaning but not too much that it would impede rinsing.
- Sink Two—Rinse: The second sink is continuously replenished with clean water by a slow-running faucet. The excess water flows out through a tall standpipe positioned in the sink's drain. The glasses are dipped into the water heel in and heel out, allowing the interior of the glass to completely fill and then empty back into the sink's reservoir. The glasses should be double or triple dunked to ensure complete rinsing.
- Sink Three—Sanitize: The third sink contains hot water and sanitizer and is where the clean, rinsed glass is dunked in the same heel-in and then heel-out manner as done in sink two. National food service sanitation guidelines and local health codes for sanitizing must be followed. The level of sanitizer should be checked regularly to maintain concentra-

tions at local health code standards. The effectiveness of the sanitizer may be pH dependent and subject to water source variability. Therefore, this variable may also require monitoring. Enough sanitizer must be dosed for effectiveness but not so much as to taint the glass.

A fairly common sanitizer is a chlorine-based solution. These sanitizers leave residual chlorine in the glass, which in turn reacts with the beer to form very unpleasant flavors. If a sanitizer must be used, a chlorine sanitizer should be avoided. Some bars are now using glass rinsers to both remove sanitzer residues and chill the glass before pouring (Fig. 5.2).

Drying

The glasses should be placed upside down in a stainless steel drying basket or on a deeply corrugated sanitary surface that allows proper drainage and airflow so that residual sanitizer dissipates before refilling (Fig. 5.1 #5). Glasses should not be drained or stored upside down on a flat rubber mat or towel. The glasses should not be towel dried, because towels can leave lint and contaminate the glass with germs or grease.

Figure 5.2. Rinsing a beer glass with a cold-water rinser at the bar. The rinse removes sanitizer residues and chills the glass prior to filling it with beer. (Courtesy BridgePort Brewing Company)

Storing

When handling beer clean glasses, it should be remembered that the bottom of the glass belongs to the server and the top of the glass belongs to the customer. Fingers should not touch the rim or interior of the glass. Glasses should be stored in an area free of dust, smoke, and odors. Depending on the temperature of the beer that will fill the glass, the glasses may be stored in a cooler. In such cases, the cooler should be dedicated solely to glasses and never contain food that will transmit odors onto the glass surface. Glasses should only be placed in the cooler when totally dry so that any aromas present in the cooler do not adhere to them. Glasses should never be frozen in a freezer, since this imparts an "ice tray" note and freeze the beer when filled. (Although ice beer is an acceptable style of beer, it is the brewer who should make it, not the bartender.) A serious flaw in handling glasses is to take wet glasses still coated by a film of sanitizer and freeze them. The sanitizer also freezes and remains in the glass to taint the beer that will be poured into it.

Testing for Beer Clean Glasses

The following are four simple tests to judge the effectiveness of a cleaning regime (Fig. 5.3).

Sheeting Test

If the glass is filled with clean water and then turned upside down and the water drains in a uniform sheet off the interior of the glass, it is beer clean (Fig 5.3 row 1). If the water sheets unevenly or leaves droplets, the glass is covered by an invisible film or soil that will adversely affect the beer's appearance and taste.

Head Retention Test

If the pourer is able to build in the glass a solid foam collar that remains standing for a minute or so with no bubbles clinging to the interior walls, the glass is beer clean (Fig 5.3 row 2). If the head quickly falls or bubbles cling to the interior of the glass, there is still an invisible film coating the glass. Remember that glassware that has been stacked can have interior scratches where bubbles will form and also give the appearance of not being beer clean.

Lacing Test

If after pouring the beer, the foam lacing clings to the side of the glass, leaving successive rings of lace to mark the volume of beer emptied with each sip, the glass is beer clean (Fig 5.3 row 3).

Salt Test

To conduct this test, a cleaned glass is rinsed with fresh water and quickly drained by turning it upside down so that a sheet of water remains on the interior surface. With the sheet still present, table salt is sprinkled over the interior sides. If the salt sticks to the entire surface evenly, the glass is beer clean (Fig 5.3 row 4). If the salt falls to the bottom or sticks in random patterns, the glass is not beer clean.

Pouring Beer

With a beer clean glass in hand, a server is prepared to pour the beer. The appropriate pouring technique is dependent on the beer style, the glass, and the level of carbonation. In this section, the proper technique for a classic pour from a bottle and from a draft faucet is described, in addition to some unique techniques for individual beer styles.

Figure 5.3. Four tests for beer clean glasses. Glasses on the left side are close to clean. Glasses on the right side are beer clean. **Row 1,** Sheeting test. **Row 2,** Head retention test. **Row 3,** Lacing test. **Row 4,** Salt test. (Courtesy Diversey, Inc.)

Bottled and Canned Beer

Classic Pour

The classic pour is used for the vast majority of beer. The interior of the glass may be sprayed with cold water from a special beer glass rinser to chill the glass and rinse away dust or residues, or the glass may be filled dry. Practices vary by style and culture. Germans generally rinse their glasses, but certain British and Belgian styles are best poured into a dry glass. An effective device to rinse the glass can be installed near the tap. It consists of a perforated flat disk that sits on top of a sprayer valve. When an inverted glass presses down on the disk, the valve opens and the sprayer flushes the glass with cold water, which is allowed to drain while the glass is still inverted.

To achieve the classic pour:
- Hold the glass at a 45° angle.
- Pour the beer down the side of the glass.
- Never let the bottle or faucet touch the glass or the beer in the glass.
- Gradually tilt the glass upright and let beer pour into the center of the glass.
- Manipulate the glass angle to produce a 1-inch foam collar.

Pilsner Pour

In northern Germany, they brew a delicate, dry, bitter pilsner with a spritzy character not unlike champagne that is served in a stemmed glass resembling a champagne flute. The ritual to dispense the beer is so drawn out that it has been labeled the "7-minute pour". The idea is to build a long-lasting, thick, frothy head that stands inches above the rim. The stiff crown of foam is built by a succession of three violent pours that whips up a huge head of foam. After each pour, the head is allowed to partially fall and then it is built up again with each succeeding pour.

To achieve the pilsner pour:
- Rinse the glass with cold water to cool the glass and rinse any foam-damaging residue.
- Hold the glass straight up by the stem with the rim about 6 inches below the bottle or faucet.
- Pour about 50% the contents of the beer directly into the center of the glass.
- As the foam nears the top of the glass, stop pouring.
- Wait until the foam partially collapses.
- Pour half of the remaining beer violently into the center of the glass again.
- Wait again until the foam partially collapses.
- Pour the remaining contents of the bottle into the glass.
- The mousy foam collar should stand stiff with three to four fingers of foam, including about two fingers of foam above the rim.
- If filling a glass from a draft faucet, follow the same procedures above but use estimated fill volumes similar to those poured from a botte.

Unfortunately, few customers or bartenders outside of Germany or the Czech Republic have the patience or time to wait through this drawn-out protocol. It might be advisable for servers to ask first if the customer is willing to wait or allow the tradition-conscious drinker to pour their own beer from the bottle.

Weizen Pour

Southern German wheat beer contains 20–30% more carbonation than the typical lager. Therefore, careful pouring and a large tall glass are needed to fit the beer and its massive foam collar into the glass. *Weizen* is packaged in half-liter bottles and the beer is bottle conditioned. The yeast that created the secondary fermentation and settled in the bottom of the glass is swirled and decanted into the glass, which provides full body, soft mouthfeel, and bready flavor. The glass is typically rinsed with cold water to chill the glass and remove dust. A warm glass or dust causes the carbon dioxide to break out of solution and foam excessively. If the pourer is too rambunctious and builds the head too quickly, it will be impossible to fit the whole contents of the bottle into the glass without setting the beer aside and waiting for the foam to collapse.

To achieve the *Weizen* pour:

- Rinse the glass with cold water.
- Tilt the glass at a 45° angle.
- Pour the beer gently down the side of the glass without touching the glass to the bottle.
- When the glass is more than half full, start bringing the glass upright if more foaming is needed.
- With about two fingers of beer left in the bottle, stop pouring and swirl the beer to suspend the yeast.
- Pour the suspended yeast and beer into the upright glass.
- There should be about two to three fingers of foam below the rim and one finger of foam above the rim.

Opening a Bottle with Cork and Cage

Highly carbonated Belgian-style ales are commonly in the same type of bottle that holds champagne. Beer is bottled under much lower levels of carbon dioxide pressure than is champagne, so the risk of a rocketing cork is lower. However, wine lacks the protein and hop compounds that make beer foam stable. Therefore, the rapid evolution of bubbles in champagne causes mostly a rapid succession of bursting bubbles, while beer builds a bigger and bigger head of foam that can spew out of the bottle.

The procedure to open a corked bottle of Belgian ale is the same as that for opening champagne.

- Make sure the bottle is properly chilled to reduce internal gas pressure.
- With the left hand, grab the bottle neck with the palm and fingers, placing the thumb over the cage.
- With the right hand, unscrew the cage and then grab the bottle near the bottom.
- Slide the left hand up the neck and around the cage.
- Never take the left hand off the cage to prevent an accidental and possibly injurious discharge.
- With the right hand, turn the bottle, while the left hand works the cork out of the neck.
- The goal is for the cork to quietly "pop" into the left hand and not shoot across the room.
- If the beer starts to foam, tilt the bottle to a 45° angle. The increased surface area in the neck should allow more room for the gas to disperse and not foam.

Draft Beer

The steps to execute the classic pour from a standard beer faucet are below (Fig. 5.4).

- Chill the keg to proper serving temperature.
- Place a beer clean glass under the faucet at a 45° angle.
- Grab the faucet handle at its lowest point and then fully open the faucet with a crisp snap forward.
- Let beer run down the side of the glass to minimize foaming.
- Gradually tilt the glass upright and let the beer pour into the center of the glass.
- Manipulate the glass angle to produce a 1-inch foam collar.
- Never let the faucet touch the glass or the beer in the glass.
- Quickly shut the faucet to prevent waste.

A variation on the standard faucet is the creamer faucet, which has a two-way handle. Filling starts by following the same steps as above. However, when the glass is about three-fourths full, the pourer pushes the handle backwards to a second operating position that is only 75–80% open. The restriction in flow creates a sheering effect that causes a breakout of carbon dioxide and the formation of a "creamy" head.

Figure 5.4. Proper pour of draft beer from a standard faucet. (Courtesy Micro Matic USA, Inc.)

Stout Pour

Irish stout and certain English ales are dispensed using a mixed gas (beer gas) that is 70–75% nitrogen and the remainder carbon dioxide. The keg pressure is set at a high level (30–40 pounds per square inch [psi]) and the beer is pushed through a special stout faucet that forces the beer through a five-hole restrictor plate the size of a small button. The friction created as the beer shoots through the tiny holes causes the gas to break out of solution, causing thousands of tiny bubbles to cascade to the top of the glass. The side of the glass slows the speed of the outer bubbles, while the center bubbles float upward at a faster rate, causing a current that pulls the outer bubbles to the center. As the bubbles are pulled inward, it creates the puzzling perception that the outer bubbles are floating downward. The traditional stout glass is tulip shaped to help accentuate the flow of bubbles down and to the center. Stout dispensed in this fashion is referred to as nitrostout and is lightly carbonated (1.5 vol/vol carbon dioxide) so it to mimics the soft texture and creamy head produced by a beer engine serving traditional cask ales (described below).

To achieve a consistent stout pour:
- Take a dry, room-temperature, tulip-shaped, 20-ounce imperial pint.
- Tilt the glass to a 45° angle under the faucet and pour the beer down the side.
- Stop pouring when the glass is three-fourths full.
- Never let the faucet touch the glass or the beer in the glass.
- Place the glass on the bar to settle completely for a minute or two.
- Now position the glass upright under the faucet and pour the beer into the center.
- Top off until the foam creates a flat dome that sits just above the rim.

Widgets

Several brewers also produce nitrogenated, "nitro", bottled or canned stout and ale that pour like the draft beer engine version with the same creamy texture. A special widget produces the draft effect. A widget is a hollow, nickel-sized plastic ball that is blow molded with nitrogen. A laser burns a minute hole through the ball wall, and the ball is dropped into the can before filling. As the can is filled, liquid nitrogen is also added. After canning, the beer is pasteurized. The heat increases the pressure in the can, forcing beer inside the widget. When the can is opened and the pressure released, the beer shoots out the tiny hole in the widget, releasing the nitrogen from the solution just like a restrictor plate in a faucet.

Pouring a widget beer involves the following.
- Slowly open the can to gradually release pressure.
- Immediately pour the beer gently into a 16-ounce glass held at a 45° angle.
- Fill the glass to the rim, and wait for the beer to settle to add the last one-half ounce of beer.
- The beer should look the same as a pour from a stout or nitro faucet.

Note, that while the Irish use 20-ounce glasses in a pub, the nitro-stout cans are 14.9 ounces and are made to pour into a 16-ounce pint glass. The 20-ounce glass works with the can, but it does not produce the same look since there is excess headspace.

Cask Ale

Cask-conditioned or "real" ale is the traditional style of British ale. In reality, all beer was "cask" beer before the invention of pressurized dispense in the late nineteenth century. Cask ale is a tradition preserved in the United Kingdom, where the unique character produced by the cask is stilled highly valued. The Campaign for Real Ale (CAMRA) is an organization dedicated to the preservation of cask ale.

A cask differs from a keg in that it is not pressurized and does not have built-in fittings for connection to a standard faucet. Instead, the cask is connected by driving the tap with a mallet through the keystone on its front end. The top bung port must also be tapped so that air (or carbon dioxide through a cask breather) can enter as the beer is withdrawn. The beer is poured via gravity by simply opening the tap or by connecting the tap to a beer pump termed a beer engine, which pumps the beer from the cellar to the bar (Fig. 5.5). The brewery fills the cask with uncarbonated beer and adds sugar to create carbonation through a secondary fermentation caused by yeast remaining in the unfiltered beer (see Chapter 2). The cellarman at the pub must determine when the cask has reached the proper carbonation level and the beer has dropped bright through the settling of the yeast, dry hops, finings, and haze. Only then is it ready to dispense.

The beer is pumped to the spout by pulling the beer engine handle. The spout is often shaped like an inverted "U", called a swan neck, which allows the spout to be placed near the bottom of the glass. Pumping entrains air, which is about 80% nitrogen and creates the signature creamy nitro-head. A nozzle similar to a shower head, called a sparkler, is sometimes added to the spout to enhance the frothiness. Sparklers are most common in northern England, but their use is opposed by some consumers who believe the aeration strips flavor from the beer. The swan neck is the only spout that should be placed inside a beer glass. For hygiene, only clean glasses should be filled, and after each pour, the spout must be wiped off with a clean damp towel dedicated solely for this purpose.

For proper pouring through a beer engine:

- If pouring the first beer of the day, first pump out all the beer that has been sitting in the lines overnight and discard it.
- Place the spout near the bottom of a clean dry glass.
- Pull the handle to start filling the glass.
- Before the second pump, make sure the spout is above the beer. If the spout is in the beer, pushing back the handle sucks beer from the glass into the spout.
- Keep the spout near the surface of the beer as the beer rises in the glass.
- After filling, wipe off the spout.
- At the end of the night, the spout should be wiped with sanitizer and then wiped again prior to the first pour the next day, or ideally, the inside of the spout should be rinsed to reduce bacterial contamination and keep the beer tasting fresh longer.

Figure 5.5. Pouring a pint of cask-conditioned ale using a beer engine. (Courtesy BridgePort Brewing Company)

Beer-Appropriate Glassware

Based on the unique character of different beer styles, various forms of style-specific glassware were developed that best present the flavors, carbonation, and appearance of that style. Some retailers and consumers scoff at the notion that beer requires style-specific glassware. Although specialized glassware for wine, distilled spirits, and mixed drinks are readily accepted and used, retailers frequently use a universal beer glass (usually a shaker pint). Ironically, the different sizes of bottles and carbonation levels alone demand a variety of glasses for the proper pouring of beer. Besides enhancing flavor, glasses also raise the image of beer in the eyes of the consumer and contribute toward making beer drinking a special experience to be relished.

German- and Continental-Style Glasses

German beer culture recognizes that proper glassware enhances the character of beer, and strong traditions have evolved regarding style-appropriate glasses. A German who is served a wheat beer in a lager mug is likely to ask whether wine is to be served in a coffee cup. There are unwritten rules for drinking beer, and the Germans expect them to be followed.

Pilsner Glass

The German pilsner glass (*Pokal*) is set on a pedestal (Fig. 5.6). Some versions have a short stem similar to a wine glass, while others have no stem with a base that sits directly on top of the pedestal. The shape of the glass can range from an elongated tulip to a straight-sided vase. The look is elegant and sophisticated. The thin diameter allows for the passage of light and enhances the beer's pale brilliance. High-quality examples of these glasses are as delicate and refined as the finest wine glasses. When crowned with a luxurious head of foam standing well above the rim, the appearance is truly impressive.

Figure 5.6. Pilsner glassware. (Courtesy Rastal GmbH & Co. KG)

Tumbler

The German tumbler (*Becher*) is used for a wide range of lager beers, from pale lager to *Märzen* to bock to *Dunkel* (Fig. 5.7). If there was only one choice of glass in which to serve German lager (including pilsner), the tumbler would be the appropriate compromise.

Mug

The modern German beer mug (*Krug*) (Fig. 5.8 left) is typically made out of glass and has a handle. It is also a universal lager glass but is more associated with beer halls and beer gardens serving draft beer. The glass is thick and sturdy to withstand enthusiastic toasting and also serves to insulate the beer on a warm afternoon. The glass is often dimpled, especially in the 1-liter size, called a *Mass*, served at Oktoberfest (Fig. 5.8 middle). A full *Mass* of beer weighs 2.5 kilograms or about 5.5 pounds. To lift this giant, drinkers slip their whole hand through the handle and wrap the thumb and fingers around

Figure 5.7. German tumbler. (Courtesy Rastal GmbH & Co. KG)

Figure 5.8. Left, Mug (*Krug*). **Middle,** *Mass*. **Right,** Stein. (Courtesy Rastal GmbH & Co. KG)

the mug. It is incorrect to call the glass version a stein, which refers specifically to the less common ceramic mug (Fig. 5.8 right). The popular souvenir version of the stein has a metal lid. Although seen infrequently in commercial use, the lid helps ward off marauding insects and also gives protection from falling chestnuts, the fruit of the thick shade trees traditionally planted in beer gardens.

Bavarian *Weizen* Beer Glass

Bavarian wheat beer, or *Weizen*, is a highly carbonated ale that comes in half-liter bottles (i.e., 16.9 ounces). The glass is approximately 23 ounces (700 milliliters), or 35% larger than the bottle, so it can hold the beer's massive head (Fig. 5.9). *Weizen* is also packaged in kegs, but because this style is bottle conditioned, it frequently is served from the bottle. The glass has a heavy base to add stability to its long, vaselike shape. In the United States, many suppliers incorrectly label this glass style pilsner.

Figure 5.9. *Weizen* beer glass. (Courtesy Rastal GmbH & Co. KG)

Kölsch and *Alt* Beer Glasses

Ales from the regions around Cologne (*Kölsch* beer) and Dusseldorf (*Alt* beer) are served in relatively small, straight-sided glasses that look similar to a highball glass except for their thin base and narrower diameter (Fig. 5.10). *Alt* and *Kölsch* are commonly served on draft in volumes under 12 ounces. Pub culture in these cities dictates that an empty glass is a signal to the waiter to deliver a new full glass. The waiter keeps track of the beer count with a pencil mark on the patron's coaster.

Figure 5.10. Left, *Alt* beer glass. **Right,** *Kölsch* beer glass. (Courtesy Rastal GmbH & Co. KG)

Berliner Weisse Beer Glassware

Berliner Weisse is served in a shallow, wide bowl (Fig. 5.11). The beer is a pale, highly carbonated, wheat beer of modest alcohol content made from a mixed fermentation of ale yeast and lactic bacteria that provide its tart flavor. A sweet raspberry or woodruff syrup is mixed with the beer to counter the sour flavor. Its resemblance to sparkling wine may have been the inspiration behind the wide-rimmed glass resembling a champagne bowl. Its similarity to fruit lambic may also suggest a connection to the bowl-shaped goblets of Belgium.

Belgian-Style Glasses

It is not surprising that the numerous styles of Belgian beer have

Figure 5.11. *Berliner Weisse* beer glassware. (Courtesy Rastal GmbH & Co. KG)

spawned a multitude of different glasses. Although Belgians use a wide variety of glassware, they seem less rigid in strictly pairing a certain shape with a particular beer style. The same creativity applied to the development of their beer styles is evident in their choice of glassware. Furthermore, while other countries fill their glasses to the rim, Belgians often leave empty headspace in a manner similar to how a wine glass is filled.

Goblet or Chalice

The large surface area of the shallow bowl of the goblet or chalice easily releases the aromas of the beer and dissipates the high carbonation level typical of many Belgian beers that might otherwise foam over in a narrower glass (Fig. 5.12). This is the same principle employed in the wide, shallow-bowled glasses for champagne. The bowl also provides a large surface area underneath where the drinker's hand can hold the glass and warm the contents if so desired. Once the proper temperature has been achieved, the glass can be gripped by the stem to slow further warming. Because the chalice has been used in Christian worship, it is not surprising that this style of glassware is used with abbey and Trappist beers.

Figure 5.12. Goblet or chalice. (Courtesy Rastal GmbH & Co. KG)

Snifter

The snifter's short height, large body, and narrow opening allow for the aromas to be trapped in the glass (Fig. 5.13). Like brandy, the aromatic esters and complex alcohols of strong Belgian ale or barley wine can be fully appreciated in a snifter. As with the goblet, a cupped hand underneath can warm the beer to fully release the flavor volatiles. Any complex, aromatic, or high-alcohol beer brewed for sipping like Scotch whisky or brandy can be served in a snifter.

Figure 5.13. Snifter. (Courtesy Rastal GmbH & Co. KG)

Tulip

The tulip has a flared opening that spreads the beer over the tongue to enhance the appreciation of the malt and hops (Fig. 5.14). Many Belgian styles are highly carbonated, and the flared opening also allows the beer to flow easily underneath the foam and into the mouth. The bulbous bowl and narrowing center allow for collection and retention of the aroma. The tulip may be short and squat, like a goblet, or long and thin, like a pilsner flute.

Figure 5.14. Tulip. (Courtesy Rastal GmbH & Co. KG)

Wit Beer Glassware

A *wit* beer is meant to be enjoyed cool, and the chunky tumbler's thick glass provides good insulation (Fig. 5.15). The glass should be held with the fingers on only two of the six sides (or better yet on the points) to minimize heat transfer from the hand. The wide mouth allows for full release of aromas from the estery yeast and orange and coriander spices.

Figure 5.15. *Wit* beer glassware. (Courtesy Rastal GmbH & Co. KG)

Flute

Highly carbonated lambics have the same tart-sweet contrast of a demi-sec (slightly sweet) champagne. It is not surprising that these beers are poured into flutes just like sparkling wine so their sparkling effervescence can be enjoyed rising up through the long, narrow glass (Fig. 5.16).

British-Style Glasses

British ales, especially traditional cask-conditioned ales, are lower in carbonation relative to the majority of German and Belgian beers. In certain styles, the head is also more stable because it is entrained with nitrogen from a beer engine, stout faucet, or widget. The foam collar is subdued and does not rise above the rim, which makes the easy-drinking wide mouth of a British pub glass more than capable of containing the head on British bitter, Irish stout, Scottish ale, or American pales ales. The ales are served at cellar temperature, so thick-sided glasses are especially needed to insulate the beer from the drinker's warm hand.

Figure 5.16. Flutes. (Courtesy Rastal GmbH & Co. KG)

Traditional Brits still drink out of a 20-ounce imperial pint (568 milliliters), such as the bulge-waisted nonic (Fig. 5.17 left), or the more metric-friendly drinker may use a half-liter pub glass that looks like an up-

Figure 5.17. **Left,** Nonic. **Middle,** Stout. **Right,** Dimpled mug. (Courtesy Rastal GmbH & Co. KG)

side-down pear (Fig. 5.17 middle). The flared upper third of each glass helps keep the glass from slipping through the hand. If keeping a tight hold is really important, there is also a dimpled pub glass with a handle (Fig. 5.17 right). It is shorter and squatter than a German glass *Krug* and would certainly be less effective in retaining its contents during a round of glass-crashing toasting than the narrower, taller German version.

Miscellaneous Glassware

Not all bars and restaurants carry style-appropriate glasses, nor can a patron expect the owner of a specialty beer pub to have the perfect glass for each of the hundreds of beers carried. In these situations, one must remember that glasses were made for beer, not beer for glasses, and compromises should be made.

The 16-ounce highball glass is a reasonable compromise for most lager beers and British-style ales (Fig. 5.18). A pilsner and most Belgian-style ales are compatible with a 16-ounce wine glass (Fig. 5.19). Any strong aromatic beer, such as barley wine, Belgian *dubbel*, imperial stout, or *Eisbock*, is perfectly suited for a brandy snifter (Fig. 5.20).

The 16-ounce shaker glass has generally become the national beer glass in America (Fig. 5.21). Not because it is so special, but because it is so practical. Originally designed to fit over a stainless steel shaker for mixing drinks, this sturdy workhorse is now used for water, iced tea, soft drinks, Bloody Marys, and of course beer. While the shaker is a serviceable compromise for most beer styles, its thick walls and heavy weight make the drinking experience less enjoyable than those with style-specific glassware. Shakers are often stored stacked, and when filled, they come with a distinctive array of carbon dioxide bubbles that have come out of suspension where the base of the glass on top has made scratch marks. How special does it make the beer drinker feel when he or she just paid for an expensive specialty beer and then sees soft drinks, tea, or milk in the same glass? How many $100 bottles of wine would a restaurant sell if the wine was poured into an iced tea glass?

Figure 5.18. Sixteen-ounce highball glass. (Courtesy Rastal GmbH & Co. KG)

Figure 5.19. Wine glass. (Courtesy Rastal GmbH & Co. KG)

Figure 5.20. Brandy snifter. (Courtesy Rastal GmbH & Co. KG)

Serving Temperature Guidelines

The serving temperature for a beer style is discussed only as a guideline and presented as a range to reflect commonly accepted temperatures that ultimately depend on personal preference. However, temperature affects the perception of sweetness, bitterness, aromas, carbonation, and mouthfeel. It is the simultaneous experience of each of these factors combined that creates drinking enjoyment. There are some generalized guidelines on how temperature affects flavors and how a serving temperature can change a beer's character (Table 5.1). They can be used in choosing the appropriate serving temperature.

In general, ales are more aromatic and less carbonated than lagers, so they are typically consumed warmer than lagers. From a general perspective, these two main categories of beer usually fall within these temperature ranges: ale (45–55°F/7–13°C) and lager (40–50°F/4.5–10°C).

Figure 5.21. Sixteen-ounce shaker. (Courtesy Rastal GmbH & Co. KG)

Table 5.1. How Temperature Affects Beer Flavor and Character

With Increasing Temperature	With Decreasing Temperature
Sweetness increases	Dryness increases
Bitterness diminishes	Bitterness intensifies
Aroma increases	Aroma decreases
Carbon dioxide solubility decreases	Carbon dioxide solubility increases
Mouthfeel becomes smoother	Mouthfeel becomes sharper

Example 1: Pilsner

A northern German pilsner is dry and delicate, with a bitter finish accentuated by moderately high carbonation and a crisp, snappy mouthfeel. Late-kettle hopping can produce some noble hop aroma. The lager yeast produces low aromatics, which are secondary to this style. A lower serving temperature accentuates these desirable qualities that define the style.

Example 2: Bock

Compared with pilsner, bock is higher in alcohol, sweeter, maltier, lower in bitterness, and less carbonated (yet still lively) and has a smoother, rounder body. The lager yeast used has a low flavor impact so that malt and alcohol aromas are readily evident. To reveal the malty sweetness and aromas, bock should be served slightly warmer than pilsner.

Example 3: Barley Wine

Barley wine is an ale that is high in alcohol and residual sweetness. It has a very full, smooth mouthfeel that is accented at higher temperatures. The beer is also massively aromatic from the ale yeast and high gravity, which produce high levels of esters and aromatic alcohols. Hop and malt aromas are also predominant. Carbonation is modest so as to not interfere with the luscious texture of the beer. A higher serving temperature best highlights these attributes in barley wine.

Example 4: American Lagers

American lagers, standard and light, are crisp, light bodied, and refreshing. They are clean tasting and without intense hop or fermentation aromas. A lower serving temperature accentuates the crisp, refreshing carbonation and its light, thirst-quenching body.

There are some general serving temperatures based on the criteria above (Table 5.2).

Table 5.2. Serving Temperatures for Different Beer Styles

Temperature	Style	Lower Range ←	→	Upper Range
35–40°F (2–4.5°C)	American lager	Light lager		Standard lager
40–50°F (4.5–10°C)	European lager	Pilsner	*Dunkel*	Bock
40–50°F (4.5–10°C)	*Wit, Weizen*	Wit		*Weizen*
45–55°F (7–13°C)	Belgian ale	Golden ale	*Tripel*	*Dubbel*
45–55°F (7–13°C)	British ale	Pale ale	Stout	Real ale
50–60°F (10–15.5°C)	Strong beers	*Doppelbock*		Barley wine

Chapter 6:
Beer and Food

Gary Namm and Stephen R. Holle

Beer is a versatile and enjoyable companion to food and a traditional part of feasting in world cuisines throughout history. For the beer steward, the earlier chapters about brewing ingredients, flavors, and styles make up the building blocks for matching beer with food. Of course, palates are individual; if one does not like porter, for example, one may not enjoy the beer regardless of how well it is paired with food. On the other hand, the right mix of beer and food flavors may help the beer steward lead the drinker to a new appreciation of porter because of the pairing.

Beer Is Food

Although many people consider beer to be just a beverage, during earlier centuries, beer was an integral part of a nourishing meal. Brewing has been closely linked to baking, and beer has been called liquid bread. Like bread, beer provides carbohydrates, protein, vitamins, and minerals. Moreover, beer is safe to drink because the brewing process eliminates pathogens in the drinking water and the alcohol, hops, and acids preserve freshness and quality.

Beer Is Refreshment

Beer is pure refreshment. It is consumed to quench thirst, cool down, and lift spirits. Because it is delicious, affordable, and widely available, beer is a favorite drink at family gatherings and public celebrations. Beer drinkers understand that it is acceptable to quaff beer in hearty gulps to quench thirst and refresh their palate. Before discussing the finer points that make beer a great companion with food, it is instructive to emphasize the following two aspects that form the essence of beer's relationship with food.

Thirst Quenching
Most beers are low in alcohol, spritzy, and served chilled, which makes beer an excellent thirst quencher. Beer is also nourishing. For these two reasons, beer has accompanied food to refresh and sustain active people when they are hungry or thirsty. Throughout history, farmers, laborers, and other physically active people have chosen beer to drink as part of their meals. Even in today's white-collar societies, beer is the preferred partner

Figure 6.1. Beer owns the grill, including toasty stout with grilled burgers. (Courtesy L. Saunders, www.beercook.com; photo by Enji)

with food at picnics, tailgate parties, sporting events, and festivals, where meals are combined with sunshine, warm weather, and physical activity (Fig. 6.1).

Palate Cleansing

Several components of beer act as palate cleansers; first, carbonation lends acidity and effervescence to beer to cleanse the palate of the mouth-coating effects of fats, oils, eggs, and strong food flavors. Second, bitterness cuts through grease, fatty meats, and heavy sauces. Third, Acidity and alcohol refresh the mouth for the enjoyment of individual flavors from a variety of foods served during a meal.

Principles of Pairing Beer and Food

- Impact: pairing beer with foods of like flavor intensity
- Match: pairing beer with foods of similar flavor
- Contrast: pairing beer with foods of different, but compatible, flavors and textures

Impact

Impact refers to balancing the intensity of a beer with the intensity of food in terms of flavors, aromas, and mouthfeel. This principle is important if the goal is to prevent the impact of the beer from overwhelming the impact of the food, or vice versa.

For example, the impact of hop bitterness in an American standard lager with 12 bitterness units is less than the impact of a German pilsner with 30 bitterness units, even though the malt, alcohol content, and yeast flavors may be similar. The fermentation-derived banana and clove flavors of a Bavarian *Hefeweizen* create a greater impact than a *Kölsch* with only subtle hints of fruitiness. The citrusy and resinous aroma of a dry-hopped American pale ale is much bolder than that of an Irish red ale, which uses no aroma hops. The impact of a high-alcohol beer is greater than one low in alcohol. The viscosity of a high-gravity *Heller Bock* supplies greater mouthfeel than that of a highly attenuated low-carbohydrate beer. Finally, the dark-roasted coffee character of a stout supplies more impact than that of a *Schwarzbier*, which has only a hint of roast character. These are just a few examples of impact comparisons found between beer styles.

In similar fashion, oven-roasted chicken supplies less impact than Tabasco-drenched buffalo chicken wings. Smoked brisket is more intense than roast beef. Salad with zesty

Italian dressing is spicier than one with simple vinegar and oil. Broccoli covered in a creamy cheese sauce is more mouth coating than simple steamed broccoli.

Balancing impact helps ensure that the flavors of the beer and food are identifiable and enjoyable both separately and as a combination. The intense bitterness and citrusy hop aroma of India pale ale would not overwhelm the peppers and spices in Mexican or Thai food but would obliterate the delicate flavors in white fish. The neutral malt character and citrus flavors of a Belgian *wit* would complement the delicate herbs and lemon flavors in a shrimp salad but be buried by the sweetness and spices in a smoked slab of sauce-slathered pork ribs. An American standard lager with its clean, refreshing character allows the delicate flavors of baked whitefish to shine through, but the smoke and spicy, roasted flavors of blackened catfish might match up better with the dark malt and spicy fermentation flavors of a Belgian *dubbel*.

Restaurateurs do not always create beer lists to complement their menus, and frequently the beer offering consists of a majority of low-impact beers. Sometimes, this is a reflection of distribution and cost efficiencies. However, all is not lost. A refreshing, American standard lager or light lager is still thirst quenching and palate cleansing, which allows it to be an enjoyable pairing with many high-impact dishes. In fact, some beer drinkers may prefer beer flavors to remain in the background and the flavor of the food to take center stage. Critics of beer may cite its commonness and simple drinkability as evidence that beer lacks the pedigree to accompany fine dining, thus making it fit only for ordinary cuisine, such as pizza and burgers. Within the range of styles, there are numerous examples of light, easy-drinking brews as well as complex, bold, and aromatic beers of impressive alcoholic strength suitable for aging. Beer is unique in that it is incredibly flavorful, even at alcohol levels one-third that of wine and one-tenth that of spirits. When brewed to alcohol levels approaching wine, the impact of beer can become massive. Beer is so incredibly diverse in impact and flavor that it can create an excellent pairing with cuisine from any nationality, intensity level, or flavor profile.

Match

An obvious pairing technique is to identify a major flavor in food and then match it with a beer possessing the same flavor attribute, or vice versa. In the culinary trade, this is known as bridging, or finding the key ingredient to match flavors. One brewer describes this process as matching flavor "hooks" (Oliver, 2003; p. 56). Moreover, if more than one flavor hook can be found, the synergism is magnified. However, matching flavors can also have an undesirable effect when the compounded flavors become overwhelming. Pairing a sugary beverage with an ultrasweet dessert may create a sickeningly sweet combination. Similarly, matching an acidic drink with a sour dish may create an unpleasant intensification of tartness. Fortunately, beer flavor rarely goes to the extreme end of the sweet and sour scale because hops balance malt sweetness and only a few beers, such as lambic, have enough acid or are highly attenuated enough to create intense sourness on the palate. In the event a flavor match is unpleasant, choosing contrasting flavors may be more appropriate (discussed later).

The following three sections and accompanying tables present a summary of major flavor components derived from malt, hops, and fermentation. While various flavors are listed for each source, these flavors do not exist in isolation. The entire spectrum of flavors in the beer must be considered in finding a suitable match with food. For example, pale malt produces flavors of lower impact than does dark malt, all other factors being equal. However, if a pale beer has any combination of high bitterness, broad hop aroma, high alcohol, or assertive fermentation flavors, the impact of the beer may be anything but low. When considering the descriptions of the following ingredients, assume that the discussion is preceded by "all things being equal".

Malt

Malt character is one of the most straightforward beer flavors to identify and match because the identification by taste is also partially validated by color. Pale malt (and, consequently, pale beer) provides the most neutral flavor and the lowest impact, with flavor and impact increasing with increasing color, as Table 6.1 illustrates. Color can only partially validate malt flavor because beers with the same color do not always have the same malt flavor. A beer made with 10% amber-colored crystal malt and one made with 1% dark-roasted malt may have the same copper color, but the taste may be completely different. The former is likely to have a rounder, caramel sweetness, and the latter, a sharper, more acrid flavor with hints of roastiness. Malt is also the source of sweetness, but the brewer controls the amount of residual sugar by manipulating mashing and fermentation parameters. Beer color is not an indicator of sweetness.

Table 6.1. Malt Types and Examples of Corresponding Flavors in Beer

Malt Type	Impact	Flavor
Pale	Low	Cereal, grain, bread, sweet, honey
Amber	Moderate	Biscuit, toasty, nutty, caramel, toffee
Dark/roasted	High	Burnt, bitter, chocolate, coffee, smoke

Figure 6.2. Crisp Bohemian pilsner and seared seafood brochettes make a tasty pair. (Courtesy L. Saunders, www.beercook.com; photo by Enji)

Pale Malt

Beers made with pale malt tend to have neutral flavors and are often paired with low-impact foods, including low-intensity salads, eggs (including quiche and omelets), soup, chowder, fish (especially white fish), shellfish (especially lobster, crab, clams, and mussels), mild cheeses, and poultry (Fig. 6.2).

Amber Malt

Amber malts exhibit flavors that range from biscuit and toast on the light end of the amber color scale to nutty, caramel, and toffee as the malt color deepens. The heat of cooking food creates similar flavors in bread crust; roasted nuts; roasted, grilled, and barbequed meats; burritos, enchiladas, tacos, and chili; stew and goulash; wild game; and sausages. Other food matches with amber malt include mushrooms, lentils, and nuts because of the dark flavors (discussed later) in both the food and beer.

Dark/Roasted Malt

The impact of dark malts ranges from moderate to intense. Varieties with low to moderate alcohol strength (e.g., Irish dry stout, brown porter, oatmeal stout, *Schwarzbier*) usually have moderate roasted character and a dry to modestly sweet finish. These beers are often paired

Figure 6.3. The luscious flavors of dark and heavier beers accompany the bitter sweetness of chocolate desserts. (Courtesy Weisses Bräuhaus)

with hearty foods, including roasted meats, sausages, and stews. As the impact of stouts and porters increase with the rising levels of alcohol, sweetness, and roast character (e.g., foreign stout, Baltic porter, imperial stout), either alone or in combination, they enter into a new flavor realm, emphasizing chocolate and coffee flavors that match desserts and rich foods. An imperial stout matches both the sweetness and chocolate flavors in chocolate dessert, providing a dual flavor match (Fig. 6.3). The roasted coffee flavors allow stouts and porters to match foods that are traditionally served with coffee. Beers with smoked malt (*Rauchbier*) obviously match the smoked flavors in ham, bacon, and barbeque or in other hearty meats cooked on the grill.

Hops

Bitterness

Bitterness creates one of the most readily identifiable flavor components in beer. Low bitterness contributes a low impact and high bitterness provides a high impact. For this reason, strong bitterness matches the intensity of hot, spicy dishes. Bitterness is rarely the primary flavor in food, so beer bitterness typically matches the impact of spicy food; however, certain herbs, spices, and vegetables have a bitter component. A bitter beer may complement the bitterness in certain herbs and greens, such as arugula, radicchio, and radish. Furthermore, the character of beer bitterness can vary between beers to create different impact impressions. A pilsner made with nonalkaline water and noble German hops may have a delicate bitterness in comparison to the assertively coarse bitterness in pale ale brewed with non-noble hop varieties. The different perceptions of bitterness may be desirable characteristics for each respective beer style, but the beers may create a different impact when paired with food. The beer steward must understand that a beer's perceived bitterness level is influenced by its maltiness, sweetness, and body. For this reason, familiarity with both the beer's tested bitterness level (international bitterness units; see Chapter 7) and its perceived palate bitterness when tasted without food is essential before suggesting it in a food pairing.

Aroma

While nearly all commercial beers contain some amount of hop bitterness, not every beer contains recognizable hop aromas from the essential oils. Beers with hops added late in the wort boil or beers that are dry hopped have recognizable hop aromas. In addition to aroma differences between hop varieties, beers that are dry hopped have more pronounced, grassy, or herbal character than non-dry-hopped beers.

The descriptors in Table 6.2 are readily recognizable as common flavors in a variety of foods, especially salads, salad dressings, sauces, and glazes. Interesting food pairings based on hop aroma can match similar aromas or magnify the aromatic character of the meal by simply adding additional complementary aromas to heighten the olfactory experience.

Table 6.2. Common Hop Aromas in Beer[a]

Citrusy	Esters	Floral	Herbal	Spicy	Sylvan (Woody)
Grapefruit	Pineapple	Geranium	Fresh hop	Sandalwood	Cedar, pine
Bergamot	Pear skin	Lavender	Grassy	Oak moss	Woody
Lemon	Sweet	Rose	Green	Astringent	Earthy
Lime	Fruity	Neroli			

[a] Source: www.barthhaasgroup.com/images/pdfs/hop%20varieties.pdf.

Other Beer Flavors and Ingredients

In addition to hops, certain beers have added flavors among their list of ingredients, including fruit, honey, citrus, and spices. These beers can be matched with foods having the same ingredients. For example, chocolate or coffee is sometimes an ingredient in stout and porter, which makes these beers perfect for dessert pairings. Certain beers are also flavored with herbs and spices reminiscent of gruit, such as orange peel, coriander, nutmeg, lemon grass, grains of paradise, and heather. *Kriek* (cherry), *framboise* (raspberry), and other fruit lambics are excellent with creamy desserts, such as cheesecake, that are drizzled with fruit sauce. The fruit flavors in the beer match the sauce and the tart background of the beer cuts the richness of the cheesecake.

Fermentation Flavors

Different yeast strains and fermentation conditions create a multitude of flavors in beer that provide opportunities for flavor matches with food (Table 6.3). Among other factors, ale yeast strains, high alcohol content, and warm fermentation conditions tend to produce a greater amount of esters and aromatic alcohols. Belgian ales, especially strong ones, are particularly renowned for their high levels of esters, phenols, and fusel alcohol flavors. Fruity beer esters can be a good match with salads or even desserts. Bavarian *Hefeweizen* is well known for its banana ester, isoamyl acetate, and clovelike phenol, 4-vinyl guai-col. A Belgian *tripel* with hints of banana and citrus might be a good partner to a salad with lemon zest. A *saison* with its peppery spiciness pairs well

Table 6.3. Common Fermentation-Derived Flavors in Beer

Esters	Phenols	Alcohols/Oxidized	Other
Pear	Pepper	Raisin	Sour
Banana	Clove	Sherry	Vinegar
Citrus	Smoke	Alcoholic rum	Barnyard–horsey
Apple	Vanilla	Spicy	Earthy
Aniseed		Winelike	Butterscotch

with a hard, sharp cheese covered by a spicy rind (Fig. 6.4). A rich, sweet, raisiny Belgian *dubbel* can match a dessert with the dark flavor of raisins, prunes, or other dried fruits.

Ethanol is fairly neutral in flavor and makes up the vast majority of alcohol in beer. However, the small amount of aromatic alcohols (i.e., fusel or higher alcohols) can have a big impact on beer aroma. These alcohols, which are spicy and rumlike, are found in beers of high alcohol content, such as an imperial India pale ale, and might complement a spicy Cajun dish. Alcohol is susceptible to oxidation and can create the same oxidized flavors in beer that are found in intentionally oxidized wines, such as sherry or port. Barley wines and old ales are sometimes aged like wine to soften the mild astringency in the malt and develop an increased depth of flavor by oxidizing ethanol to create vinous, raisin, rum, and sherry flavors. Meat prepared with a sherry-based sauce or raisin-rum bread pudding is a suitable pairing for a barley wine.

Sour fermentation flavors are often associated with wild yeast and other microflora that produce acid. *Gueuze* and barrel-aged Flemish red or brown ales exhibit a wide range of sourness from intense in *gueuze* to moderate in the Flemish red and brown ales. Sour beers can match vinegar or citrus in salads, ceviche, sauerkraut, and pickled foods. Earthy, barnyard, and horsey flavors are typically associated with *Brettanomyces* yeast often found in Belgian ales, especially those aged in untreated oak barrels. These beers can be paired with earthy mushrooms and rind-washed cheeses.

Figure 6.4. You don't have to cook to enjoy beer and food pairings—it is as easy as slicing cheese and offering "liquid bread", such as barley wine. (Courtesy L. Saunders, www.beercook.com)

Bright vs. Dark

Food and beer can also be divided into two groups of flavors: bright and dark (Oliver, 2003; pp. 52–53). The premise is that bright flavors should be paired with other bright flavors and dark with dark. Bright flavors include dry briskness, refreshing acidity, and citrus and fresh fruity flavors. Bright beers include pale ales with citrusy hops; fruity Bavarian *Hefeweizen*; crisp, dry pilsners; and refreshing *Kölsch*. Dark flavors include chocolate, toffee, caramel, coffee; dark fruits such as raisins, plums, currants, and olives; sweet spices such as cinnamon and nutmeg; and umami flavors in mushrooms, truffles, and peppers; and cultured, fermented, and smoked foods. Dark beers include many types of ale, especially Belgian varieties, that have yeast-derived phenolic flavors of clove, nutmeg, pepper, smoke, and tobacco. The horsey character of *Brettanomyces* yeast is also included, as well as plum and raisin flavors in strong beers, especially those aged in oak barrels. Grassy, woody hop flavors belong on the list of dark flavors, along with amber and roasted malts. Dark color is not necessarily a determinant of dark flavors because pale artisanal ale may have phenolic yeast flavors and grassy herbal hop character (Oliver, 2003; pp. 52–53).

Contrast

Contrast is a common approach to food pairing, such as hot and cold, sweet and sour, and sweet and salty. Contrast can elevate the intensity of flavors or cause them to subside into a more balanced marriage. For example, a sweet drink may complement a sweet dessert, but in some combinations, the pairing may become overly sweet and cloying. In such cases, contrast might be a better approach. Conversely, pairing a sour drink with dessert could produce a balanced contrast, while the dichotomy may simply make the drink taste too sour, or vice versa. A common rule in wine and food pairing is to avoid pairing a dry acidic wine with a sweet dessert. Instead of the acids in the wine balancing the dessert's sweetness, the dessert changes the perception of the wine to an unflattering sourness. Therefore, a complementary approach is usually followed, pairing sweet wines with sweet desserts. The same effect could result when pairing a bitter dry pilsner with something sweet. Instead of the bitterness balancing the sweetness, the contrast transforms the delicate pilsner into an unpleasantly bitter, thin-bodied beer.

Astringency and Richness

Astringency is commonly experienced in tea and red wine when the tannins in these beverages cause a rough drying sensation in the mouth. Tea and coffee drinkers may add cream because the richness from its fat and sugar offsets the drink's astringency. Tannic red wines are frequently paired with fatty meats for this reason. Astringency is typically an off-flavor in beer, and brewers use techniques in mashing to avoid extraction of astringent tannins from the grain husks. However, dark-roasted malts are known for their bitter astringency, which is recognized as a signature characteristic in stouts and porters. These beers are often paired with rich creamy cheeses and desserts, such as ice cream. The sweeter, full-bodied versions of stout (milk or cream stout) and Baltic porter are more compatible than drier versions (Irish stout). Full-bodied stouts and ice cream can even be paired to make a float. Chocolate desserts are an especially popular pairing with stout and porter because not only do the roasted malt phenols balance the richness in the dessert but the chocolate and coffee flavors in the beer complement the same flavors in the dessert.

Salt and Bitterness

Bitterness offsets the satiating effects of malt sweetness, thus enhancing the thirst-quenching character of beer. Beer is well known as a partner to salty snacks, such as pretzels, nuts, and popcorn, because salt stimulates thirst and beer is a thirst quencher. Consequently, dry, bitter beers, such as pilsner, can be paired with other salty foods, such as salami and caviar. Evidence also exists that salt suppresses bitterness in beer (Breslin and Beauchamp, 1995) and can tone down the intensity of the beer's bitterness.

Bitterness and Richness

An important reason for the wide popularity of hops as an ingredient in beer is its ability to offset the bland fullness that a malt only beer would have. This relationship is also evident in chocolate. Chocolate has a bitter taste that is more pronounced in semisweet dark chocolate than in sweet milk chocolate. Bitterness also lightens the satiating and coating effects of fat on the palate. Therefore, beer offers a good counterbalance to rich foods containing fat or both fat and sweetness. The bitterness of American pale ale may reduce the satiating richness of fatty pork ribs covered in sweet barbeque sauce (the caramel malt may also match the caramelized flavors created in the ribs). For rich fatty meats without sweet sauces, spices, or roasted flavors, a dry, pale, bitter beer such as pilsner or a strong Belgian golden may be appropriate.

Spicy Heat and Sweetness

Malty sweetness and the soothing weight of viscosity are beer attributes that subdue the heat of spicy hot dishes (Fig. 6.5). Beer's ability to combine rich malty flavors in a moderately alcoholic base possessing the high impact of spicy bitterness gives it an advantage over wine when paired with hot, spicy food. Wine creates impact primarily with tannins, acidity, and alcohol. Spicy heat in food makes wine tannins feel rough and unpleasant and the alcohol feel hot (Oliver, 2003; p. 53). Sweet wines can provide the balancing contrast, but they are generally unable to match the impact of the spices, so the wine flavors are often overwhelmed.

Acid Cuts Oil and Richness

Beer with an average pH of about 4.3 is only mildly acidic compared with other beverages, such as wine, with a pH of about 3.5. Wine drinkers use the acidity of wine to cut through oils, heavy cream sauces, and mouth-coating eggs. Champagne is popular with brunch for both its acidity and carbonation because it can attack oily sausages and mouth-coating eggs covered in rich hollandaise sauce. A dry, bitter pilsner with little residual sweetness to mask its acidity can accomplish the same task, especially when backed up by its effervescence and focused bitterness. There are also beers with higher acidity, approaching that of wine, including (in order of increasing acidity) *wit*, Flemish red and brown ales, and lambic. *Wit* is a highly attenuated beer with a dryness that helps accentuate the acid in the beer. The tartness is further emphasized by citrus flavors added from orange peel and coriander. Therefore, *wit* is

Figure 6.5. Who says beer can't match the acidity of tomatoes? Try a malty Vienna lager or Oktoberfest. (Courtesy L. Saunders, www.beercook.com; photo by Enji)

tart, citrusy, and fruity. These characteristics allow it to not only cut the oil in salad dressing but also match the citrus, herbal, and fruity character of the greens and seasonings. Flemish red and brown ales owe their tartness to acid-producing microflora contained in the wood of barrels used for aging. Lambic, with a pH similar to wine, gets its tartness from acid-producing microflora from spontaneous fermentation and conditioning in barrels. Lambics taste much tarter than wine, so the impact of their acidity should be considered when pairing with food. Lambics may be paired with oily salmon or creamy sweet cheeses.

Miscellaneous Topics

High Levels of Alcohol Intensify the Spicy Heat in Food

This is more of an issue with wine and spirits than with beer because high-alcohol-content beers are typically less attenuated, which allows the residual sweetness to ameliorate the unpleasant contrast between alcohol and spice. Highly hopped, bitter beers can intensify the sensation of chilies and hot peppers as well (Fig. 6.6).

Salt Neutralizes Acidity

A salty dish may lessen the tartness of a sour beer.

Figure 6.6. Curried vegetable and onion salad melds with the spicy flavor of an imperial wheat ale. (Courtesy L. Saunders, www.beercook.com)

Match Beer and Food from the Same Region

Popular pairings of food and beer from a particular country or region are interesting to explore since the traditional affinity of the match probably exists because the impact, match, and contrast of the food and beer work. For example, dry stout and oysters is a popular combination that originated in Ireland.

Share a Bottle and Match a Different Beer with Each Course

Most beer is packaged in bottles ranging from 12 ounces to one-half liter. Beer's small containers and affordability allow for matching several different beers with different courses during a meal. Two or three diners can easily split one 12-ounce bottle over a salad/appetizer, another beer for the main course, a third for dessert, and possibly a fourth for an after-dinner digestif. All in all, the diners will only consume between 16 and 24 ounces of beer. A wine glass is perfect for sharing these smaller portions.

Aperitifs

Aperitifs are enjoyed before a meal because alcohol stimulates the appetite. Because sweet viscous drinks are filling, aperitifs are typically dry, bitter, acidic, and effervescent, either alone or in combination, making them refreshing and not satiating. Liquors and fortified wines, such as vermouth, are aperitifs. Champagne is a frequent aperitif because it is dry, effervescent, and acidic. A dry, delicate German pilsner contains many of the same characteristics, but it substitutes bitterness for acidity to be refreshing on the palate. Fruit and nonfruit lambics are aperitifs because of their effervescence and tartness. Fruit lambics are often served in a champagnelike flute. *Saisons* and strong, dry, golden Belgian ales also have the dryness, effervescence, and bitterness to make good aperitifs, presented in flutes or stemmed glassware.

Digestifs

Digestifs are enjoyed after a meal because the alcohol is thought to aid digestion. Brandy, grappa, whisky, and fortified wines are common digestifs. (Mixtures of special herbs known as bitters have also been combined with alcohol because of the curative power attributed to bitters to settle the stomach.) Barley wine, *Doppelbock*, quadruple Belgian ales, and Scotch ale are beers high in alcohol and suitable as digestifs; they should be served in snifters or goblets to concentrate aromatics and highlight tawny colors.

Proper Glassware and Serving Temperature

Beer flavor is optimized when it is served at the proper temperature and in the proper glassware (see Chapter 5), just as the enjoyment of food is enhanced when it is presented at the right temperature and in the proper serving ware. Elegant, style-appropriate glassware not only improves the aroma, flavor, and appearance of the beer, but it also heightens the anticipation of the drinker that he or she is about to enjoy a memorable dining experience because great meals are accompanied by great beer. When the beer steward presents beer in a thoughtful, stylish manner, not only is the enjoyment of the beer and meal increased, but the image of beer is elevated as well.

Cooking with Beer

Beyond menu pairings, chefs also use beer as an ingredient in food to bring uniqueness and flavor to the menu. The following are a few ways chefs are using beer to create a variety of dishes (see also www.brewersassociation.org/attachments/0000/2095/Beer_and_Food_Flyer_MDC.pdf, www.craftbeer.com/pages/beer-and-food/pairing-tips/pairing-chart, and www.beercook.com).

- Beer can be used as an ingredient to add bitterness, acid/tartness, or sweetness.
- A moderately hopped beer adds lightness to a batter used to deep-fry fish or chicken.
- A quick sauce for sautéed or roasted food is made by using a low-bitter beer to deglaze a pan. (Care should be taken not to reduce the beer, because it then becomes excessively bitter.)
- Pale beers and low-bitter beers are the perfect ingredient for dressings; acidic beers are even being substituted for vinegar. Heartier amber or brown beers are great for sauces or marinades for grilled or barbecued meat.
- The acids in beer can create a marinade to tenderize meat and malt enhances surface caramelization and browning when cooking on the grill or making pan-seared preparations.

- Beer can add richness to meat gravies and hearty soups, particularly cheese soups. However, reheating soups and stews can intensify hop bitterness, so a less-hoppy style should be chosen.
- Although mussels steamed in wheat beer are classic, beer can also be used for steaming other seafood and fresh food items for added flavor. Bratwurst cooked in beer before going on the grill is another classic.
- When it comes to dessert, a strong, rich beer may be substituted for other clear liquids in cakes or pastries, or a fruity beer can add another layer to a fruit compote or sauce. An ice cream float can even be made by adding a scoop of ice cream to a glass of imperial stout.

Conclusion

When beer drinkers have a basic knowledge of the many flavors in beer, they have the basic tools to explore a limitless number of beer and food combinations. The principles in this chapter are intended to inspire the beer steward to explore flavors, not to set unbreakable rules. Similarly, a road map shows a variety of routes to reach one's vacation destination. However, it is the driver's prerogative to choose the most enjoyable route that provides the best opportunity to explore new sights along the way. Likewise, in exploring beer with food, beer drinkers will pursue beer and food combinations that are of most interest to them. Learning to explore the possibilities that beer offers with food is more important than deciding in advance that there are only a few predetermined pairings that one must choose.

Selected References

Breslin, P. A. S., and Beauchamp, G. K. 1995. Suppression of bitterness by sodium: Variation among bitter taste stimuli. Chemical Senses Journal 20:609-623.

Brewers Association. 2007. American Craft Beer and Food: Perfect Companions. Brewers Publications, Boulder, CO.

Brewers Association websites:
www.brewersassociation.org/attachments/0000/2095/Beer_and_Food_Flyer_MDC.pdf
www.craftbeer.com/pages/beer-and-food/pairing-tips/pairing-chart

Calagione, S., and Olds, M. 2008. Food fight—Beer and wine square off across the table. All About Beer 29(2) May.

Ishikawa, T., and Noble, A. C. 1995. Temporal perception of astringency and sweetness in red wine. Food Quality and Preference 6:27-33.

Jackson, M. 1997. Beer Companion, 2nd ed. Duncan Baird Publishers, London, U.K.

Jackson, M. 1998. Ultimate Beer. DK Publishing, Inc., New York.

Mosher, R. 2009. Tasting Beer. Storey Publishing, North Adams, MA.

Oliver, G. 2003. The Brewmaster's Table: Discovering the Pleasures of Real Beer with Real Food. Harper Collins Publishers, New York.

Panovská, Z., Šedivá, A., Jedelská, M., and Pokorný, J. 2008. Effect of ethanol on interactions of bitter and sweet tastes in aqueous solutions. Czech Journal of Food Science 26(2):139-145.

Saunders, L. 2009. www.beercook.com.

Simon, S. A. 2002. Interactions between salt and acid stimuli: A Lesson in gustation from simultaneous epithelial and neural recordings. Journal of General Physiology 120(6):787-791.

water is so famous that many pale ale brewers add gypsum and other water salts to "Burtonize" their water to capture the classic character of Burton ales.

Pilsen in the Czech Republic is famous for the birth of the pilsner beer style, which is pale in color with a high level of delicate bitterness. The production of a pale-colored lager was possible because Pilsen's extremely soft water did not require dark malt to counteract alkalinity. The lower alkalinity also produced a more delicate bitterness and a paler color. Brewers of pilsner-style beer frequently remove alkalinity to capture the classic pale color and clean bitterness associated with this style that soft water allows.

Today, brewers have the technology to remove dissolved minerals, odors, flavors, and contaminants from water. Nearly any water supply can be treated to make it compatible for not only brewing but for making any style of beer. Water treatment methods such as ion-exchange and reverse osmosis can effectively demineralize the water, to which the brewer can add the desired water salts in the proportions that best fit the style of beer. Munich, Germany, has alkaline water and was famous in the nineteenth century for its dark brown lagers. However, as Munich brewers gained the technology to remove the alkalinity, the character of the local beers changed along with consumers' taste for lighter-colored beers. The change in the local character of the beer from dark to light was so extensive that Munich is now best known for its pale lagers, and the once common dark lager, or *Dunkel*, is rarely found.

Malt and Adjuncts

Malt is the soul of beer because it defines its very essence—a fermented beverage made from grain. Malt is grain that has undergone controlled germination to produce the enzymes that convert grain starch to sugar in the brewhouse. After germination, the green malt is carefully dried to preserve the enzymes. At the end of the drying process, heat is applied to remove unwanted vegetable and grassy flavors and to produce various degrees of color and desirable flavors ranging from sweet to malty, caramel, coffee, and burnt.

Malt takes a major role in determining the strength, color, and flavor of beer. All other factors being equal, as the amount of malt increases, so does the alcoholic potential of the beer. Likewise, as the malt increases in color, so does the beer's color. Furthermore, the type of grain and the malting processes it underwent have an influence on beer flavor that is as significant as those from hops and yeast.

Barley is the commercial grain most widely used for malting. It has the right combination of size, carbohydrates, proteins, husk, germination characteristics, enzymes, and flavors to efficiently make good-tasting beer. Other grains are also used in brewing and are frequently mashed in combination with barley for the unique characteristics they impart. In certain areas where barley does not grow well, indigenous beers are brewed from local grains, such as sorghum or corn/maize.

The different types of base malts, specialty malts, and adjuncts that provide the fermentable sugars to make beer and malt flavors that determine beer style are summarized below.

Base Malt

Base malts (also known as pale or brewer's malt) are enzyme-containing malts that make up the majority of the total malt weight. Base malts are dried and kilned using moderate heat to preserve enzymes that would be denatured by excessive heat, especially moist heat. Therefore, base malts also tend to be pale in color. Base malt is used to provide starch and supply a large source of the enzymes to not only convert its own starch to sugar but also to convert the starch of the specialty malts and adjuncts when they are mashed with the base malt. Specialty malts (discussed below) are used in smaller percentages to supply specific color and flavors to the wort. Base malt can be compared with the ingredients that go into the foundation of a sauce to which the chef adds other ingredients (specialty malt) to add flavor and color (Table 7.1).

Table 7.1. Base Malts[a]

Type	Color (°L)[b]	Hue	Flavor	Style
Pils	0.8–1.1	Very light yellow	Very mild	Pilsner, *Kölsch*
Vienna, pale ale	3.2–4.0	Yellow	Mild malty	Pale ale, Vienna lager
Munich	8–12	Orange	Pronounced malty	Bock, Oktoberfest, *Alt*
Wheat	2.2–3.0	White to gold	Floury	*Weizen*

[a] Source: Gruber, 2006; Kramer, 2006.
[b] Malt color is measured from a wort extract made through a controlled miniature mashing and lautering process. The unit of measure used in North America is degrees Lovibond (°L). Other standard measurements, such as Standard Research Method (SRM) and European Brewing Convention (EBC), are used internationally and serve the same purpose as °L. The correlation between malt color and beer color is not straightforward, since a lot depends on how the malt is used. Therefore, malt color is merely a relative measurement used by brewers to determine its potential impact on beer color. (Beer color is discussed further in Chapter 9.)

Barley

Barley produces the most common base malt because it is rich in extract and enzymes and has husks that allow for efficient wort separation. After germination, base malt is prepared by reducing the moisture content of the green malt from 45 to 20% using forced air of 130°F (55°C). Additional heat of 160°F (71°C) reduces the moisture content to 10%, and then the malt is kilned at around 180°F (82°C) to develop malt flavor and color and render the malt stable for storage by reducing the moisture content to around 4%. There are two major types of base barley malt used in the United States: two-row and six-row. The two barleys are identified by the number of vertical rows of kernels attached to the grain head. Two-row barley is the predominant European malting barley and is valued for its plump extract-rich kernels, low protein content, and mild flavor. Six-row barley is used more frequently in North America because it grows well in the hot, dry conditions of the midwestern prairies. Compared with two-row barley, six-row barley has thinner kernels, less extract potential, higher protein, more enzymes, and perhaps a grainier flavor owing to its greater amount of husk material. The high husk and enzyme content of six-row barley make it ideal for converting enzymeless and huskless adjuncts (see Adjuncts section below).

Pilsner, or *Pils*, malt (Fig. 7.2) is base malt that is subjected to lower kilning temperatures (160°F [71°C])

Figure 7.2. *Pils* malt is germinated and then very lightly kiln dried to preserve its very pale color. (Courtesy Weyermann Specialty Malting Company)

to minimize color formation and produce a very mild flavor appropriate for the delicate, clean-tasting, pale beer style in which it is used. English pale ale malt and its German cousin, Vienna malt, are kilned at a higher temperature (195°F [90°C]) to produce a more intense malt flavor and deeper golden hue.

High-Kilned Malt

High-kilned malts are produced in the same manner as base malt but the final kiln temperature is higher (215°F [102°C]) to produce darker, more aromatic malt. Common names are aromatic malt and, especially, Munich malt because it is similar to the amber malts that produced the brown lager beer common in Munich 100 years ago. Munich malt is often used as a specialty malt, but it contains enough enzymes to convert itself and can make up 100% of the grain bill in some cases. High-kilned malts produce an amber color and a malty sweet to toasty flavor.

Wheat

While 100% barley base malt is used in certain styles, such as pilsner, it is impractical to use 100% wheat malt because the kernels have no husk to provide a filter bed during wort separation. Therefore, when wheat malt (Fig. 7.3) forms the base malt of a style, such as Bavarian *Hefeweizen*, no more than 60–70% wheat malt is used, with the balance being barley malt to provide husks for lautering. Wheat makes good bread dough because it is high in sticky protein that holds the dough together. The protein has the same binding effect on beer bubbles, and wheat beers are known for their stable foam and hazy appearance derived from the malt protein.

Figure 7.3. Wheat is malted and can be kilned dry or roasted to add color and flavor. (Courtesy Weyermann Specialty Malting Company)

Sorghum and Millet

While they are not common brewing grains in western nations, sorghum and millet grow well in warm climates and are important malts in commercial beers in Africa, where they are also still used in various indigenous beers. In the West, malted sorghum and millet are receiving increased interest because they lack the protein gluten, found in wheat, barley, and rye, that causes gastrointestinal irritation in persons with celiac disease. Other gluten-free grains include rice, corn, and oats, but they are not easily malted.

Specialty Malts

Specialty malts are subjected to higher heat than base malts to create melanoidins through a browning reaction between malt proteins and sugars, which is similar to the chemical reaction that produces caramel. The amount of heat and moisture content of the green malt is manipulated to produce different colors and intensities of malt flavors. The high heat denatures enzymes, so specialty malts must be mashed with base malts for starch conversion.

Caramel or Crystal Malt

While still moist after germination, caramel malts (Fig. 7.4) are heated to mashing temperatures (140°F [60°C]) to allow the enzymes to convert the starches to sugar. After conversion, they are kilned to remove the excess moisture and crystallize the sugar. For this reason, the malts are sometimes referred to as crystal malts. Depending on the amount of heat, caramel malt flavors range from sweet, caramel, and toffee to burnt sugar and raisin, and colors range from gold to mahogany (Table 7.2). Caramel malts are typically used at a rate of 5–15% in the mash because of their intense flavors and lack of enzymes.

Figure 7.4. Caramel malt is stewed within its kernel to give it sweetness and then roasted to give it caramel, toffee, and nutty flavors. (Courtesy Weyermann Specialty Malting Company)

Table 7.2. Caramel Malts[a]

Type	Color (°L)	Hue	Flavor	Style
Caramel-10	8–12	Light golden	Sweet	Pale ale, pale lager
Caramel-20	18–22	Golden	Sweet toasty	Amber ale, lager
Caramel-40	35–45	Light red	Sweet toffee	Amber ale, red ale, lager
Caramel-60	55–60	Red to dark red	Roasted, slightly burnt sugar	Bock, Oktoberfest, dark ale
Caramel-80	78–85	Dark red	Burnt sugar	Barley wine
Caramel-120	100–120	Deep red	Burnt sugar, coffee	Porter, barley wine
Special B	135–145	Mahogany	Burnt sugar, raisin, prune	Barley wine, abbey ales

[a] Source: Gruber, 2006.

Dry-Roasted Malt

Dry-roasted malt (Fig. 7.5) is prepared in a way similar to base malt except that in the final step the malt is subjected to an extremely high temperature in a roaster similar to that used to roast coffee beans. Dry-roasted malts are not held at mashing temperatures while moist like caramel malts so they lack the same degree of sweetness and have a dryer, grainer flavor; but, like caramel malts, they have no enzymes. Colors range from amber/orange to brown and black. As the color increases, flavors change from nutty, toasted, biscuit, coffee, and cocoa to acrid smoke (Table 7.3). The flavor and color impact of dark-roasted malts can be intense. Chocolate and black malts rarely make up more than 5–10% of the mash and may be used at rates less than 1%.

Figure 7.5. Black malt is made by roasting pale barley malt to an almost burnt appearance that adds intense color and astringent coffee-like flavor. (Courtesy Weyermann Specialty Malting Company)

Table 7.3. Dry-Roasted Malts[a]

Type	Color (°L)	Hue	Flavor	Style
Amber malt	25–32	Orange	Nutty, toasted, cracker	Alt, Scottish ale, nut brown ale
Biscuit, brown malt	50–60	Orange	Warm bread	Brown ale
Chocolate malt	300–325	Deep red	Chocolate	Porter, brown ale
Dark chocolate malt	375–425	Deep red, brown	Dark chocolate	Porter, stout
Black malt	500–550	Deep red, brown	Smoky, acrid	Stout (or for color in other styles)

[a] Source: Gruber, 2006.

Adjuncts

Adjuncts are any nonmalted product that is added to a mash or a beer. These products are divided into two groups: nonmalted grains or other starches and sugar. There are many reasons to use adjuncts, including to lighten color/flavor, increase or decrease body, improve foam, and increase wort strength (i.e., alcohol content).

Lighten Color/Flavor

Germination and kilning create a range of flavor and color compounds that are lacking in raw grain or simple sugar. Being unmalted, grain adjuncts supply only starch. Using them or processed sugar in the mash increases the alcohol potential of the beer but with less flavor impact than malt. Adjuncts are primarily used in certain styles (e.g., American pale lager) to produce beers that are paler, less satiating, and snappier in taste.

Increase or Decrease Body

During malting, enzymes are created that also break down the structural proteins and carbohydrates of the kernel. When nonmalted grain is added to the mash, it adds large molecular proteins and carbohydrates that have not been broken down. As a result, they are carried into the beer, increasing its viscosity, mouthfeel, and body. On the other hand, certain adjuncts, such as sugar, rice, and corn grits, are processed to remove protein. As such, when they are added into the mash, or in the case of sugar sometimes into the wort, they lighten a beer's viscosity, mouthfeel, and body.

Improve Foam

For the same reason that sticky proteins in bread flour hold the carbon dioxide produced by baker's yeast, which causes the dough to rise, protein helps stabilize beer foam. High-protein adjuncts such as wheat are especially used for this purpose.

Increase Wort Strength

Dry sugar crystals or syrups can be added to the wort kettle to increase extract strength, especially for brewing high-alcohol beer.

Adjuncts are important ingredients that create the unique flavors that define many styles of beer enjoyed by millions of beer drinkers throughout the world. In Germany, however, the *Reinheitsgebot* continues to prohibit the use of raw grains and sugar. In some regions, the local grain, such as corn/maize, which cannot be easily malted, is used and provides a way for the brewer to economically use local materials to create a unique style of beer. Strong Belgian ales frequently include sugar to increase alcohol content without adding body or sweetness and employ raw wheat to improve head retention. These adjuncts are used because they add characteristics that have come to define the beer's style. Adjuncts are frequently used to lighten the body, flavor, and color, either alone or in combination, in American lagers. Use of an adjunct does not necessarily reduce the cost to produce a beer. For instance, the cost of rice per pound can be higher than that of many malts. Ultimately, it is the brewer who decides whether or not to craft his or her beer using an adjunct.

Unmalted Grains

Corn

Corn is native to North and South America and is commonly used as an adjunct in the Western Hemisphere. Corn is difficult to malt because it contains lots of oil (think corn-based margarine and cooking oil) that can go rancid when malted. In South and Central America, unmalted corn has been used to make an indigenous beer called chicha. Because the raw corn has no enzymes, the corn grits are chewed to mix in saliva and then expectorated into a pot. The amylase enzymes in the saliva convert the starch to sugar, and the mixture is fermented into beer.

In commercial brewing, unmalted corn grits that have had the oil- and protein-containing germ removed are mixed with malt after they have been flaked or cooked to gelatinize their starch to expose it to malt enzymes. Before advances in barley breeding and farming made low-temperature European two-row barley more available in North America, six-row barley was the predominant malting barley. Six-row barley contains more protein than two-row barley. The protein causes beer haze and problems in mashing and wort separation. It was therefore advantageous for brewers to use the locally abundant corn grits to dilute the six-row malt protein. Furthermore, six-row malt is enzyme rich and contains lots of husk material to aid in the conversion and filtration of the enzymeless and huskless grits.

Figure 7.6. Rice is grown in California and the southeastern United States. It is used to make beer pale and light bodied. (Courtesy Anheuser-Busch InBev)

Rice

Rice (Fig. 7.6) is used much like corn and is especially recognized for its ability to produce a light-colored, light-bodied, and crisp-tasting beer.

Wheat

Because of its high protein content, wheat is a popular adjunct to enhance the foam stability of beer and create haze. Wheat is a popular adjunct in Belgian-style beers. Many strong Belgian ales combine wheat and high carbonation to produce their characteristic thick, mousy head. *Wit* beer (white beer) uses wheat to throw a pale, floury-looking white haze from which the beer gets its name.

Oats

Rolled oat flakes, just like those in oatmeal, can add viscosity and mouthfeel and are frequently used to make full-bodied stouts, often named oatmeal stout.

Barley

Raw barley can be used to lighten the color of an all-malt beer, but it is probably best known in its dark-roasted form. Roasted barley gives Irish stouts their opaque black color and dry finish.

Sugar

Beet, cane, or corn sugar can be used to increase the alcohol content of beer without adding body, flavor, or residual sweetness. For this reason, Belgian brewers often use sugar in their strong ales. In contrast, German *Doppelbocks* are made only from malt because of the *Reinheitsgebot*. Because mashing leaves some complex unfermentable sugars (dextrins) in the beer, these strong German beers typically have a trademark level of sweetness and body. Sugar is also used in cask ale to create a secondary fermentation for bottle conditioning and carbonation. Other types of sugar, such as honey, molasses, maple sugar, or even fruit, can be used as a source of both extract and flavor.

Hops

Hops are the cones of the female hop plant (Fig. 7.7). These cones have lupulin glands filled with resins that contain bitter alpha acids and aromatic oils (Fig. 7.8). Alpha acids contribute bitterness to beer, offer protection against beer-spoilage microbes, and support foam stability in the glass. The oils provide fragrant aromas. These desirable contributions from the bitter acids and aromatic oils have combined to make hops the primary flavor agent in modern commercial beer.

Consistently managing the flavors derived from hops is one of the most challenging aspects of the brewer's art. Hops and hopping techniques not only influence the flavor and quality of beer but also differentiate brands and beer styles. Although hopping may have been largely an art in centuries past, increased knowledge of hops and how to use them has transformed hopping into both an art and science.

This section describes the history of hops, the flavors hops contribute to beer, and how hop varieties and brewing methods produce the wide range of important flavors in various beer styles.

The History of Hops

Hops are often ascribed a poetic, almost mystical role, as in "the kiss of the hops". If

Figure 7.7. Hop cones ripening on the vine. Hops grow up to 18 feet high on twine each season from a perennial rootstalk. (Courtesy S. Presley)

Figure 7.8. Cross section of a hop cone. Note the bright yellow lupulin that houses the hop bittering resins and aromatic oils. (Courtesy Anheuser-Busch InBev)

barley malt is the "soul of beer", then hop is its spice. This is a good analogy because hops are a minor ingredient in beer (usually less than 5% of the total recipe weight) that has a disproportionately important role in its aroma, flavor, stability, and appearance.

Why are hops so important? In centuries past, when most beers were brewed on a small scale in kitchens or monasteries, many different herbs were used to add flavor to the brew, including hops. In addition to their distinctive flavor, hops also helped preserve the flavor of beer.

In earlier times, brewers did not understand that beer became sour because of infection by acid-forming bacteria. However, they did observe that souring occurred less frequently when hops were added. The improved flavor stability of hopped beer was due to the powerful antibiotic nature of the hop bitter acids against certain beer-spoilage bacteria, while having little, if any, effect on the action of yeast. Consequently, hops may have come into widespread use because of their preservative qualities, with their flavor characteristics possibly being of secondary importance. In any case, hops became the predominant flavoring agent in beer. Modern microbiology and sanitation in the brewery have reduced the importance of the antibiotic action of hops, which in part has allowed for a corresponding reduction in bitterness levels in many modern examples of beer (see Hopping: The Brewer's Art and Science below).

The history of hops and their use in beer has been the topic of much research, but there is no consensus of when hops were first cultivated and used in beer. The earliest written evidence of hop cultivation was made in 736 A.D., with a reference to a hop garden in the Hallertau district of Germany. The first written report of hops used in beer dates to 1079 A.D.

Prior to the use of hops, a wide variety of herbs and spices, called gruit, were used to flavor beer. Some of the most common were juniper berries, ginger, caraway seed, aniseed, nutmeg, cinnamon, sweet gale, mugwort, yarrow, heather, and marsh Labrador tea. The following quotation demonstrates that there were economic as well as public safety reasons to switch from gruit to hops.

> "In the middle ages brewing beer was a primitive science, but by the 15th century it was also becoming a very lucrative industry. Brewers looking to make greater profit often used cheaper ingredients of mixed variety to achieve their financial goals. Unscrupulous brewers would add fruit, herbs, eggs, tree bark, fish bladders and who knows what else to their beer. As a result, beer was frequently foul tasting and occasionally poisonous." (Beer Church)

The transition from gruit to hops was difficult and slow and required several centuries. The hop was even condemned in England in the fifteenth and sixteenth centuries as a "wicked

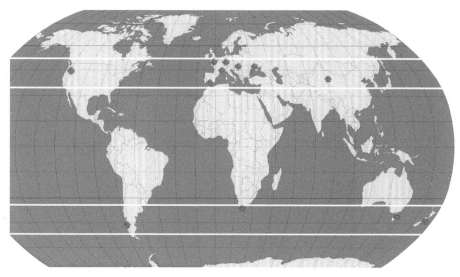

Figure 7.9. World hop-growing areas are predominately within the 35–50° north latitudes. Hop-growing latitudes are outlined in yellow. The red dots indicate major hop-growing areas. (Courtesy John I. Haas)

and pernicious weed" (Bamforth, 1998; p. 101). Despite the vigorous campaigns against their use, hops eventually prevailed, until it became virtually the only herb used in the flavoring of the vast majority of beers worldwide.

Hop Cultivation

The cultivated hop, *Humulus lupulus*, is indigenous to the temperate zones of the Northern Hemisphere between the latitudes of 35°N and 50°N. It is found wild in western Europe, Asia, and North America and, in 2007, was cultivated in some 28 countries, primarily in the Northern Hemisphere. The majority of the world's commercial hop production occurs between latitudes 35° and 55° either north or south of the equator. Theses latitudinal bands are preferred because the development of hops for brewing is optimized by the amount of sunlight received at these latitudes (Fig. 7.9).

The hop plant is a hardy, climbing perennial that produces annual vines

Figure 7.10. Field of hops maturing in the summer sunshine. (Courtesy Anheuser-Busch InBev and S. Presley)

Figure 7.11. Hop harvesting begins with cutting the vine off at the rootstalk and at the top of the trellis. (Courtesy HopUnion LLC)

Figure 7.12. After the cones are stripped from the vines, they make their way through a series of conveyors and sorting machines to separate out leaves and stems. (Courtesy HopUnion LLC)

from a permanent rootstock. They are propagated vegetatively by rhizomes (underground stems) or stem cuttings. The annual shoots emerge in early spring and twine around supporting strings or wires in a clockwise direction. Plants grow to a height of 15–25 feet in a single season (Fig. 7.10). The cones of the female plant contain thousands of yellow, resin-filled lupulin glands that hold the bitter alpha acids and aromatic oils that are of value in brewing. In the United States, shoots emerge in late February and early March, and flowering occurs in late June to mid-July. By mid- to late July, the first signs of cones appear, and by mid- to late August, the hop harvest starts by cutting the vines from the rootstock (Fig. 7.11), followed by removing the cones (Fig. 7.12). In late fall, the hop's rootstock goes dormant, not to reawaken until spring, when shoots reemerge to repeat the cycle of growth that can continue for years.

It is important to harvest hops at the peak of maturity to ensure optimum resin content. After harvest, the hop cones are dried in a kiln to prevent spoilage in storage (Figs. 7.13 and 7.14). Dried hops are typically compressed into 200-pound (90-kilogram) bales in large presses, wrapped in protective fabric, and put into cold storage because heat and oxygen cause deterioration of the hop bitter acids and aromatic oils (Fig. 7.15).

Although baled hops (also called cone hops or leaf hops) were the traditional form of hops worldwide, their use has declined in favor of compressed hop pellets, liquid extracts, and hop oils because these products are more stable, provide greater product con-

Figure 7.14. Hop cones are dried to between 8 and 10% moisture. The entire batch is left in a cooling pile for about 12 hours to equalize moisture throughout the bed. (Courtesy Anheuser-Busch InBev)

Figure 7.13. From the sorting conveyors, the cones are loaded into a kiln for drying. The bed of hops is about 2–3 feet deep, and drying each lot with 140–150°F (60–65.5°C) air takes about 8 hours. (Courtesy HopUnion LLC)

Figure 7.15. Cooled, dried hops are compressed into 200-pound bales and wrapped with a burlap blanket, sewn tight, marked, and tested. (Courtesy HopUnion LLC)

sistency, are less costly to store, and are easier to handle and use with modern brewing equipment (Figs. 7.16 and 7.17).

One example of a processed hop product is a special hop extract used for the prevention of the skunky or light-struck aroma that occurs in beer exposed to ultraviolet light. Ultraviolet light reacts with the bitter acids in beer to produce free radicals that then react with the sulfur compounds dissolved in beer to produce a skunky aroma. Since brown glass offers protection against this light, it has become the preferred glass color for beer bottles. Brewers using clear and green glass who want to protect their beer from developing this skunky aroma must use a modified liquid hop product that has had the light-struck potential eliminated.

Figure 7.16. Hops can be processed in pellets for more efficient use in the brewhouse. The pelleting process involves milling the cones into a rough powder, pressing the mixture through a die, and then packaging the pellets in air-tight metal or plastic. As pellets, the hops keep better and disperse easily into the wort in the brew kettle. (Courtesy Anheuser-Busch InBev)

Figure 7.17. Hops in the typical forms of use: whole cone, pellet, and hop extract syrup. Hop bittering resins and oils can be refined to a pure syrup. (Courtesy Anheuser-Busch InBev and S. Presley)

World Hop Production

Hops are cultivated commercially in about 28 countries (Barth-Haas Group, 2007). Germany was the largest hop grower in 2009, followed by the Unites States and China (HGA, 2010a) (Table 7.4).

U.S. Hop Production

In earlier times, U.S. hop production was centered in New York and Wisconsin (for details of the history of hop growing in the United States, see Barth et al., 1994). However, for many reasons, including pests and disease, production moved west along the same latitude to dryer climates in California, Washington, Oregon, and Idaho. Today, the latter three states grow about one-quarter of the world's hop acreage. About 75% of the 2009 U.S. hop acreage was grown in Washington's Yakima Valley, about 15% in Oregon's Willamette Valley, and 10% in Idaho around Boise and Bonners Ferry (HGA, 2010b).

Table 7.4. World Hop Acreage and Production in 2009[a]

Country	Hop Acreage	% World Acreage	Production (pounds)	% World Production
Germany	43,902	33	68,894,000	29
United States	40,126	30	91,491,000	38
China	14,322	11	35,494,000	15
Czech Republic	12,479	9	14,109,000	6
England	2,669	2	3,197,000	1
Rest of Europe	16,222	12	20,780,000	9
Rest of the world	3,991	3	6,927,000	3
World totals	133,711	100	242,892,000	100

[a] Source: HGA, 2010a.

Hop Varieties

Hundreds of named hop varieties exist worldwide and more are being released each year by various hop breeding programs. In 2007, the number of hop varieties grown commercially worldwide was about 40 (Barth-Haas Group, 2007). Hops are classified into two major categories according to their major roles in beer production: bittering hops and aroma hops.

Bittering Hops

Bittering hops are those varieties containing a high percentage of alpha acids, which contributes the bitterness to beer, which balances the malt sweetness. The alpha acid content in commercial hops ranges from 2 to 15% by weight, with bittering hops usually containing 8% or more alpha acids. It is economical to use high-alpha-acid hops for bittering beer because the brewer can use a smaller amount to achieve the desired bitterness. The amount or character of aromatic oils in bittering hops is of lesser concern to the brewer, since bittering hops are boiled in the wort for long periods of up to 1 hour or longer, which drives off the volatile aroma constituents through steam distillation.

Aroma Hops

Aroma hop varieties are valued for their volatile oils, also called the essential oil. Hop essential oil is estimated to contain more than 300 different chemical entities that are produced late in the ripening phase. Hop variety is an important determinant of hop essential oil content. The primary components of the oil are hydrocarbons (myrcene, caryophyllene, humulene, and farnesene), oxygenated components (geranyl esters, geraniol, and linalool), and sulfur compounds (Stevens, 1987; pp. 42–54). The various concentrations of these oils determine the unique aromas associated with the different varieties of aroma hops. Typical hop aromas have their own flavor descriptions (Table 7.5).

Aroma hops are prized for the amount and character of their hop oils and typically contain a lower percentage of bitter alpha acids. To preserve the volatile aromas of the hydrocarbon fraction, aroma hops are typically added during the last 10 minutes of the boil or even after the boil has ended. Unlike bitter alpha acids that must be boiled to dissolve them in the wort, essential oils are soluble at room temperature.

For this reason, hop aroma can be contributed to the beer by adding hops postfermentation in the conditioning tank or in the cask in a process known as dry hopping. Dry-hopped beer normally contains more aroma than beers hopped only with late-kettle hops, and the character of the aromas may be different. Dry-hopped beers may be more herbaceous, pungent, or grassy tasting since even a short period of boiling for late-kettle hops can reduce these flavors. This is a major difference between German pilsners flavored only with late-kettle hops and dry-hopped British and American ales. The traditional hop aroma in Ger-

Table 7.5. Common Hop Aromas in Beer[a]

Citrusy	Esters	Floral	Herbal	Spicy	Sylvan (Woody)
Grapefruit	Pineapple	Geranium	Fresh hop	Sandalwood	Cedar, pine
Bergamot	Pear skin	Lavender	Grassy	Oak moss	Woody
Lemon	Sweet	Rose	Green	Astringent	Earthy
Lime	Fruity	Neroli			

[a] Source: www.barthhaasgroup.com.

man pilsners is often described as noble because of the fine, delicate, and flowery nature of the hop aroma. Therefore, aroma hops from Germany are often referred to as noble hops.

The distinction between bittering and aroma hop varieties is not always clear cut. Some hop varieties may be used for both bittering and flavor. German brewers seeking a very delicate hop character may even use low-alpha-acid aroma hops for bittering because they believe that the quality of the bitterness contributed by aroma hops is more delicate and noble than that of traditional bittering hops.

How Brewers Impart Hop Character to Beer

Bitterness

Hop bitterness is imparted to beer when the heat of boiling in the wort kettle converts the insoluble bitter alpha acids to a soluble form through a process called isomerization. The longer hops are boiled, the greater the amount of bitter acids that are isomerized, or dissolved. Therefore, bittering hops are most often added at the beginning of the boil. Many factors besides heat, including wort strength and pH, affect the solubility of the bitter acids. Furthermore, because dissolved bitter acids are concentrated in beer foam, any time during the brewing process when beer foams, bitter acids may be deposited in the collapsed foam left in tanks or equipment. (This is the reason that beer foam tastes more bitter than beer.) Bitter acids also attach to yeast and protein particles that are removed from beer in the whirlpool or in the filter. Consequently, only 30–40% of the bitter acids in the hop resins make it into packaged beer. Brewers must pay close attention to the entire brewing process to produce a consistent level of bitterness.

The bitterness level in beer is measured in international bitterness units (IBU, or simply BU), which is the number of milligrams of isomerized alpha acids in 1 liter of beer, or simply parts per million. The IBU level can vary between styles (Table 7.6), as experienced in an American light lager with 4–7 IBU, a German pilsner with 24–36 IBU, and an American India pale ale with 40–65 IBU.

Aroma

Volatile hop essential oil is generally conceded to be the primary source of hoppy aroma in beer, but controlling the desired hop aroma is one of the most elusive challenges in brewing. Hop oil is a complex mixture of many different flavor components. The proportion of these entities in the oil can vary by crop year, between varieties, and among lots of the same hop variety.

Hop essential oil also contains a complex oxygenated fraction (geranyl esters, geraniol, and linalool), which includes compounds that survive into the finished beer. As previously stated, heat volatizes the aromatic oils

Table 7.6. Bitterness of Typical Beers of Various Styles[a]

Style	International Bitterness Units (IBU)
American light lager	4–7
American standard lager	6–9
German *Märzen*	15–20
German pilsner	24–36
Bavarian *Hefeweizen*	10–15
American wheat ale	10–35
English bitter ale	20–35
Pale ale	28–40
India pale ale	40–65
Scottish ale	15–25
Barley wine	>50
Stout	20–40

[a] Source: Brewers Association, 2010.

in the hop resin; therefore, aroma hops are added during the last 10 minutes of the boil, in the whirlpool, or even in the conditioning tank. The extraction of flavor from hops occurs through various complex and often little understood chemical reactions, including these oxygenated fractions. Therefore, brewers may add hops at various points during the brewing process because of the different chemical reactions that take place depending on the amount of heat and the length of time the hops are exposed to heat. First wort hopping involves adding hops to the wort kettle while the wort is being

Figure 7.18. Many craft brewers dry hop beer, which is adding hops into the already fermented beer. This process adds fresh hop oil for interesting and intense flavors and aromas. (Courtesy BridgePort Brewing Company)

collected from the lauter tun before boiling commences. Brewers may also boil hops for 1 hour, 30 minutes, or 10 minutes, or other time frames, since each type of time-and-heat combination produces different flavor characteristics. Dry hopping involves adding hops in the conditioning tank or in the cask just before it is delivered to the pub in order to contribute hop oil to the beer and create fresh green, grassy, and herbal varietal aromas and flavors. Many American brewers practice dry hopping by adding fresh hops to fermented beer in cellar tanks (Fig. 7.18). At this point, there is no heat to volatize and drive off the aroma. Finally, brewers can also add a processed form of hop essential oils to the beer before packaging to produce hop aroma.

Hopping: The Brewer's Art and Science

From the foregoing, it can be appreciated that hops, hop products, and hopping techniques are powerful tools that affect the flavor and quality of beer to differentiate brands, create new brands and styles, and aid in the marketing of brands. Although hopping may have been largely an art, it can now justifiably be called both an art and science because of the huge amount of scientific research and technology that has gone into the understanding and control of hop flavor.

The art and science of hopping encompasses many factors, including the amount of hops, time of hopping, number of hop additions, type of hop products, hop varieties (and blends thereof), brewing process, and finishing process that the brewer combines to produce the desired bitterness and aroma consistent with the style of beer.

Bitterness is readily recognizable and is a defining characteristic of beer that varies between styles and even within style categories based on consumer preference. Bitterness varies considerably from country to country and from beer style to beer style. For example, European lagers may range from 15 to 40 IBU, U.K. ales from 16 to 50 IBU, U.S. lagers from 8 to 15 IBU, Australian lagers from 14 to 18 IBU, and German pilsners from

Table 7.7. Worldwide Hopping Rates[a]

Brewing Year	Hopping Rate (g α/hL[b])
1995	6.3
1997	6.1
1999	5.7
2001	5.5
2003	5.2
2005	5.0
2007	4.8

[a] Source: Barth-Haas Group, 1999–2006, 2007.
[b] Grams of isomerized alpha acids per hectoliter of beer.

25 to 35 IBU (EBC, 1997; p. 3). For this reason, beer styles are partly defined by bitterness levels.

The worldwide trend in beer bitterness has been toward lower and lower bitterness levels. Between 1995 and 2007, the estimated worldwide hopping rates declined by 24%, from 6.3 grams of alpha acids per hectoliter to 4.8 grams of alpha acids per hectoliter (Table 7.7). However, a significant number of American craft brewers have headed in the opposite direction by creating new versions of super hoppy beers, such as double or imperial India pale ales, with enormous amounts of bittering hops (and aroma hops) that produce IBU levels approaching 100.

As stated several times above, one of the most elusive problems in brewing is to brew beer with a consistent level of bitterness and hop aroma. Although much is known about hop varieties, including extensive analytical data, hop flavor (especially aroma) is elusive, such that the selection and use of hop varieties still requires the artistic skill of the brewer.

Yeast

Brewer's yeast is a single-cell fungus that feeds on wort sugars in a process called fermentation, which transforms wort into beer through the production of alcohol, carbon dioxide, and minor metabolic by-products that make powerful contributions to flavor.

There are hundreds of different strains of brewer's yeast that are valued individually for the unique flavor characteristics they impart and the role they play in defining beer styles. While different yeast strains are a factor in making wine and distilled spirits, they are not emphasized to the same extent in identifying style as they are in brewing. In fact, the two major categories of brewer's yeast define the two major categories of beer: ale and lager.

History of Yeast

Although the action of yeast in fermentation was readily observable by early brewers with the appearance of carbon dioxide bubbles and alcohol, individual yeast cells were too small for the naked eye to see. Their presence was only recognizable as a creamy mass of krausen on top of fermenting beer or as the gooey sludge left in the bottom of brewing vessels. Early brewers probably unwittingly developed techniques for adding yeast to wort to initiate fermentation based upon what worked rather than their understanding of yeast and fermentation.

Throughout history, brewing and bread making were closely linked. It was understood that leavening caused dough to rise, but it was not understood that fermenting yeast was the actual leavening agent. Early brewers understood this cause-and-effect relationship and used half-baked bread loaves containing yeast to initiate fermentation in the wort they produced. This technique was prevalent in ancient Egypt and Sumeria. Airborne yeast also inoculated wort when the fermentation vessels were left open. Porous clay brewing pots or wooden vats also harbored yeast from prior fermentations and could restart fermentation when these containers were refilled with wort. Fruit, the skins of which naturally contain yeast, was used as an ingredient and caused fermentation to occur. (A similar practice is still used today by some wine makers to produce wines using only the naturally occurring yeast on grape skins.) Finally, brewers also must have observed that, when the thick sludge from the bottom of fermentation vessels was added to a new batch of wort, the fermentation proceeded more efficiently and predictably.

A brewing ordinance from Munich in 1551 mentions *Hepffen* along with barley, water, and hop. This is a clear indication that brewers had identified *Hefe*, the modern German name for yeast, as an ingredient in beer even though its identification as a single-cell fungus was not yet understood. It was not until 1868 that Louis Pasteur identified yeast as the organism responsible for fermentation. In 1890, Emil Hansen of the Carlsberg Brewery in Denmark demonstrated how to isolate pure strains of yeast so that fermentation could be conducted free of wild yeast or other microorganisms.

Prior to this time, the inability to isolate pure yeast strains meant that the brewing yeast could contain multiple yeast strains that produced various flavor profiles. Therefore, the flavor of beer could vary from one batch to the next. Furthermore, beer-spoilage bacteria that turned beer sour could be carried forward from fermentation to fermentation.

Some historians credit medieval German monks with devising a method to extend the stability of beer by fermenting it at low temperatures. By brewing only during the winter or in cellars cooled by ice cut from frozen lakes, they unknowingly selected for yeast genetically capable of working in the cold. Since most bacteria are inactive at low temperatures, the fermentation proceeded without meaningful intrusion of souring bacteria as long as the beer stayed cold. They stored (or *lagered* in German) the beer in cold caves to clarify it and mellow or mature its flavor. The cold-fermenting yeast became known as lager yeast, and the beer produced was named lager beer.

Improved sanitation and the ability to pitch pure yeast strains eventually allowed warm-fermented ales to achieve the same flavor stability, but the distinction between the two types of yeast still exists. Ale (*Saccharomyces cerevisiae*) and lager (*Saccharomyces pastorianus*) yeast are each prized for their unique flavor characteristics.

What Is Brewer's Yeast?

Yeast is a simple, microscopic, single-cell fungi about ten times larger than bacteria (Fig. 7.19). Brewer's yeast sustains itself by feeding on sugar and other wort nutrients so it can grow and reproduce through a process called budding, in which the yeast cell divides into two new cells. By feeding on sugar through a process called fermentation, it produces alcohol and carbon dioxide as primary waste products, plus trace amounts of other metabolic by-products that can be powerful flavor compounds, such as acids, esters, fusel alcohols, and phenols.

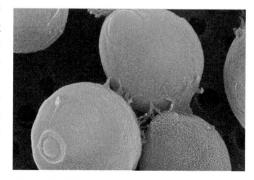

Figure 7.19. Yeast cells. (Courtesy A. Speers)

Yeast is a living organism that needs the right nutrients and environmental conditions to feed and reproduce. Among these nutrients are sugar, nitrogen, unsaturated fatty acids and sterols, minerals and vitamins, and oxygen. The type of sugar available to the yeast is important because it affects the body and sweetness of the beer. Common sugars fermentable by brewer's yeast consist of one, two, and three sugar molecules in size, such as glucose (table sugar), maltose, and maltotriose, respectively. Sugars of up to three glucose units in complexity are fermentable by brewer's yeast, but larger molecules of four glucose units and larger are not. These nonfermentable sugars, called dextrins, remain intact and add body and sweetness to beer.

Fortunately, wort produced from malt generally provides all of these nutrients in sufficient quantities for yeast health and growth. The exception is oxygen, which the brewer simply dissolves in the wort when yeast is added, or pitched, into the wort. Oxygen is important to yeast for metabolism, reproduction, and especially building cellular membranes.

Beer Fermentation

The primary goal in fermentation is to produce alcohol, but the brewer must also produce a consistent-tasting product batch after batch. To achieve this, the brewer must create the ideal combination of nutrients (i.e., wort), oxygen, and environmental factors (particularly temperature) that produce healthy, active yeast that can be repeatedly pitched into successive batches and still produce a consistent beer flavor. Properly sustaining, propagating, and managing yeast is extremely important in producing high-quality and consistent-tasting beer.

After boiling, clarifying, and cooling the wort, the brewer fills the fermenter and aerates the wort with sterile air or pure oxygen immediately before, or just after, the yeast is added to the fermenter (also known as pitched). For the first few hours, the action of the yeast is unobservable as the yeast takes up oxygen. Oxygen is needed to build cell membranes in preparation for yeast cell reproduction. Cells reproduce by budding, whereby a bump forms on the outer cell wall that grows into a daughter cell and eventually breaks free from the mother cell. Reproduction, or doubling, continues until the optimum cell density is reached or until the necessary nutrients, fermentation conditions, or both, are no longer present to support reproduction. Brewers pitch yeast at a rate between 5 and 25 million cells per milliliter of wort—yes, that is a whole bunch of cells! In a typical fermentation, yeast cells increase their numbers to a peak cell count between 80 and 120 million cells per milliliter.

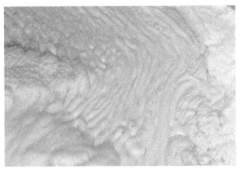

Figure 7.20. Initial creamy formation of foam on freshly fermenting lager beer. (Courtesy K. Ockert)

After the yeast cells have prepared themselves by multiplying and creating an anaerobic environment through the uptake of oxygen during the first 12–24 hours, the yeast cells start to actively ferment. There is a progression that the foam formations take as fermentation proceeds (Figs. 7.20–7.23). Ale yeast usually ferments at 59–72°F (15–22°C) and lager yeast ferments at 46–59°F (8–15°C). The most active, or primary, phase of fermentation is easily observable by the krausen of foam that forms on top of the fermenting beer. Rapidly escaping carbon dioxide bubbles that carry yeast cells, protein, and hop residue to the surface of the fermenter form the krausen. In open ale fermenters, this debris is often skimmed off and disposed of one or more times. When a clean krausen forms, the yeast is then skimmed off and collected for repitching in subsequent batches. The propensity of ale yeast to rise to the surface is one reason why ale yeast is sometimes referred to as top-fermenting yeast. After about 1 week, primary fermentation ends when 80 or 90% of the fermentable extract has been consumed. The krausen falls with the diminished release of carbon dioxide as fermentation slows. A large portion of the yeast that was in suspension flocculates and settles to the bottom of the fermenter, from where it can be removed.

Lager yeast creates the same krausen effect as ale yeast; however, when fermentation nears conclusion, the lager yeast has a greater propensity to settle to the bottom of the tank, from where it is harvested. This is why lager yeast is sometimes referred to as bottom-fermenting yeast. In reality, the distinction between bottom- and top-fermenting yeast is becoming less relevant with the increased attention to sanitation, which has led to fermenting both ales and lagers in closed fermenters. These closed fermenters often have a bottom cone that collects the yeast after it drops. Conical vertical fermenters are now widely used for both ale and lager yeast fermentation and harvesting.

The young beer is then transferred to a conditioning tank with enough yeast still in suspension to complete maturation of the beer. In the conditioning tank, the yeast completes fermentation of the remaining fermentable sugars (i.e., fully attenuate) and cleans up young beer flavors, such as acetaldehyde and diacetyl. Conditioning periods last from 1 to 4 weeks, with ales undergoing maturation at the shorter end of the range and lagers at the longer end. Although technology is allowing for decreasing conditioning periods, some specialty beers (especially those high

Figure 7.21. Fermentation foam turns rocky as the fermentation grows active and carbon dioxide is released. (Courtesy K. Ockert)

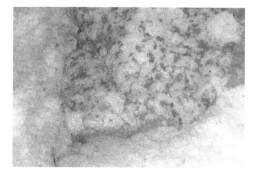

Figure 7.22. As fermentation begins to decline, bitter resinous material forms on the top of the foam and is commonly skimmed off or sticks to the top of the fermenter. (Courtesy K. Ockert)

Figure 7.23. At the end of fermentation, the yeast cools and drops to the bottom of the fermenting tank, leaving a sheet of large bubbles behind. (Courtesy K. Ockert)

in alcohol) may still mature, or lager, for several months. Maturation periods for ales are shorter than for lagers because ales ferment and condition at higher temperatures, which support greater metabolic activity that allows the yeast to clean up young "green" beer flavors more rapidly. Lager yeast metabolism is slower because of the lower temperatures needed to produce its signature character, which in turn requires longer maturation periods. Lagers traditionally mature at temperatures between 30 and 46°F (–1 and 8°C).

During its growth and fermentation phases, yeast consumes nutrients in the wort that were extracted during mashing. By manipulating mashing variables, such as malt type, time, temperature, and water volumes, the brewer controls the sugar concentration, nutrients, nitrogen levels (protein and amino acids), and fermentability of the wort. These wort constituents influence how the yeast converts wort into ethanol, carbon dioxide, and especially secondary metabolites that determine the beer's character. The yeast strain and fermentation parameters are also important in producing the unique flavors that define the beer style and brand. In summary, brewers create the desired beer characteristics by manipulating a host of dynamic variables, including the life cycle of a living organism—yeast.

Brewers select yeast based on its ability to
- Rapidly convert all fermentable sugars to alcohol and carbon dioxide,
- Consistently produce the same aromas and flavors batch after batch, and
- Withstand the stresses of propagation, storage, and repitching without loss of vitality, viability, or genetic stability.

Fermentation Parameters and Effects on Flavor

Brewing a consistent beer is much more complicated than just following the same recipe over and over again. To brew consistently requires managing the metabolic activity of two living organisms, germinating grain and fermenting yeast. In fermentation, it is essential that the brewer create a favorable environment to support a healthy population of yeast that will grow and ferment in a predictable manner. This environment includes nutrients and fermentation parameters that, if varied even slightly, could change the branded taste that consumers expect. Therefore, the brewer's ability to produce a consistent beer batch after batch is dependent upon the ability to recreate the same wort and fermentation conditions regardless of the changes that nature and maltsters create.

The following is a short list of important fermentation parameters that the brewer must manage to produce consistent-tasting beer.

Wort Composition

Effective wort production produces a balance of nutrients required by yeast for reproduction and fermentation. For example, if the water does not contain enough calcium or other minerals, if too little oxygen is dissolved in the wort, or if the mashing process fails to release enough amino acids from the malt or create the needed balance of fermentable and unfermentable sugars, the yeast may not grow to the optimal population of healthy cells, which could result in an incomplete fermentation and the production of unwanted flavors.

Temperature

Lager yeast has the ability to ferment at low temperatures, ale yeast does not. The slower yeast metabolism created by lower temperatures allows lager yeast to produce fewer esters and fusel alcohols than that of ale yeast. In general, whether using lager or ale yeast, increasing the temperature of fermentation can increase the level of esters and fusel alcohols. Brewers manipulate temperature to influence the flavor compounds produced by yeast.

Oxygenation

Controlling the level of aeration or oxygenation of the wort provided to the yeast is critical for the formation of yeast cell membranes to support cell growth and health. If insufficient oxygen is available to the yeast, fermentation may be incomplete and produce increased levels of unwanted flavors. However, brewers sometimes limit but not fully restrict aeration to produce desired flavor traits, especially esters, which tend to increase as the level of oxygen in the wort decreases. It is important to point out that this is the only step in the brewing process where the introduction of oxygen is acceptable. Its inclusion at any other part of the process, especially packaging, can lead to unwanted stale flavors.

Yeast Management

Increasing the pitching rate tends to increase the level of attenuation and decrease the level of esters. Using unhealthy, nonvital, or impure yeast may produce excess diacetyl, sulfury off-flavors and incomplete fermentation of sugars. Therefore, breweries are especially protective of their yeast to avoid contamination by other microbes, guard against mutation, and maintain the vitality and viability of the cells. For this reason, breweries periodically propagate a new population of yeast from a pure culture stored in its laboratory or purchased from a commercial yeast bank. This periodic renewal from a pure culture reduces the risk of contamination and ensures that the yeast strain has the correct genetic characteristics to produce the desired beer flavors.

Table 7.8 lists certain brewing parameters and their potential effects on beer flavor. These causes and effects are complex and interrelated and are relationships that are left to brewers to deal with. For nonbrewers, this list simply demonstrates the importance of yeast in creating a wide range of beer flavors and the many factors that influence the creation and intensity of these flavors. Fermentation flavor compounds are discussed in greater detail in Chapter 9.

Table 7.8. Brewing Parameters and Their Potential Effects on Beer Flavor

Parameter	Effect
Wort gravity ↑	↑ Esters, ↑ alcohols
Oxygen ↑	↓ Esters, ↓ H_2S, ↓ SO_2 ↑ fusel alcohols
Fermentation temperature ↑	↑ Esters, ↑ fusel alcohols
Amino acids (nitrogen) ↑	↑ Esters, ↓ fusel alcohols
Pitching rate ↑	↓ Esters, ↓ H_2S, ↑ attenuation
Yeast viability ↓	↑ Diacetyl, ↑ H_2S, ↓ attenuation
Yeast growth ↑	↑ Diacetyl production and reduction, ↓ esters, ↓ SO_2
Fermenter depth ↑ or top pressure ↑	↓ Esters

Conclusion

This section has demonstrated the importance of yeast in making beer and creating the unique flavors that define individual beer styles. Because fermentation involves coaxing a living organism to produce a specific amount of alcohol and flavors, brewers must manage this dynamic process with skill and focused attention to produce consistent results. Yeast is often listed as an ingredient in beer and has been listed as such in this chapter along with water, malt, and hop. In reality, yeast is much more than an ingredient. It also works alongside the brewer to create beer from water, malt, and hop.

Selected References

American Society of Brewing Chemists (ASBC). 1992. Appendix II: Nomenclature of hop resin fractions and components. In: Methods of Analysis of the ASBC, 8th ed. ASBC, St. Paul, MN.

Bamforth, C. 1998. Beer: Tap Into the Art and Science of Brewing. Insight Books, Plenum Press, New York.

Bamforth, C. W. 2006. Scientific Principles of Malting and Brewing. American Society of Brewing Chemists, St. Paul, MN.

Barth, H. J., Klinke, C., and Schmidt, C. 1994. The Hop Atlas: The History and Geography of the Cultivated Plant. Joh. Barth & Sohn, Nuremberg, Germany.

Barth-Haas Group. Home. www.barthhaasgroup.com. Joh. Barth & Sohn, Nuremburg, Germany.

Barth-Haas Group. Varieties & Products. www.barthhaasgroup.com. Joh. Barth & Sohn, Nuremburg, Germany.

Barth-Haas Group. 1999–2006. The Barth Report, Hops 1998/1999 to 2005/2006. Joh. Barth & Sohn, Nuremburg, Germany.

Barth-Haas Group. 2007. The Barth Report, Hops 2006/2007. Joh. Barth & Sohn, Nuremburg, Germany.

Beer Church. Beer Info: Beer History: The Reinheitsgebot. www.beerchurch.com. Beer Church, Seattle, WA.

BetaTec Hop Products. www.betatechopproducts.com. Washington, DC.

Bradee, L., Duensing, W., Halstad, S., Klimovitz, R., and Laidlaw, A. 1999. Adjuncts. Pages 75-98 in: The Practical Brewer, 3rd ed. J. T. McCabe, ed. Master Brewers Association of the Americas, St. Paul, MN.

Brewers Association. 2010. Brewers Association 2010 Beer Style Guidelines. www.brewers association.org/pages/publications/beer-style-guidelines

Briess Malt & Ingredients Co. Products. www.brewingwithbriess.com/Products/Default.htm. Briess Malt & Ingredients Co., Chilton, WI.

Briggs, D. E., Boulton, C. A., Brookes, P. A., and Stevens, R. 2004. Hops and The chemistry of hop constituents. Pages 227-254 and 255-305 in: Brewing: Science and Practice. Woodhead Publishing Ltd., Cambridge, England, and CRC Press, Boca Raton, FL.

Cargill, Inc. Brewers base malt. www.cargill.com/food/na/en/products/malt/brewers-base-malt/index.jsp. Cargill, Inc., Minneapolis, MN.

European Brewery Convention (EBC). 1997. Hops and Hop Products. EBC Manual of Good Practice. Fachverlag Hans Carl, Nuremberg, Germany.

Gales, P. W., ed. 2007. Brewing Chemistry and Technology in the Americas. American Society of Brewing Chemists, St. Paul, MN.

Gruber, M. A. 2006. Specialty malts. Pages 55-72 in: MBAA Practical Handbook for the Specialty Brewer—Vol. 1: Raw Materials and Brewhouse Operations. K. Ockert, ed. Master Brewers Association of the Americas, St. Paul, MN.

Hop Growers of America (HGA). 2010a. USAHops 2009 Statistical Report. HGA, Moxee, WA. www.usahops.org.

Hop Growers of America (HGA). 2010b. Hop Farming. www.usahops.org. HGA, Moxee, WA.

Hopsteiner. Hop Varieties. www.hopsteiner.com/varietiesus.html. S. S. Steiner, New York.

HopUnion. Hop Variety Characteristics Booklet. www.hopunion.com/hvcb/. HopUnion, Yakima, WA.

Kramer, P. 2006. Barley, malt, and malting. Pages 15-54 in: MBAA Practical Handbook for the Specialty Brewer—Vol. 1: Raw Materials and Brewhouse Operations. K. Ockert, ed. Master Brewers Association of the Americas, St. Paul, MN.

Neve, R. A. 1991. Hops. Chapman & Hall, London.

Moir, M. 2000. Hops—A millennium review. Journal of the American Society of Brewing Chemists 58:131-146.

Roberts, T. R., and Wilson, R. J. H. 2006. Hops. Pages 177-280 in: Handbook of Brewing, Second Ed. F. G. Priest and G. G. Stewart, eds. CRC Press, Taylor & Francis Group, Boca Raton, FL.

Stevens, R., ed. 1987. An Introduction to Brewing Science and Technology, Ser. II, Vol. 1: Hops. The Institute of Brewing, London.

Wikipedia contributors. 2010. Gruit. Wikipedia, The Free Encyclopedia. http://en.wikipedia.org/wiki/Gruit.

Yakima Chief. 2000. Hop Varietal Guide. www.yakimachief.com/hopvarieties/ycivarieties.pdf. Yakima Chief, Inc., Sunnyside, WA.

Chapter 8:
Draft Beer

Neil Witte and Stephen R. Holle

Draft beer, when handled properly, can offer beer drinkers the pinnacle of freshness and quality. Compared with bottled or canned beer, draft beer is rarely pasteurized, is typically kept cold after leaving the brewery, picks up less staling oxygen during filling, and is usually consumed shortly after leaving the brewery. When all these conditions come together, they add up to fresh beer in the consumer's glass. Unfortunately, some retailers do not understand that beer is a perishable product and that draft systems must be diligently maintained to protect beer quality. This chapter discusses the general principles for serving draft beer. The goal is not to turn the reader into a draft system technician. Designing and installing a system should be hired out to a trained professional. However, tavern owners, managers, bartenders, and others that handle draft beer should be knowledgeable of some basic principles required to install, operate, and maintain their systems.

What Is Draft Beer?

Prior to the development of the modern draft system, beer was stored in wooden casks that were lined with pitch to provide a protective barrier between the wood and the beer. The beer was dispensed without pressure by opening a spigot at the bottom of the cask through which beer flowed by the force of gravity. In 1797, Joseph Bramah invented a mechanical pump, or beer engine, that allowed the cask to be placed in a cool cellar and pumped to the spigot by pulling on the tap handle. The casks were unpressurized and air simply filled the headspace as the beer left the cask. Ideally, the tavern drained the cask in a few hours since the beer would gradually lose its carbonation in this unpressurized environment. Furthermore, because the air caused staling and carried beer-spoilage microbes, freshness and quality also deteriorated rapidly.

In the late 1800s, brewers developed methods to pressurize kegs with inert carbon dioxide gas, which not only maintained the carbonation level but also protected the beer from staling and spoiling. By the early twentieth century, metal replaced wood as the material of choice for kegs for reasons of hygiene, durability, and pressure tightness. Today, in the United Kingdom, beer is still served from unpressurized casks (both metal and wooden) for reasons of tradition and taste. Pubs dispense these traditional unfiltered ales, known as real ales, from casks via a beer engine.

The focus of this chapter is on draft beer served from a modern, pressurized, stainless steel keg with a single opening, or tap well, at the top (Fig. 8.1). It is tapped for dispense by locking a proprietary male coupler into the tap well. The coupler is connected by

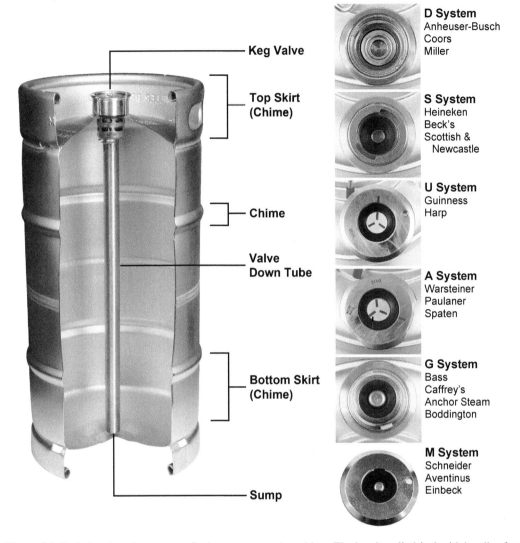

Figure 8.1. Left, Interior of a common Sanke one-quarter-barrel keg. The keg is cylindrical with handles for use when lifting. The keg valve is at the top of the keg and extends inside with a tube that comes to within about one-quarter inch of the bottom of the keg in a small well for almost complete emptying. **Right,** Keg valve systems. (Courtesy Micro Matic USA, Inc.)

flexible plastic tubing to a gas cylinder and to the dispense faucet, or tap as it is frequently referred to in the trade. A stainless steel tube or spear connected to the tap well extends to the bottom of the keg. Gas flows through the coupler and into the top headspace of the keg as the beer is withdrawn up the spear, through the coupler, and to the dispense faucet. The pressure in the headspace above the beer provides the driving force to push the beer from the keg to the faucet and maintain the beer's level of carbonation.

Some breweries have marketed bottles or cans as "draft" beer because, like most draft beers, the contents have not been pasteurized. Typically, these packaged beers have been protected against microbes by aseptic filtration, which serves to protect the beer from microorganisms that can spoil it. This process is sometimes marketed or described as "cold" filtration, even though all beers are cold when filtered. Certain nitrogenated canned beers containing widgets (small, liquid nitrogen-charged devices in the can that create a dense head of nitrogen-filled bubbles when the can is opened) may also be described as "draft" since the widget's action helps create the creamy head produced by a beer engine or stout faucet.

Challenges in Maintaining a Draft System

As the quality of draft systems has improved, so have demands on them. In the past, when tavern owners served only one or two draft beers, kegs turned over daily, ensuring that fresh beer was always on tap. As the number of beer brands increased and retailers added more taps to meet demands for greater variety, kegs emptied more slowly and the length of draft lines increased as refrigerated space near the bar became insufficient to accommodate the greater number of kegs.

As the number of faucets/taps and the length of draft lines increase, so does the diligence required to maintain beer quality. Slow turnover and long draft lines expose beer to greater risks of staling and spoiling. Multiple faucets/taps and long runs also make draft systems more complex, increasing the potential for operating problems.

Dispense Gas

Carbon dioxide is the most common dispense gas used because it is an ingredient in beer, is relatively inexpensive, and provides the constant internal carbon dioxide pressure needed when dispensing beer to maintain its desired level of carbonation. Because carbon dioxide is inert, it also provides a protective environment in the headspace that preserves freshness and flavor. Nitrogen is another inert gas sometimes used in conjunction with carbon dioxide. While the familiar hand air pump used at picnics is more than adequate to dispense beer consumed within a few hours, air should never be used in a commercial draft system because it causes oxidative staling and may contain airborne contaminants that can cause the beer to spoil.

Counterpressure gas plays four important roles in a balanced draft beer system:
- It is neutral in aroma and taste.
- It preserves flavor and freshness.
- It maintains the appropriate carbonation level.
- It propels the beer from the keg to the faucet at the proper flow rate.

Neutral in Aroma and Taste

Suppliers of dispense gas obtain their product from various sources using different processing methods. The care with which the supplier processes it determines its purity (exclusion of oxygen) and whether or not it contains any off-aromas or -tastes that can remain in or are inadvertently added into the gas.

Preserves Flavor and Freshness

When beer is poured, dispense gas pushes beer out of the keg and fills the headspace, where it stays in contact with the beer until the keg is empty. Any impurities in the gas can damage the beer flavor. Even the intrusion of a minute amount of air in the gas carries with it staling oxygen. The introduction of air into the gas stream can lead to the risk of infection from airborne microbes. Therefore, reliable sources of pure carbon dioxide and nitrogen are necessary to protect flavor and freshness.

Maintains Appropriate Carbonation Level

Carbon dioxide is an ingredient that contributes acidity and a refreshing effervescence to beer. Brewers carefully control the carbon dioxide content to fit the desired beer style and flavor profile. It is the responsibility of retailers to regulate the keg gas pressure to ensure that the desired level of carbon dioxide remains in the beer until the keg is empty.

A carbon dioxide cylinder with a properly functioning pressure gauge and gas regulator is a basic requirement for this task. At a constant temperature, the carbonation level increases as the gas pressure on the keg increases. Since kegs are expected to be kept at a constant temperature, it is important to supply a constant and correct gas pressure to the keg.

As a general rule, beers have a carbonation level that requires about 12 pounds of carbon dioxide pressure per square inch gauge (psig) at 38°F (3.3°C). Some beers, such as *Hefeweizen*, are carbonated to a higher level and require higher carbon dioxide pressure. Other beers, such as English ales, are less carbonated and require less pressure. A beer distributor should provide the proper gas pressure and temperature to the retailer based on the brewer's specifications and the retailer's dispense system's design.

The loss of carbonation due to inadequate pressure develops slowly and speeds up as the keg empties. Consequently, the loss of carbonation is more noticeable with the last pour than with the first. Likewise, overcarbonation develops in the same way when excess pressure is applied.

Propels Beer from Keg to Faucet at Proper Flow Rate

Kegs leave the brewery with the ideal gas pressure to maintain the proper carbonation level. As beer is poured, the keg pressure drops as the gas in the headspace expands to fill the void left by the exiting beer; thus, carbon dioxide passes out of solution to equalize the pressure between the headspace and the beer. Without the addition of external gas and pressure, the internal pressure becomes insufficient to propel the beer and maintain the correct carbonation level.

When the pressure to maintain the proper carbonation level is equal to the pressure needed to push the beer from the keg to the faucet at the proper flow rate, the draft system is considered to be balanced.

Ideal Gas Pressure

Prior to system adjustments, the gas pressure required to maintain the desired level of carbonation is not likely to be the same as the pressure needed to propel the beer to the faucet at the proper rate. Making adjustments in the dispense system so that the gas pressure fulfills both goals is called balancing the system.

The carbon dioxide content in beer is typically measured in volumes of carbon dioxide per one volume of beer. Most draft beers contain about 2.5 volumes of carbon dioxide. When a keg of beer contains 2.5 volumes of carbon dioxide, it means 2.5 keg volumes of uncompressed carbon dioxide gas are dissolved in the beer. Because the solubility of carbon dioxide in beer is dependent on temperature, the ideal gas pressure changes with beer temperature. The solubility of gases in liquid is inversely related to temperature, which means carbon dioxide is more soluble in cold beer than in warm. (Anyone who has been sprayed when opening a hot can of beer has experienced this principle.)

A chart like the one in Appendix B is used to determine the ideal gauge pressure. For example, an American lager has a carbon dioxide level of 2.5 volumes and a dispense temperature of 36°F (2.2°C). What pressure should be applied to maintain the desired volume of carbon dioxide at the given temperature? By locating 36°F (2.2°C) on the left side of the chart and following the horizontal row to 2.5 volumes, the chart indicates that the corresponding pressure is 10 psig. For an English-style pale ale at 50°F (10°C) with 2.0 volumes of carbon dioxide, the ideal gauge pressure is 11 psig. Finally, a Bavarian *Hefeweizen* with a carbon dioxide content of 3.1 volumes at 42°F (5.6°C) would require an ideal gauge pressure of 20 psig.

Because atmospheric pressure varies with elevation/altitude, adjustments to the ideal gauge pressure chart must be made to compensate for it. The basic rule adds 1.0 psig for every 2,000-foot increase in elevation. In the example above, if the keg of American lager were in Denver at a 5,280-foot elevation, the 10 psig at sea level would need to increase by 2.5 psig to 12.5 psig (5,000 feet × 1 psig/2,000 feet = 5,000 psig ÷ 2,000 = 2.5 psig). If the same beer were in a ski resort at 10,000 feet above sea level, the gauge pressure would need to increase by 5.0 psig to 15 psig (10,000 ÷ 2,000 = 5 psig).

The Proper Pour

While it is important to maintain the proper carbonation level, it is also important for the beer to pour at an efficient rate without excessive foaming. The industry standard is a flow rate of 1 gallon per minute or about 2 ounces per second. A slower flow rate slows service, frustrating both customer and bartender, while a faster rate is likely to cause foaming problems. By this standard, a 12-ounce pour should be completed in approximately 6 seconds, including the creation of a 1-inch head of foam.

A beer faucet should be operated in only two positions—closed or wide open. A partially open faucet produces turbulence that results in excessive foaming and beer waste. If the beer does not pour at the correct rate or produces excessive foam, the system is unbalanced. Excessive foaming is one of the most common causes of beer loss and wasted revenue, thanks to the bartenders' tendency to let beer overflow the glass to flush out the unwanted foam. Such losses can be eliminated by maintaining a balanced system and operating the beer faucet correctly. Excessive foaming can also occur if the glass interior is scratched, dirty, or contains ice particles that formed due to refrigeration while wet (see Chapter 5 and the description of beer clean glasses).

Proper Operation of a Beer Faucet
- Chill the keg to the proper serving temperature.
- Place a beer clean glass under the faucet at a 45° angle.
- Grab the faucet handle at its lowest point and fully open the faucet with a crisp snap forward.
- Let the beer run down the side of the glass to minimize foaming.
- Gradually tilt the glass upright and let the beer pour into the center of the glass.
- Manipulate the glass angle to produce a 1-inch foam collar.

- Never let the faucet touch the glass or the beer in the glass.
- Quickly shut the faucet to prevent waste.

Handling and Storage of Kegs

Handle with Care

Kegs are not as robust as they appear, even though the stainless steel construction might indicate resistance to dropping and bouncing. Kegs dent and the delicate valves and beer spear inside are easily damaged. Damaged kegs are harder for the brewer to clean. If damage is severe enough, it can cause nucleation sites where carbon dioxide comes out of suspension more rapidly and causes foaming problems. Get help when moving beer kegs, a full one-half-barrel keg weighs about 165 pounds!

Store Kegs Cold

Kegs are rarely pasteurized. For this reason, it is important to keep them cold at all times to stave off the effects of spoilage microbes and reduce the rate of staling oxidation. Ideally, kegs should be kept in a clean, flavor-neutral, beer-only cooler. When they are kept in a refrigerated area that stores food, care must be taken to ensure that food aromas do not enter into them when they are tapped or when lines and fittings are left open.

Order with Enough Lead Time

Kegs may warm up to above serving temperature during transit. The combination of increased temperature and rough handling seen in beer deliveries causes beer to foam. For these reasons, kegs should sit in the cooler for 24 hours to cool down and settle before being tapped for dispense.

Turnover

Before storing, each keg should be marked with an easily visible delivery date to help with proper stock rotation. The cold keg should be stored no longer than 30–60 days before tapping. Suppliers should provide expiration or pull dates for each beer. These dates are important to maintaining quality and consistency in the beers served. After tapping, the keg should be emptied in 5 days or less. In those cases in which it is not practical to do so, the retailer should maintain especially rigorous cleaning and maintenance protocols and should taste each extended-storage beer daily to monitor its flavor and freshness. If a beer tastes outside its normal character, it should be taken off tap and held for review with the selling agent. When using a picnic tap or beer engine that uses air to fill the headspace, the beer should ideally be enjoyed in 1 day before it becomes unacceptably flat or oxidized because of its unbalanced pressure and contact with air.

Unfiltered Beer

Certain unfiltered beers, such as *Hefeweizen*, are intended to be served cloudy or turbid. However, with extended storage and low temperatures, the haze and yeast that created these desirable characteristics drop to the bottom of the keg, leaving the beer clear or bright. For intentionally turbid beers, the retailer should store these kegs upside down in the cold room before tapping. It is a good practice to frequently invert or gently rock the keg throughout its serving duration to help resuspend the yeast and other solids that have settled over time.

Balancing the System

Since there can only be one ideal gas pressure to maintain the carbonation level, carbon dioxide pressure alone should not be used to speed up or slow down the flow of the beer at the faucet. If the pressure is increased to speed up the flow, the beer gradually becomes overcarbonated and foams excessively when poured. If the pressure is decreased to slow down the flow, the beer gradually goes flat and reduces pouring efficiency. Therefore, the ideal gas pressure to maintain the carbonation level should always be applied to the keg. Adjustments to achieve desired flow rates should only be made to the delivery system. Doing so produces a controlled, efficient, and cost-effective pour that maintains beer quality.

Three ways to balance a system include adjusting the flow resistance, installing beer pumps, and using mixed gas. A typical draft system is shown in Figure 8.2.

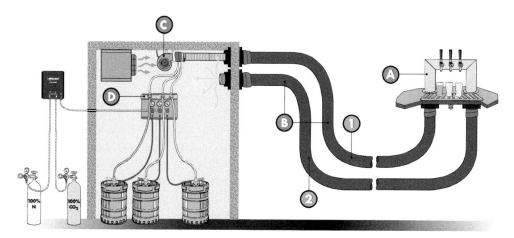

Figure 8.2. A typical draft installation with a faucet station (**A**) cooled by chilled forced air, a beer line and cold-air supply duct (**B1**) cooled by a blower (**C**), and a warmed-air return (**B2**) to the cold box. A beer gas blender (**D**) supplies a mix of carbon dioxide and nitrogen, pushing the beer to the kegs. (Courtesy Micro Matic USA, Inc.)

Adjusting Flow Resistance

As the beer flows from the keg to the faucet, the pressure in the line falls because friction between the beer and the line creates resistance. A balanced system should have sufficient resistance in the system so that the drop in pressure reduces the flow rate to 128 ounces per minute when beer exits the faucet. Too much resistance results in an insufficient flow rate. Too little resistance results in an excessive flow and foaming. Factors that produce resistance in a draft system include the tube diameter; the system run length (i.e., tubing length); gravity (when beer is pushed upward); and the roughness of the tubing surfaces.

Surface roughness depends on the tubing material. There are three common tubing materials, listed in descending order of roughness: polypropylene (commonly called vinyl); barrier tubing; and stainless steel.

If the flow rate at the tap is too fast, the line resistance must be increased. This can be accomplished by using smaller diameter tubing, increasing the length of the tubing, or using a tubing material with a rougher surface. In fact, in short-draw systems in which the keg sits directly under the faucet and has a relatively short tubing length, a narrow, three-sixteenth-inch-diameter tube, known as a choker, is often used for the entire line. Chokers are used in most under-the-counter/short-draw installations and are usually no longer than a few feet in length. For comparison, 1 foot of three-sixteenth-inch choker tubing has a flow resistance equivalent to 15 feet of three-eighth-inch tubing.

Beer Pumps

It is common for long-draw systems, especially those that move beer to an upper floor, to have more resistance than the ideal gas pressure can overcome, even with tubing adjustments. For these installations, a beer pump installed in the tubing delivery line is a good solution. Beer pumps can be powered by compressed air, pressurized carbon dioxide, or electricity. The gas used to drive a pneumatic pump never contacts the beer. Because the beer is moved by mechanical pumping, the pump propels the beer without altering its carbonation level.

Pneumatic beer pumps are typically mounted on the cooler wall near the keg (Fig. 8.3). Beer is supplied to the pump from the keg at the ideal gas pressure. The beer pump supplies the additional pressure to push the beer to the faucet. The beer flow is controlled by adjusting the force of the pump.

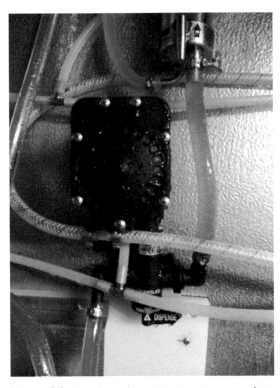

Figure 8.3. Very-long-draw systems may use a beer pump driven by carbon dioxide to supply beer out of the keg on demand. The keg is kept at a constant optimal pressure with carbon dioxide or mixed gas. When the faucet is opened at the bar, the pump delivers beer at the proper rate to the beer glass. (Courtesy BridgePort Brewing Company)

Mixed Gas

A combination of carbon dioxide and nitrogen gases can be used to facilitate delivery of beer that must travel in long runs or up several floors in elevation. When nitrogen is mixed with carbon dioxide, the ideal gas pressure must be increased to maintain the desired volume of carbon dioxide because the mixture has a lower percentage of carbon dioxide. It is this additional pressure that is used to overcome the resistance in long runs or vertical climbs. Because nitrogen is about 100 times less soluble than carbon dioxide, very little nitrogen goes into solution, so the character of the beer is not changed. Tavern owners should consult a professional to determine the proper ratio of nitrogen and carbon dioxide in the blend and the ideal gas pressure to apply with the mixed gas before attempting to use it. There are still mixed-gas systems in use that combine compressed ambient air with gas from a cylinder. These should only be used in high-volume, quick-turnover venues, such as stadiums, since such a system introduces the staling factor of oxygen into the beer.

Retailers have two options in obtaining mixed gas.

- Buy gas from a vendor who blends the proper ratio of gases in a single cylinder.
- Install an on-premise gas blender that blends the proper gas ratio from separate nitrogen and carbon dioxide cylinders (Fig. 8.4).

There are also several important operating features to consider with an on-premise blender.

- Blend settings should be tamper resistant so that untrained employees cannot tweak the system.
- The blender should shut down when either gas supply runs out to prevent damage to the beer from exposure to only one gas.
- The blender should have the flexibility to produce at least two blends for dispensing regularly carbonated beers and nitrogenated beers.

Figure 8.4. Long-draw bars up to 25 feet away, where high pressure is needed to push the beer or where a nitrogenated beer is served, may use a beer gas blender. The blender uses a preset mix of carbon dioxide and nitrogen gas so that the beer can be pushed at high pressures without over- or undercarbonating. (Courtesy BridgePort Brewing Company)

Nitro-Beer Gas

The draft industry uses a standard mixed gas of 75% nitrogen and 25% carbon dioxide to dispense nitrogenated beers such as Irish stout. This gas is commonly referred to as 75/25, beer gas, or Guinness gas. Irish stouts and some English ales with low carbonation levels (usually below 2.0 volumes) are dispensed with mixed gas through a special stout faucet. The stout faucet is designed to operate under a pressure between 30 and 40 psig that helps force the beer through the small holes in a restrictor plate, which causes the nitrogen to break out of solution and form a compact head. The stout faucet replicates the effect of a sparkler on a hand pump (or beer engine) that entrains nitrogen into the head of traditional cask ales. The result is a beer with a smooth, noncarbonated texture and creamy nitrogen foam composed of small, stable bubbles.

The 75/25 blend is not intended for balancing a system. Its sole purpose is to produce a pour that is characteristic of certain traditional ale styles. The 75/25 blend should not be used to dispense more common beers having 2.5 or greater volumes of carbon dioxide because the gas has too little carbon dioxide to maintain the proper carbonation level at normal pressures and makes the beer go flat.

Cooling the Lines

Beer must be kept cold as it travels from the keg to the faucet. If the beer warms up, the carbon dioxide becomes less soluble, breaks out of solution in the lines, and foams excessively when poured. There are four basic methods of cooling the draft lines: using a direct-draw system, forced air system, glycol-chilled system, or cold plate/jockey box.

Direct Draw

The simplest method to cool the draft lines is using a direct-draw system in which the draft lines are fully contained inside the keg cooler, with the faucets mounted on the outside wall of the cooler or on top of a hollow tower directly above it. Because the tower is open to the cooler below, cold air can circulate around the draft lines leading to the faucet.

Forced Air

Forced air is used when draft lines must exit the cooler to reach a faucet that is a short distance away. In a forced-air system, the draft lines run through an insulated chase that is 3–6 inches in diameter. The chase is cooled by a fan in the keg cooler that blows chilled air through the ductwork and back to the cooler through a return chase. Forced air is effective if the total run does not exceed 25 feet (less 5 feet for each elbow bend) and if the refrigeration cooling unit can handle the extra cooling load. Forced-air systems can be problematic if the cooler doors are opened frequently or the chase runs through a hot environment, such as a kitchen or basement boiler room.

Glycol Chilled

Chilled glycol is used for draft systems longer than 25 feet. Glycol is a food-grade solution that is mixed with water and chilled in a refrigerated reservoir. The glycol solution is continuously circulated through cooling lines that are bundled with beer lines inside an insulated housing called a python because of its snakelike appearance. For effective temperature maintenance, the glycol should flow in the opposite direction of the beer flow and for the entire length of the run.

Cold Plate/Jockey Box

A jockey box is a converted picnic cooler that has a beer faucet attached to the side. Inside the cooler is either a hollow, stainless steel cold plate or a coil of stainless steel that is connected to the faucet. The beer line runs into the cooler and connects to the cold plate or coil, which is immersed in ice. The beer is chilled as it flows through the plate or tubing in the ice bath to the faucet. Jockey boxes are commonly used for temporary beer dispense at outdoor festivals and picnics.

Draft System Hygiene

Beer is a food, and like any food, everything it contacts must be kept clean to prevent spoilage or flavor changes. Beer contains organic materials (e.g., carbohydrates, protein, hop resins, and yeast) and minerals that can create deposits on tubing walls. Wild yeast, bacteria, and mold can also find their way into a draft system, creating a biological film on tubing walls, haze, and unwanted flavors that include sourness, vinegar, phenols, butter, and rotten eggs. Any of these defects apparent in beer are indicators of a dirty draft system.

Draft System Cleaning

The following seven variables are important considerations in designing an effective cleaning program.

- The amount of soil in the draft system
- The frequency of cleaning
- The cleaning chemical selection
- The concentration of the chemical solution
- The temperature of the chemical solution
- The mechanical or "scrubbing" action of the chemical solution
- The contact time of the chemical solution in the draft line

Amount of Soil in the Draft System

As the level of soil and contamination in a system increases, so must the frequency and rigor of the cleaning process increase. Effective cleaning practices that leave the system in good condition not only protect beer quality but also reduce the time and difficulty of subsequent cleanings.

Frequency of Cleaning

Beer faucets, tubing, hoses, coils, taps, and vents must be thoroughly cleaned at regular intervals. Unless local regulations require more frequent cleaning, once a week is desirable and once every 2 weeks a must. A frequent cleaning cycle provides additional insurance against the development of dirty lines and the negative effect they have on the beers' appearance and flavor. A longer cycle between cleanings can result in excessive soil and biological matter buildup that cannot be removed by a regular cleaning regimen.

The frequency of cleaning needs to increase with the turbidity of the beer and with increased line temperature. Both conditions accelerate the accumulation of soil and growth of unwanted microbes, if present. Draft lines handling slow-selling beers are often at greatest risk because beer sits in them for extended periods. The lines that deliver these slow-moving/selling beers are candidates for a more frequent cleaning schedule.

Cleaning Chemical Selection

An FDA-approved, food-grade, alkaline cleaning solution containing sodium hydroxide, potassium hydroxide, or both, should be used for the removal of the organic soils, such as protein, yeast, mold, and bacteria, that can accumulate in beer lines. Alkaline solutions may also contain chelators for the removal of the mineral buildup, known as beer stone, and wetting agents that help the detergent penetrate and remove soil. Although chelators are somewhat useful in removing beer stone, an acid cleaner is more effective against it and other inorganic soils that may form in the line. If beer stone is an issue, a quarterly acid cleaning should be performed in addition to the regular alkaline cleaning. Consult with your draft beer specialist for direction on what acid and what strength to use before proceeding with such a cleaning.

Great care should be taken when using any line-cleaning chemical. Caustic and acid cleaners cause severe burns on human tissue. Suppliers can provide material safety data sheets (MSDS) that outline proper chemical handling procedures. Users must always follow these guidelines and wear the designated personal protective equipment (PPE) detailed in them. Great care should also be taken to ensure that all chemicals are completely rinsed from the system to protect against injury to customers and adulteration of the beer. Proper and safe storage of the chemicals between use is necessary to ensure they are not mishandled or contaminated. Storing them in their original containers with labels intact is required by law. Chlorine or chlorinated products leave a chemical flavor behind and should never be used in draft line cleaning.

Concentration of the Chemical Solution

The proper concentration of chemicals is critical for effective cleaning. At too low of a concentration, the chemical does not remove the buildup on the walls of the system. At too high of a concentration, chemicals and money are wasted and cleaning efficiency can actually be reduced. An effective cleaning solution contains 2–3% caustic, with 2% used for regular maintenance and 3% for neglected or hard-to-clean systems. The manufacturer should provide mixing instructions for the desired caustic or acid concentrations.

Temperature of the Chemical Solution

A warm cleaning solution (e.g., between 80 and 125°F [21 and 41°C]) is more effective than a cold one. While a hot solution is even more effective, temperatures above 125°F (41°C) are not recommended because fittings may loosen, burst, and create safety hazards. Extremely high temperatures can damage vinyl lines.

Mechanical or "Scrubbing" Action of the Chemical Solution

Cleaning is more effective using mechanical scrubbing. An electric pump creates this effect by causing turbulence as it rapidly circulates solution through the lines. In this arrangement, the pump delivers the warm cleaning solution from a reservoir (usually a bucket or sink) through the lines and a return loop back into the reservoir, where it is continuously reintroduced back into the lines.

Cleaning with a pressurized pot, or static line cleaning, involves filling the draft lines with chemical via a pressurized canister and allowing it to soak the system. Because the canister setup provides very little scrubbing action, it is less effective than a recirculating system and requires more contact time. Furthermore, this method is only effective in systems shorter than 15 feet in length.

Increased mechanical scrubbing can be achieved through the use of small sponge balls that are pumped through the beer lines with the cleaning solution. The abrasive action that they provide facilitates the removal of built-up soils and makes the cleaning solution more effective. However, sponge cleaning is incompatible with systems that have line restrictions that might trap the sponge, resulting in additional cost and lost time locating and extracting them.

Contact Time of the Solution in the Draft Line

The longer a cleaning solution is in contact with a dirty surface, the more effectively it cleans. Generally, recirculating cleaning solution for 10 minutes produces effective cleaning. For static cleaning, the soak time should be increased to 20 minutes. These time standards are based on normal soil loads. For heavily soiled lines, the exposure time must be increased in relation to the severity of soil buildup. However, consideration must be given to the fact that plastic lines are not indestructible and incur damage when subjected to exceedingly lengthy soak times. If a line is soiled to the point where a normal soak period does not clean it, it needs to be replaced rather than be subjected to chemicals that can denature it and further complicate the problem.

Other Cleaning Issues

The longer the beer line, the harder it is to clean. Resistance in a long-draw system can reduce the velocity and scrubbing effect of circulating cleaning solutions. It is also more difficult to maintain temperatures to keep the solution warm over the entire run, especially if using pressurized pots with a volume that is inadequate to fill the entire system. Cleaning solution must contact the entire draft system to be effective; therefore, particular attention should be given to the volume and temperature needed to adequately clean split lines, tight fixtures, valves, FOB stops (see below), beer pumps, and other narrow or

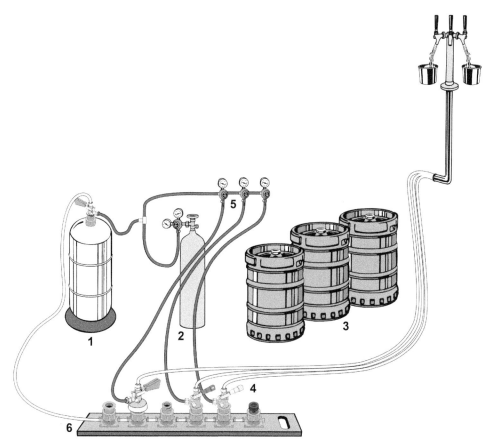

Figure 8.5. This in-place and portable cleaning system cleans multiple taps at one time in a short-draw system. A sodium hydroxide-based solution is recommended for the regular cleaning. An acid-based cleaner is recommended every third or fourth cleaning. Each time the beer lines are cleaned, it is important to clean the faucets and keg couplers. **1,** Cleaning bottle. **2,** CO_2 cylinder. **3,** Beer kegs. **4,** Keg couplers. **5,** Secondary regulators. **6,** Mounting board with sockets. (Courtesy Micro Matic USA, Inc.)

Figure 8.6. It is recommended to circulate the cleaning solution for at least 10 minutes in a long-draw system. This requires a motorized cleaning pump (an example is shown). Circulating solution is 80 times more effective than static (soaking) line cleaning. (Courtesy Micro Matic USA, Inc.)

hard-to-reach surfaces. If possible, the line cooling system should be shut down when cleaning to help maintain the temperature to keep the chemical solution warm. While the faucets are cleaned during the biweekly cleaning, it is also good practice to break down the faucets and soak the parts in cleaning solution as part of the normal cleaning regime. Cleaning options and equipment for short-draw and long-draw systems are shown in Figures 8.5 and 8.6.

Equipment Selection

Fittings

Stainless steel parts and fittings are recommended for draft systems because they are resistant to cleaning chemicals and do not impart off-flavors, deteriorate, discolor, or develop surface pits under normal use. Brass should not be used because cleaning chemicals can create pits on brass surfaces that are hard to clean. Brass can also impart metallic flavors to the beer. While many brass parts may be coated with chrome plating, the plated surface can wear away over a relatively short period of time, exposing the bare brass and creating cavities that are hard to keep clean.

Tubing

Vinyl is used in areas where a flexible hose is needed to bend around corners or fixtures and, especially, in chokers and jumper lines that attach the keg coupler to a wall mount. Vinyl has the propensity to absorb flavors, such as root beer and fruit beers, that may taint the next product dispensed through them. It is not particularly strong or hygienic because vinyl develops cracks and pits that harbor spoilage microbes. For these reasons, vinyl tubing requires regular replacement and should only be installed in easily accessible areas.

In recent years, manufacturers have created barrier tubing to address the shortfalls of vinyl. Barrier tubing is a plastic tubing lined with a smooth, inert, glassy material that is less permeable to gases, less absorbent of flavors, and easier to clean. It is also less prone to cracking and pitting than regular vinyl tubing and needs less frequent replacement. A recent development is the use of silver in the barrier lining, which creates an effective antimicrobial lining that is very effective in prohibiting the growth of the anaerobic beer spoiler *Lactobacillus brevis*. Stainless steel is also an excellent tubing material because of its robustness and hygienic properties, but its high cost may make its use less practical.

Regardless of the tubing chosen, it must be made of an approved food-grade material and be flavor neutral. Before it is put into use, it must undergo a rigorous first cleaning to remove any residual manufacturing compounds, soils, and microorganisms. The final test to qualify the tubing for use is the quality of the beer it delivers into the glass.

FOB Stops

When an empty keg is changed out, a retailer may lose beer left in the line between the keg and faucet, which can be a considerable expense with long lines. A FOB stop, which stands for "foam on beer", is a mechanical float that is connected to the outgoing draft line near the keg (Fig. 8.7). When the keg empties, the float is no longer suspended and drops, shutting off the beer flow to the faucet while keeping the line packed with beer. The keg can then be changed with a minimal loss of beer. Care must be taken to keep this piece clean so that its use does not introduce spoilage organisms into the beer line. A draft system with a secondary gas regulator, beer pump, and FOB stop is shown in Figure 8.8.

Figure 8.7. To minimize beer loss when a keg empties, a FOB stop may be used. The FOB has a stopper inside its housing and, as the beer level finally drains down at the end of the keg, it keeps gas and foam from being sent to the bar. (Courtesy Bridge-Port Brewing Company)

Figure 8.8. A system incorporating a secondary regulator to maintain the proper keg pressure, a beer pump for a long draw, a FOB stop, and a set of keg coupler cleaning cups for easy line cleaning. (Courtesy BridgePort Brewing Company)

Dispense Gas Storage

Retailers can purchase carbon dioxide and nitrogen in portable cylinders or bulk storage tanks. Nitrogen can also be produced on site by generators that separate nitrogen from compressed air using membranes or molecular sieves. Oil-free compressors should be used since they prevent the possibility of lubricants entering into the gas during compression.

Gas Purity

Because of staling caused by oxygen and the deleterious effects of other impurities, the industry standards specify that nitrogen have a minimum purity of 99.7% and carbon dioxide a minimum purity of 99.9%. Gas suppliers should be able to provide a certificate of analysis for each batch of gas purchased.

Gas Filters

Gas cylinders may be contaminated through improper cleaning, filling, maintenance, or storage or from liquid that backs up into them because of a faulty check valve. The gas itself may contain contaminants from its source or processing that can negatively affect aroma and taste. For these reasons, in-line gas filters may be used as a last line of defense to remove these impurities before the gas enters the keg.

Series Kegs

Beers that sell in high volumes create service interruptions when the kegs are emptied and changed several times per day. One solution to this problem is to connect the kegs in a series. In such a setup, dispense gas pushes beer from the first keg into the second keg through its gas inlet port, which forces beer out of the second keg into a third keg and so on, until it is finally directed to the faucet. In this way, multiple kegs can be linked together to create a larger volume of a beer for extended dispensing without having to frequently retap the beer. This is often done in sports venues.

There are problems inherent with this method. One of the most disruptive problems can occur when beer enters a keg that is not completely full, sprays into the headspace, and creates foam. Quality issues can also develop when full kegs are rotated into the series without the entire series being replaced. Partial rotation always retains some old beer in the system, which can have a negative impact on the beer in the entire series. To maintain quality and consistency in this type of system, all kegs in the series must be completely emptied and replaced with fresh ones on a regular basis as determined by experience and beer quality. If the entire series is not emptied at the predetermined schedule, the number of kegs connected together must be reduced to make it happen.

Split Lines

Some retailers pour beer at multiple faucets from a single keg. This setup is operational but not ideal. When multiple faucets from one keg are opened at the same time, foaming occurs when a substantial drop in pressure is caused by the inability of the counterpressure gas to rapidly replace the beer. Beer pumps or high-pressure mixed gas are well suited for split lines since they are designed to maintain a suitable pressure in the line throughout the pouring. Even if foaming is controlled, the flow rate can drop to an unacceptable level if too many faucets are opened at the same time. To minimize this problem, no more than two faucets should be run from the same keg. Table 8.1 is a trouble-shooting guide for common draft system problems.

Table 8.1. Common Draft Problems[a]

Condition	Temperature	Pressure	Equipment	Improper Pour	Glassware
Wild Beer					
Beer, when drawn, is all foam or is too much foam and not enough liquid beer	Too warm	Too high	Needs cleaning	Check pour	Ice inside of glass
Flat Beer					
Foamy head disappears quickly; beer lacks brewery fresh flavor	Too cold	Too low			Detergent film inside of glass
Cloudy Beer					
Beer in glass appears hazy, not clear	Too cold	Contaminated CO_2 gas	Needs cleaning		Needs cleaning
False Head					
Large soaplike bubbles; head dissolves very quickly	Too warm	Too low		Check pour	Household detergent and dust

[a] (Courtesy Micro Matic USA, Inc.)

Conclusion

Consumers like good draft beer. It is a product that provides the retailer with a solid profit margin and a strong source of revenue. In this chapter, the reader was presented with the basic tools needed to properly handle and care for keg beer. By following these draft beer guidelines, the reader can ensure that both the consumer and the retailer continue to enjoy this desirable type of beer. However, the information presented is not intended to make the reader an expert in draft system design and maintenance. Trained professionals are available for such advice and service and should be consulted as needed.

Selected References

American Society of Brewing Chemists (ASBC). 1949. Solubility of carbon dioxide in beer, Pressure-temperature relationships. In: Methods of Analysis, 5th ed. ASBC, St. Paul, MN.

Brewers Association. 2009. Brewers Association Draft Beer Quality Manual. http://draught quality.org/.

Holle, S. R. 2003. Draught Beer Dispense. Pages 75-80 in: A Handbook of Basic Brewing Calculations. Master Brewers Association of the Americas, St. Paul, MN.

Jurado, J. 2003. Hygienic design, installation, and maintenance standards for draft beer dispense: German progress and North America's challenge. Technical Quarterly Master Brewers Association of the Americas 40:271-279.

Micro Matic USA. 2010. Micro Matic Dispense Institute Online. www.micromatic.com/draft-keg-beer-edu/dispense-institute-online-cid-1870.html.

Chapter 9:
Beer Flavor

Roy Desrochers and Karl Ockert

Unlike almost any other class of beverages, beer comes in a seemingly endless profusion of flavors, colors, aromas, and styles. The complexity of beer flavor matches, and in many cases exceeds, wine and distilled spirits, making beer drinking a highly enjoyable sensory experience that deserves special attention. This chapter discusses how the human sensory detection organs work and how to utilize them to detect and describe the wide range of beer flavors.

The human olfactory region, most commonly known as the nose, is more sensitive than the most advanced laboratory instrument. Humans can detect some compounds at levels less than *one part per quadrillion*. That is like picking one single grain of sand out of a sand dune. In addition to our remarkable sensitivities, we can recognize flavor nuances and intensities and translate these stimuli into triggers for a myriad of emotions and memories.

We use our five senses, hearing, seeing, tasting, touching, and smelling, to evaluate the beer we are about to savor and enjoy. Print ads and television and radio advertisements commonly exploit our visual and auditory senses using descriptive images to bring their products to our attention. Each can be very effective in generating interest without actually sipping the product.

We can anticipate how a beer will taste without bringing it to our lips when we hear a description and then envision its appearance, flavor, and aroma. What does a description like "a cold, golden German pilsner, bitter and floral with a pillowy white head of foam standing just proud of the rim" conjure up in your mind? Can you taste this beer through your mind's "eye"? A visual image or photo alone of the same beer might be even more powerful given that we rely heavily on our sense of sight to interpret the world around us. In both examples, our ears or eyes form a mental image of the beer's flavor that impacts the drinking experience before we even take a sip. Since verbal and visual descriptions cause us to anticipate how a beer will taste, how a beer is described and presented can influence the consumer's willingness to try it and their enjoyment after they taste it.

Sensing Taste and Aroma

Our brain and body collaborate to sense and recognize everything around us, including tastes and smells. We use taste buds on our tongues and the olfactory region in our noses to taste and smell products such as beer. But the entire flavor experience is not just what we taste in our mouths, it is the combination of taste, smell, and the mouthfeel, such as the tingle of carbonation, astringency, fullness, and balance.

$$Flavor = Taste + Aroma + Mouthfeel$$

Taste Buds and the Tongue

We all have thousands of taste buds in our mouths, primarily on our tongues. At birth, we have more of the sweet-sensing taste buds, perhaps triggered by the intense sweetness of nourishing mother's milk. Bitter-tasting substances in nature are often poisonous and we have bitter-sensing taste buds to help warn us against ingesting bitter, potentially dangerous, items. This may explain why children prefer sweet foods and why a taste for bitter foods and beverages, such as coffee, semisweet dark chocolate, and bitter beers, are examples of an acquired taste more often seen in adults. A fifth taste sensation, umami, which is the sensation often triggered by monosodium glutamate and characterized as brothy or meaty, is not discussed here, since it is not a typical feature in positive beer flavor profiles, although overaged bottle-conditioned beers may develop these flavors as the conditioning yeast dies.

Taste buds have specific receptors for sweet, sour, salty, and bitter, and we all have these four types of taste buds all across our tongues and at the back of our mouths. Although we can detect each of these basic tastes across our tongues, we tend to taste them slightly more in some regions than in others. Most importantly for tasting beer, we tend to taste sour more on the sides of our tongues than anywhere else, and we tend to taste bitter more on the back of our tongues and throats than anywhere else. You can experience the sensations of these four basic tastes by sipping solutions of sugar (sweet), salt, lemon juice (sour), and decarbonated tonic water (bitter) and noting where you perceive them most on your tongue. Because bitterness is an important flavor component of beer, tasters need to swallow beer and allow the bitter compounds to reach all of the bitter taste buds at the back of their tongues and throats.

The body continually generates new taste buds since they can be damaged by heat, spicy and acidic foods, smoking, and other chemicals, such as strong mouthwash. Taste receptors can also be numbed and suppressed by cold. This is important to remember prior to tasting beer. Tasters should avoid exposure to these damaging influences before sampling beer.

The Nose and Olfactory System

If all we could taste were sweet, sour, salty, and bitter flavors, our foods and drinks would be very boring. Fortunately, the human body also has an ability to smell aromas that expand the boundary of flavors beyond the four basic tastes. The olfactory system, which is composed of the nose and nasal passage connected to the back of the mouth, provides our ability to smell. The human olfactory system is extremely sensitive. Not only can it differentiate between thousands of different scents, but it can also distinguish the intensity of each aroma.

This capability opens up an almost endless array of aromas and flavors in foods and beverages, especially beer. Beer has thousands of aroma compounds and it is the combination of these compounds that helps define styles and differentiate brands. You can experience the impact of the olfactory system quite simply by pinching your nose closed and licking a mint candy. Because your nose is shut, the air in your mouth that contains various aroma compounds cannot travel up your back nasal passage to your olfactory area. Consequently, only your tongue is available, and all it can detect is sweetness, compliments of your sweet taste buds. When you release your nose, the olfactory system quickly detects the cool, sharp sensation and aroma of mint. The olfactory system opens up the cupboard door for flavors and aromas that your taste buds alone cannot detect. For this reason, tasting beer with a stuffy nose reduces the aroma sensations and overall impact of any beer you are sampling. Temperature can also impact your ability to perceive aromas. For example, a very cold beer releases fewer volatile aromas to your olfactory area and the beer flavors are suppressed.

Learning to Taste and Building a Flavor Vocabulary

Tasting to recognize beer flavors is different from tasting for preference. Preference tasting is simply what it implies: determining which product is preferable to the taster. This is a matter of personal likes and dislikes and cannot be judged by anyone else; you like what you like. One person's favorite beer might rank at the bottom of the list for another. Preference tasting does not give descriptive information of a beer's flavor. This chapter focuses on descriptive tasting or how to describe the flavors you perceive in each type of beer. The goal is to describe how to evaluate a beer and describe it objectively and accurately in terms of flavor, aroma, mouthfeel, fullness, and body, thereby painting both a visual and verbal picture that can be conveyed to today's sophisticated beer customer.

A sales person or bartender who describes a beer as "good tasting" gives the consumer little information to make a purchase decision. On the other hand, tasting for recognition of flavor is an objective process with a goal of identifying beer flavors and using accurate descriptors to convey those flavors to consumers so they can select beers that match their preferences. Successfully detecting and identifying beer flavors requires practice to sharpen your senses, and communicating beer flavors to consumers requires a vocabulary that describes, for example, aroma, mouthfeel, color, carbonation, fullness, and balance. The following discussion will help in identifying common flavors in various beer styles and supplying the vocabulary to describe them.

Our taste buds and olfactory system send signals to the brain that are interpreted, labeled, and stored for reference when we taste foods and beverages. This is how we build flavor memory and a descriptive vocabulary. Flavor memory can go beyond simple taste and odor sensations and can bring images and emotions to mind. A sip of a Bavarian *Hefeweizen* may trigger thoughts of a drinking experience in a Munich beer hall even though you are sitting on your deck at home. Professional tasters develop an extensive library of descriptive terms by tasting and smelling reference standards over and over again. Building a flavor memory and vocabulary takes time and effort. However, once the objective terms for taste and odor sensations are categorized by the brain, they can be reliably called upon to describe a beer's flavor. With enough practice, just about anyone can learn to competently evaluate beer flavor.

Sometimes different people have different abilities to detect beer flavors. The lowest concentration at which a person can detect a compound is called their flavor threshold. Personal thresholds for a particular flavor may run from very high (they can't taste it very well) to very low (they are especially sensitive). Some people have "blind" spots and simply cannot detect certain flavors, while others are highly sensitive to those same flavors.

Intense or prolonged exposure to a single flavor can overwhelm the senses. This is called sensory adaptation (too much exposure) and sensory fatigue (too much intensity). Sensory fatigue and adaptation are important to remember when tasting a series of beers with various flavor intensities at one sitting and are discussed later in this chapter. Other important factors in evaluating beer are mouthfeel, fullness or body, and balance.

Mouthfeel

While taste buds detect sweet, salty, sour, and bitter, the rest of the mouth also senses physical and chemical stimulus called mouthfeel. Mouthfeel can be the burning heat of a chili sauce, the astringent pucker of cranberry juice, or the dry "rough tongue" of unsweetened ice tea. Some examples of mouthfeel in beer include the drying, tannic astringency in very hop-driven beers, the tingle in highly carbonated beers, the warming in high-alcohol beers, and the creaminess in nitrogenated ales and stouts.

Fullness or Body

The fullness, or body, of a beer is defined by its flavor complexity. The more complex the beer tastes, the more full bodied it is perceived. A good nonbeer example is milk. Skim milk still tastes like milk but is thin in flavor when compared with more complex whole milk. While cooks add salt and fats to food to increase fullness, brewers add fullness and body by increasing the amount of malted grains in the grist or by using a mashing profile to increase the unfermentable sugars that are left behind by the yeast after fermentation. Light-bodied, highly carbonated beer styles, such as pilsner and *Hefeweizen*, are generally less complex and less satiating than are higher-alcohol beers, such as imperial stout, barley wine, and *Doppelbock*. Beer fullness is generally described using the terms thin, light or dry, medium, and heavy or full bodied.

Balance

When flavors come together synergistically and harmoniously, this is called balance. In a well-balanced beer, no particular flavor stands out; in an unbalanced beer, it is easy to pick out the individual flavors. A symphony has many sections of instruments, but when the sections play in balance no particular instrument stands out from the blend of sounds. In simple terms, brewers often balance the sweetness of malted grains with the bitterness of hops. However, balance goes beyond just sweet and bitter. Caramel flavors from crystal malt in an India pale ale (IPA) can tone down the assertive citrus character of American aroma hops. Many styles adjust the balance either to the sweeter, malt-driven side, e.g., Scotch ale and bock, or to the bitter and aromatic hop-driven side, e.g., pilsner, pale ale, and IPA.

Color and Flavor

Color can be a key indicator of beer flavor. For example, a dark beer might exhibit intense burnt and toasted flavors because the roasting process that produces a dark color in malt also produces roasted, burnt flavors. However, interpreting color can also lead to wrong assumptions about fullness and alcoholic strength. Color may be a guide to beer flavor, but it is sometimes deceptive.

Flavor Intensity

While roasted barley and chocolate malt may lend luscious roasted flavors to a beer, debittered black malt and colored syrups can provide dark colors without the normally anticipated burnt toast, coffee, or burnt caramel flavor notes. Examples of dark beers without the expected roastiness are American bock and dark lager beers.

Fullness

Black stouts and porters are often thought of as heavy, sweet, full-bodied beers. However, dark roasted malts and grains contribute few of the unfermentable sugars that actually create fullness, which is more a function of the mashing process. A dark brown mild ale is perceived to be dry and thin compared with a golden full-bodied German *Maibock*.

Strength

The amount of malt and adjuncts and the formation of fermentable sugars influenced by the mashing process determine a beer's final alcohol content. Dark roasted malts provide almost no fermentable sugars and thus contribute little to the alcoholic strength of beer. Irish stout on draft may have an alcoholic strength of 4.2% alcohol by volume (ABV), while a pale IPA may contain 6.0% ABV.

Key Beer Flavors from Fermentation

Wort coming from the brewhouse is a complex solution of intense sweet and bitter flavors with various amounts of hop flavors and aromas. It tastes nothing like the final beer it will become after fermentation. During fermentation, yeast absorbs some of the bitter hop compounds and consumes most of the wort sugars to produce alcohols, organic acids, esters, and various other flavor compounds, all of which add interesting complexity and differentiates the final beer from its brewhouse wort.

Alcohols

Ethanol is the main alcohol produced by yeast in beer. It is fairly neutral in taste, although slightly sweet. Higher-molecular-weight alcohols, called fusel alcohols, are complex alcohols produced during fermentation that can increase the sweetness, body, and "warming" mouthfeel effect of high-alcohol beers. Fusel alcohols give vinous, spicy flavors and are produced by yeast at higher fermentation temperatures. Aging and slow oxidation of alcohols in beer give rise to raisin, black cherry, and sherrylike flavors.

Esters

Esters are important flavor components in beer and provide fruity aromas, such as apple, pear, banana, and citrus. Like alcohols, esters are produced by yeast fermentation and especially at higher fermentation temperatures. For this reason, warm-fermented ales usually contain more esters than cold-fermented lagers. Style-specific yeast strains noted for their ester-producing characteristics are used in producing Bavarian *Hefeweizen* and many Belgian ale styles to provide their signature fruity flavors.

Phenolic

The type and amount of phenolic compounds, noted for their spicy flavors, such as clove, pepper, and vanilla, present in beer are very dependent on the yeast strain used in fermentation. For example, ale yeast tends to produce more phenols than does lager yeast. Although phenolic flavors would be considered a flaw in many lager beers, they are highly prized in certain ales, including many Belgian ale styles and Bavarian *Weizen*.

Acidity

As fermentation proceeds, yeast reduces the pH of wort from about 5.3 to about 4.3 in the final beer by producing organic acids, such as lactic acid. The bittering acids from hops, the organic acids from fermentation, and dissolved carbon dioxide make beer a mildly acidic beverage. The acidity helps protect beer from spoilage organisms, prevents the growth of disease-causing pathogens, and adds to beer's refreshing, crisp finish. Some styles of beer, such as lambic and Flanders sour ales, use certain types of acid-producing bacteria and special yeasts to create their signature sour character. Yet, compared with wine, which has a pH of about 3.5, most beer styles would not be described as acidic or sour tasting.

Beer Flavor Groups

Beer is often described in terms of process and style. The two principle process categories for beer are lagers and ales. Within these two groups are a myriad of styles, hybrids, and off-shoots. Separating the beer family tree into lager and ale makes sense to brewers who formulate recipes and make the beer but means very little to the consumers who drink the beer. *Doppelbock* has more flavors in common to a barley wine than to its cousin the pilsner. This is not to say that malt-driven ales taste the same as malt-driven lager beers; there are differences in malt, hop, and fermentation flavors that further differentiate these styles. However, in an effort to simplify flavor descriptions for all beer styles, whether they are lagers or ales, any particular beer can be placed into one of four flavor-driven groups and a shorthand can be created to accurately describe each beer in terms the beer drinker understands. The flavor group scenario makes more sense to the beer drinker, who is looking for a particular flavor and does not care about its production process, while making it much easier for the beer professional to describe and explain.

The following flavor-driven groups utilize a beer's most prominent flavor attribute to assign its group membership. Each group uses a common list of descriptive vocabulary to characterize the flavors of the beer being described. Some beers overlap flavor groups, especially the last group, flavored beers, which use a base beer and then add some particular spice, fruit, or flavoring for a special character. For the most part, beer styles feature particular flavor notes that fit easily into one of the four groups—malt-driven, hop-driven, fermentation-driven, and flavored beers.

Malt-Driven Beers

Beers in the malt-driven group carry flavors that tip the balance toward their malted grain and adjunct components. Malt-driven flavors are primarily a function of the intensity of kilning and roasting during the malting process, the amount of malt in the recipe, and the mashing process used in the brewhouse. Malt flavors can be described in terms familiar to baking and candy, e.g., toast, bread, biscuit, honey, caramel, and toffee, as well as deep roasted flavors, including coffee, burnt toast, and smoke. Table 9.1 shows some flavors descriptors used for malt-driven beers. Note that normally, as color increases, the malt flavors may become more intense; but as described previously in this chapter, color alone can be misleading. However, malt-driven beer styles as a group tend to be fuller bodied, less bitter, less tart, sweeter, and sometimes higher in alcohol, often with raisin or sherry overtones.

Some examples of malt-driven beers are brown and mild ales, stouts and porters, *Schwarzbier*, American bock, *Dunkel* (dark lager), *Doppelbock*, and barley wine.

Table 9.1. Descriptive Vocabulary for Malt-Driven Beers

Malt Type	Flavor Type	Impact	Flavor
Pale	Baking	Low	Cereal, grain, bread, toasty, sweet, biscuit
Amber malt	Candy	Moderate	Honey, nutty, caramel, toffee
Dark/roasted	Roast	High	Burnt toast, bitter, chocolate, coffee, smoke

Hop-Driven Beers

Hop-driven flavors include hop bitterness from alpha acids and hop flavor/aroma from essential hop oils. Brewers measure bitterness in international bitterness units, or IBUs, with 40 IBUs indicating more bitterness than 10 IBUs. However, the IBUs listed on the bottle does not indicate "perceived" bitterness; a sweet, malt-driven beer with 30 IBUs tastes less bitter than a dry, light-bodied beer with the same IBUs. Bitterness can be characterized as low, mild, medium, or intense.

Hop-driven beers often include the characteristic hop flavor profiles seen in the varieties used. Hops of the same variety but from different growing areas tend to have *terrior*

properties associated with their area of origin, much the same as wine grapes. Cooler climate areas tend to produce aroma varieties with elegant and delicate aromas and flavors, while warmer areas produce bittering hops with bold and pungent aromas and flavors. European hops are commonly described as "noble" floral and spicy, American hops are commonly described as citrus or pine resin, and British hops are commonly described as sylvan or woody. Dry hopping in the cellar after fermentation accentuates the herbal, grassy aromas of hop-driven beers, especially with harvest ales using "wet hops". Table 9.2 shows some of the commonly used vocabulary describing the variety of hop flavors and aromas. A higher acidity (lower pH) goes well with the increased bitterness, and hop-driven beers tend to be low to medium bodied, less sweet, and more tart and finish sharp and crisp, sometimes with bitter linger.

Examples of hop-driven beers are pilsner, international lagers, *Alt*, pale ale, IPA, and imperial IPA.

Table 9.2. Descriptive Vocabulary for Hop-Driven Beers[a]

Citrusy	Esters	Floral	Herbal	Spicy	Sylvan (woody)
Grapefruit	Pineapple	Geranium	Fresh hop	Sandalwood	Cedar, pine
Bergamot	Pear skin	Lavender	Grassy	Oak moss	Woody
Lemon	Sweet	Rose	Green	Astringent	Earthy
Lime	Fruity	Neroli			

[a] Source: www.barthhaasgroup.com/cmsdk/content/bhg/products/pha_varietal_pg.pdf.

Fermentation-Driven Beers

Yeast transforms flavors born of raw materials in the brewhouse and has a profound impact on the beer's final character, flavor, and aroma. Yeast produces many types of flavor compounds that make beer taste different from wort, the most important of which are ethanol and carbon dioxide, but there are many, many others that can be labeled as fruity, tart, and spicy. While most beer styles utilize yeasts producing "clean", low-impact flavors, some beer styles emphasize assertive yeast flavors and may use "wild" yeasts and bacteria to produce more intensive and exotic fermentation-derived flavors. These styles form the fermentation-driven flavor group.

In fermentation-driven beers, the hop component is normally not prominent, bitterness is mild to very low, and hop flavors and aromas are not usually detectable. The malt flavor component may be subdued and the emphasis is on the spicy and fruit flavors and aromas produced from the fermentation, although the amount of malt used may be increased, resulting in higher alcohol contents and more fusel alcohol production. Fermentation-driven beers can be tart, even mouth-puckering sour. Some beer styles in this group rely on spontaneous fermentation from microbes in the air or in the oak barrels in which they are aged. Other beer styles are carefully pitched and fermented with selected strains of yeast and microbes, such as lactic acid bacteria, which produce intense tartness, or with *Brettanomyces* yeast, which produces the intriguing barnyard, horsey "Brett" character. The yeasts and bacteria used in these fermentations consistently produce desired flavor profiles that can be wonderfully complex. Table 9.3 provides some common flavor descriptors for fermentation-driven beer flavors.

Examples of fermentation-driven beers are lambic, Bavarian *Hefeweizen*, *Dunkelweizen*, and Belgian *dubbel* and *tripel*.

Table 9.3. Descriptive Vocabulary for Fermentation-Driven Beers

Esters	Phenols	Alcohols/Oxidized	Other
Pear	Pepper	Raisin	Sour
Banana	Clove	Sherry	Vinegar
Citrus	Smoke	Alcoholic, rum	Barnyard, horsey
Apple	Vanilla	Spicy	Earthy
Aniseed		Winelike	Butterscotch

Flavored Beers

Any beer style from the groups above can be made into a flavored beer. Beers in this group emphasize an added flavoring over the normal character of the style into which it has been added. Sometimes these flavorings compliment and combine the effects of fermentation-driven flavors with a fruit and spice, such as with *wit* or fruit lambic styles. Often the flavoring lends complexity and novel character to a hop- or malt-driven beer style. Descriptive vocabulary for this flavor group comes both from the base beer used and the flavoring added. Flavorings come in three main groups.

Fruits, Nuts, and Vegetables

Whole fruits, nuts, coffee, purees, juices, concentrates, dried peels, and artificial fruit flavors are used to produce flavored beers in this category. Fruit, nuts, and vegetables can be added to just about any style of beer to produce an interesting blend of flavors. Examples include cherry stout, pumpkin ale, and coffee porter.

Herbs and Spices

The flavor of a beer can change dramatically with the addition of spices and herbs, such as cardamom, coriander, peppercorn, grains of paradise, and lemon grass. Used with a subtle hand, the flavors can add complexity and nuance to highlight fermentation flavors as well as the flavors of the malt and hops. Examples include Belgian *wit*, *saison*, and other spiced ales and lagers.

Barrel Aging

The oak barrels used to age wines and spirits can also be used to age beer. French oak, normally used for aging wine, may impart some of its oak tannins and flavors if used as a new barrel, or a barrel previously used to age wine may carry over some of the wine flavors. For the most part, aging wine in barrels yields a slow oxidation process through the porous staves, softening the bitter flavors from hops and slowly oxidizing the alcohols in the beer to produce the characteristic sherry flavors of aged strong beers. The barrel may also contain certain acid-producing microbes left from the wine that ferment in the beer and produce sourness; many brewers purposefully add these microbes for the same effect. To produce *kriek* and *framboise* lambics, brewers introduce cherries or raspberries, respectively, to the barrels and age the soured beer with the fruit. West Flanders sour ales aged in barrels do not use a fruit addition but feature a firm tartness along with the oxidized flavors of the malt.

The charred American oak used to age bourbon transfers strong vanilla and caramel flavors to that spirit. Beers aged in used bourbon casks (they can by law only be used once for bourbon production) pick up those same vanilla/caramel characters. Additionally, aging in bourbon barrels produces the same kind of oxidized sherry and black cherry flavors that aging in wine barrels produces and the flavors are very complimentary to full-bodied, high-alcohol, malt-driven beer styles, such as porter, stout, and barley wine.

Tasting Progression

When tasting beers within and across the four main flavor-driven groups, it is important to taste them in a progression that allows for best evaluation. Since your flavor sensors can fatigue or become adapted to the flavors present in different beer styles, it is essential to pay attention to the tasting progression and minimize these effects. Tasting progression can be summed up as less intense to most intense. Examples include the following.

- Least assertive before most assertive
- Low bitterness before high bitterness
- Thin bodied before full bodied
- Light colored before dark colored
- Youngest before oldest
- Nonflavored before flavored

Taste the mildest and most delicately flavored samples first and try not to taste more than a few beer samples at a time without taking a break. Room-temperature, uncarbonated water is a great way to flush the palate clean and ready your senses between each beer sample. Unsalted soda crackers provide a neutral way to keep food in the stomach while tasting a series of beer samples; thereby helping the process.

How to Taste Beer

As discussed in Chapter 5, bottles and cans are *not* beer glasses. Bottles and cans do not provide the maximum visual enjoyment of a beer, nor do they allow for the full olfactory impact of the aromas released by the beer. Beer poured into a beer clean or beer ready glass delivers superior presentation and flavor compared with beer sipped from a bottle or can. When tasting and evaluating new beers, there are some steps that help in describing its appearance, aroma, and flavor. These steps can be abbreviated to "see, swirl, sniff, and sip".

1. See

Pour the beer into a beer clean 6- to 12-ounce glass and fill it about one-third full with a ½- to 1-inch foam head. (Beer clean glassware preparation is discussed in Chapter 5.) A tulip-shaped wine or beer glass is well suited for beer tasting. Look at the poured beer. Is the foam and color true to the style? Is the beer clear or hazy? Some beer is intentionally left naturally hazy because it is unfiltered or bottle conditioned, but haze in filtered beer can be a sign of age, exposure to heat, staleness, or unwanted microbial growth.

2. Swirl

Swirl the beer in the glass to force some carbon dioxide out of solution and allow volatile aromas to be carried into the headspace of the glass where your nose can detect them. This is very difficult to do with a beer bottle or can! A tulip-shaped beer glass or wine glass allows the aroma compounds to gather for better appreciation and detection.

3. Short Sniffs

Take short sniffs as the glass is brought toward your nose to begin experiencing the beer's aromas. Describe these aromas using your objective descriptive vocabulary and refrain from using words such as "good" or "bad". Is this a malt-driven beer with hints of toffee or burnt toast? Is this a flavored beer with an aroma of coriander? Try to identify, label, and describe what you are smelling.

4. Long Sniff

Bring the glass under your nose. After some short sniffs, take one or two long sniffs. Concentrate on the aroma characteristics that were detected in the short sniffs to verify their presence. Note and name what characteristics you are detecting.

5. Small Sip

Take a small sip, roll the beer around your tongue, and distinguish any bitter, sweet, and sour flavors. Take another sip and evaluate the balance, mouthfeel, and body. What flavors can you pick out? Describe the flavor characteristics that you taste and try to identify which flavor group this beer may belong to.

6. Swallow

Swallow the beer to experience the depth of bitterness and the warming sensation of alcohol on your palate and throat. What is the intensity and quality of the hop bitterness?

7. Exhale

Breathe out through your nose to help the aroma compounds, which are volatilized in your mouth through warming and agitation, reach the olfactory area. (Remember the overwhelming importance of aroma in creating flavor!) Do you sense any new aromas?

Keep track of your different taste experiences by creating records in your *Beer Steward Certificate Program Tasting Journal* and writing down your flavor and aroma descriptions, the story of the beer, and whatever numeric descriptions are available, e.g., alcohol content, bitterness units, and color units. These can be used later when describing the beer to your customers.

Off-Flavors in Beer

Brewers constantly taste their beers during the brewing and production process. They become familiar with each beer's characteristic flavor profile at each production stage so they can quickly detect flavor discrepancies that indicate problems. The Beer Flavor Wheel, Appendix C, was developed to help brewers identify both positive and negative flavors common in beer. Problem flavors are called "off-flavors" if they reach the final customer. They are normally not present in well-made beers. Additionally, some flavors that might be considered "off" by one brewer may be the signature flavor profile of another. Some flavors that are undesirable in one beer style may define the flavor profile of another style. Flavor quality means that the flavors present in a beer are those that the brewmaster intended to be there.

Off-flavors can develop after the packaged beer leaves the brewery, and these are not generally considered acceptable. Off-flavors can taint the intended character of the beer and leave the customer unhappy. This may dissuade the customer from drinking more, trying that particular beer again, or recommending it to friends. Winning back an upset customer is both difficult and a situation that is avoidable. As described in previous chapters, handling by the wholesaler and retailer can affect how these off-flavors develop and spoil an otherwise well-made beer. The primary culprits that cause off-flavors to develop beyond the brewery gate are oxidation, ultraviolet light, and draft line taints.

Oxidized and Staling Flavors

Oxidized flavors are characterized as papery, wet cardboard, oily, or cooked. Even the very best packaging equipment allows a small amount of oxygen into the beer. The desired flavors of a fresh beer can be transformed by oxidation into dull, harsh, and unappealing flavors. Time and elevated temperatures cause oxidation to accelerate, while lower temperatures slow the process. As described previously, brewers normally store and taste beer over a period of several weeks or months at 70°F (21°C) to determine the shelf life of their product. The shelf life indicates the time that the beer can be stored at room temperature and still retain approximately 70% of its fresh flavor. Storage conditions above this temperature can significantly reduce the shelf life of a beer and ultimately lower the satisfaction of its customers. Other unpleasant flavors develop as the beer stales.

Here are examples of what happens as beer stales over time.
- Fresh hop aroma is the first to go
- Bitterness dissipates and becomes harsh
- Malt flavors become raisiny and sherrylike
- Papery and wet cardboard flavors develop
- Unfiltered and bottle-conditioned beers may produce yeasty, meaty attributes

Ultraviolet Light Exposure

Both natural sunlight and artificial interior lighting produce ultraviolet spectrums that cause a reaction with natural hop components in beer and result in a "light struck" or "skunky" flavor. Humans are especially sensitive to this sulfury, light struck compound and it can be detected in *parts per trillion*. Brown bottles, cans, and kegs protect against ultraviolet exposure, as does fully wrapped paperboard packaging. Many brewers who package their beers in green or clear bottles use modified hop products that do not react with ultraviolet light, while other brewers accept this flavor as a component of their product flavor profile. Retailers can protect beer from ultraviolet exposure in their displays by using ultraviolet filters on their lighting.

<u>Draft Line Taints</u>

Dirty draft lines provide an environment for bacteria to grow and potentially taint a beer's flavor. The most common draft line taints are diacetyl and acids produced by bacteria in the line; these can give sour or popcorn butter flavors. Chemical taints caused by the use of chlorine-based cleaners and incomplete rinsing of line-cleaning chemicals give the beer soapy and medicinal flavors. Additionally, the growth of mold and mildew in the draft system transfers unpleasant musty flavors to the draft beer. A proper draft line cleaning regimen keeps these bacteria and mildews from forming and eliminates the chemical residues (see Chapter 8 for more details on cleaning a draft system).

Important Off-Flavors for Wholesalers and Retailers

Beer is a perishable product that can become stale or develop other off-flavors caused by improper treatment. If a wholesaler or retailer detects a flavor defect in a beer, the brewery, or supplier, should be informed of the problem and the product returned. The following are examples of off-flavors, and their causes, that may be prevented by the wholesaler/distributor through good beer-handling practices.

- Acetaldehyde—rotten apple or paint emulsion flavor apparent in old beer; warm storage of bottles, cans, and kegs or air contact in the draft system
- Chlorophenol—medicinal, chlorine chemical flavors; glasses not rinsed of sanitizer or plastic in the draft system that is not inert or is improperly rinsed after cleaning
- Trichloroanisole (TCA)—musty flavor; moldy draft lines and draft box conditions
- Diacetyl—rancid butterscotch or popcorn butter flavor; dirty, microbe-infested draft lines
- Light struck—sulfury skunky flavor; bottles exposed to sunlight or fluorescent light
- Stale, papery—wet cardboard or papery flavor apparent in old beer; warm storage of bottles, cans, and kegs or air contact in draft systems
- Acidic, acetic, sour—unpleasant sourness; dirty, microbe-infested draft lines and gas lines or contact with air in the keg
- Alkaline—soapy flavor; draft lines not properly rinsed of detergent cleaners
- Metallic—rust or metal flavors; exposure of draft beer to copper, brass, iron, or corroded stainless steel
- Carbonation—foamy or flat beer; improper gas pressure on the keg, making beer flat or overcarbonated

Summary

Drinkers enjoy beer because it is refreshing and flavorful and offers interesting choices in style and appearance. To satisfy today's sophisticated beer customer, we need to understand how our own sensory systems detect and recognize flavor and aroma. We further need to describe a beer's flavor sensations in a way that our customers can identify with and understand. By describing beer in terms of its flavors, beyond "malty" and "hoppy", and accurately using other flavor non-taste/smell descriptors, such as mouthfeel, fullness, and balance, beers can be differentiated across all styles and beer customers can be led to the tasting experience they will enjoy most. You can build an effective descriptive vocabulary using the four flavor-driven groups. This process elevates beer in the eyes of our customers and expands the beer market.

The beer world has never seen as much diversity in the flavor of its brands and styles as it does now. Our customers rely on us to help them understand beer and to consistently deliver to them the beer drinking experience they enjoy. We need to work hard at understanding beer flavor, and we need to communicate important flavor information to our customers so that we don't let them down.

Selected References

Desrochers, R. 2011. Lecture materials presented at the MBAA Brewery Packaging Technology Course. Master Brewers Association of the Americas, St. Paul, MN.

Furusho, S., Kobayashi, N., Nakae, N., Takashio, M., Tamaki, T., and Shinotsuka, K. 1999. A developed descriptive sensory test reveals beer flavor changes during storage. Technical Quarterly Master Brewers Association of the Americas 36:163-166.

Hughes, P. 2009. Beer flavor. Pages 61-83 in: Beer: A Quality Perspective. C. W. Bamforth, ed. Academic Press, Burlington, MA.

Lewis, M. J., Pangborn, R. M., and Tanno, L. A. S. 1974. Sensory analysis of beer flavor. Tech. Q. Master Brew. Assoc. Am. 11:83-86.

Schmidt, T. R., and Kluba, R. M. 1999. Beer Quality and Taste Methodology. Pages 381-412 in: The Practical Brewer, 3rd ed. J. T. McCabe, ed. Master Brewers Association of the Americas, St. Paul, MN.

Chapter 10:
Beer and Health

Charles Bamforth and Laine J. Murphey

In recent years there has been a surge in the number of publications relating to the benefits of the moderate consumption of alcohol. Perhaps the turning point came with the television program *Sixty Minutes*, in which the first strong touting was made for taking a glass or two of red wine daily to counter the risk of atherosclerosis (blocking of the arteries by cholesterol). Since then, the wine lobby has never been shy of using this platform to advocate their product, even though claims for beer as a healthful beverage are at least as strong.

Brewers have been much more leery of positioning their product in a context of health and well-being. There are those who firmly believe that this caution is wise, saying that to offer this proposition of healthfulness is to tempt fate by encouraging the anti-alcohol lobby to seize upon any weakness in the arguments and reinforce their own prejudices. However, there are others who are very much pushing the healthful image of beer, to the extent that certain products are now available with an overt marketing angle of "drink this and your body will reap these benefits".

One of the chapter authors advocates a middle-of-the-road approach, as exemplified in Bamforth (2004) and Bamforth (2008). It would be careless to allow the wine industry to hog all the moral high ground, and yet it is important that any claims be based on a solid scientific foundation. It is critical that there be impartial and substantiated judgment on both the merits and demerits of consuming alcoholic beverages, including beer. Recent studies have revealed that there is a real need for better education of the drinking public (Wright et al., 2008a,b).

One fundamental difference between the worlds of wine and beer, at least in the United States, is that in the former the industry is united in celebrating their product. In the brewing world, however, there is the insidious tendency for companies to attack the products of others through the medium of advertising and beyond: big brewing companies denigrating the products of others; craft brewers rubbishing the brands of the mega brewers. This is a repeating cycle that benefits no one and can lead to a profound lessening of the beverage's image in the eyes of the customer, who is left in a position of not trusting any brewer. They are left confused about what quality really is, and against such a background, how can they really believe any claims made for beer as regards the effect that it will have on their bodies?

Critically Assessing the Data

As with any food, drug, treatment, or life-style modification, it truly is important that a critical appraisal is made of all claims made regarding the impact that alcoholic beverages have on health, whether positive or negative.

In this regard, several questions should be considered when reviewing health claims. First, is the data presented statistically sound? So many of the claims made for the impact of dietary components on health are derived from studies in which aspects of healthfulness (e.g., incidence of coronary heart disease) are correlated with individuals' self-reporting of what they have or have not consumed. Two very real risks from this are misreporting by the subjects (otherwise known as lying) and also the matter of confounding factors. A likely example of the latter are instances in which studies have shown a benefit of wine in countering atherosclerosis, though not beer. There is strong evidence that most consumers of wine indulge in healthier lifestyles than do many beer consumers. So on the one hand, it may be that the similar benefits of both drinks as regards countering the blocking of arteries (discussed later) are disguised in the case of beer through a counter-impact of some other factor (e.g., smoking, higher intake of fat, less exercise, and accessing lesser-quality health care). Even more concerning would be reports directly linking the consumption of a foodstuff to some detrimental impact on the body. For example, there are reports that beer drinkers tend to smoke more. Smoking is linked to cancer and contributes significantly to atherosclerosis. Thus a correlation may be expected between beer consumption and cancer, not because beer is the causal agent but because smoking goes hand in hand with beer drinking in some societies. An analogy would be drawing a correlation between wearing a beard and becoming a bishop. Not all bishops have beards (a few are female!) but many do, so there will be some form of correlation between the two. The unthinking might say "ah, if you grow a beard there is an increasing chance that you will become a bishop". As regards "lying", this may sound a brutal term to use, but it is appropriate. Much of the data in the literature relating alcohol consumption and health is based on surveys that depend on declarations by individuals of how many drinks they have per day. Most people's tendency when faced with questioning by a doctor is to underestimate their consumption of alcohol. "How many beers do you drink?" may fetch the answer "oh, one or two per day" when the honest answer might be "three or four".

Second, are the claims made based on realistic systems? For example, is the data derived from a laboratory test, from an animal model, or by properly conducted trials with human subjects? A strong example of this would be the claims made for red wine as a rich source of antioxidants. There is no arguing that red wine does contain very large quantities of polyphenols, many of which have antioxidant potential. And they are assayed in the laboratory using diverse tests. However, just because an antioxidant (whether from wine, beer, or anything else) has strong activity in a laboratory test does not mean that it has a benefit to the body. The only true test is to do studies that show that the agent is assimilated by the body, reaches the parts where it needs to work, and once it gets there, does the job. Certainly laboratory tests with molecules, cells, tissues, and laboratory animals give much support to a case, but it is only in rigorous studies with humans, taking into consideration the concerns raised earlier, that bona fide conclusions can be made. One study in which an antioxidant was shown to be taken into the body concluded that ferulic acid was more effectively assimilated from beer than from tomatoes. Another concern is that too much of some agents in foodstuffs may be counterproductive. It is likely that there is an optimum dosage of antioxidants in the daily diet and it is not inconceivable that the quantities present in beer are actually more appropriate than the much higher levels in, say, red wine. But that is speculation. For a more comprehensive review of the subject, the reader is referred to *Beer in Health and Disease Prevention* (Preedy, 2008).

Beer Composition

Table 10.1 summarizes the nutritional elements of beer. Clearly, there is great diversity in alcohol content, from essentially 0 to >26% by volume, with an attendant range in calorific values, ethanol being the major calorie source in beer. There is also a range of carbohydrate contents of beer, depending (among other things) on the fermentability of the wort, extent of attenuation in fermentation, and use of primings. Residual carbohydrates, such as pentosan and beta glucan, with various degrees of solubility survive into beer and represent soluble fiber and putative prebiotics. Beer contains some protein, depending largely on the grist composition. Beer is relatively devoid of thiamine but can contain significant quantities of other B vitamins, notably folate. Beer contains a range of antioxidants, including phenolic acids such as ferulate, derived from the cell walls of barley and wheat, and polyphenols, derived from cereal and hops. Beer is perhaps the richest source of assimilable silicon in the diet and this may help in countering osteoporosis.

From time to time, attention has been drawn to various components in beer that may be disadvantageous to health. These

Table 10.1. The relative nutrient composition of beer[a,b]

Nutrient	Beer, regular (one 12-fluid-ounce serving)	Reference Daily Intake (Males 19–50)
Proximates		
Water (g)	327.4	3.7 liters per day
Energy (Kcal)	153	1,800
Protein (g)	1.64	56
Fat (g)	0	
Ash (g)	0.57	
Carbohydrate (g)	12.64	130
Fiber (g)	1	38
Sugars (g)	0	
Minerals		
Calcium (mg)	14	1,000
Iron (mg)	0.07	6
Magnesium (mg)	21	350
Phosphorus (mg)	50	580
Potassium (mg)	96	4,700
Sodium (mg)	14	1,500
Zinc (mg)	0.04	9.4
Copper (mg)	0.018	0.7
Manganese (mg)	0.028	2.3
Selenium (μg)	2.1	45
Silicon (mg)	10	
Vitamins		
Vitamin C (mg)	0	90
Thiamine (mg)	0.018	1.2
Riboflavin (mg)	0.086	1.3
Niacin (mg)	1.826	16
Pantothenic acid (mg)	0.146	5
Vitamin B_6 (mg)	0.164	1.3
Folate (μg)	21	400
Vitamin B_{12} (μg)	0.07	2.4
Other		
Ethanol (g)	13.9	

[a] Based on Bamforth (2008).
[b] The dietary guidelines of the U.S. Department of Agriculture (USDA, 2005) recommend a maximum of one drink per day for women and two for men, a drink being a 12-ounce serving of a regular beer or 5 ounces of wine (12% alcohol by volume). And it is stated that at this level there is no association of alcohol consumption with deficiencies of either macronutrients or micronutrients, and furthermore, there is no apparent association between consuming one or two alcoholic beverages daily and obesity.

Alcohol Absorption

"Ethanol is highly soluble in water and is absorbed much less in fat. So alcohol tends to distribute itself mostly in tissues rich in water (muscle) instead of those rich in fat.

- Two people may weigh the same, yet their bodies may have different proportions of tissue containing water and fat. Think of a tall, thin person and a short, fat person who both weigh 150 pounds. The short, fat person will have more fat and less water making up his body than the tall, thin person. If both people, in this example, consume the same amount of alcohol, the short, fat person will end up with a higher blood alcohol content (BAC). This is because the alcohol he drank was spread into a smaller water space.
- Women's bodies, on average, have more fat and less water than men's bodies. Using the same logic, this means that a woman will reach a higher BAC than a man of the same weight when both drink the same amount of alcohol."

Source: eMedicineHealth, 2010.

have included the nitrosamines, monochloropropanols, and pesticide residues. Brewers have been fastidious in addressing these issues so as to minimize levels in products. Some normal components of beer may induce symptoms in sensitive individuals, the most notable example being protein degradation products of hordein claimed to be deleterious for sufferers of celiac disease. It has not been rigorously proved that these hydrolyzed and denatured protein fragments (peptides and polypeptides) truly do cause a problem in such patients, but medical advice is invariably to avoid foodstuffs derived from wheat and barley. Hence, there is interest in beers based on grains such as sorghum, which do not contain sensitive proteins.

Positive Impacts of Beer on Health

Beer may beneficially impact the body through two mechanisms: directly by affecting bodily functions or indirectly by boosting morale and perceived well-being.

Atherosclerosis

Many of the beneficial effects of beer consumption may be due to decreases in coronary artery disease. Several studies have drawn U-shaped or J-shaped curves to illustrate the relationship between alcohol intake and coronary heart disease and all causes of mortality, respectively. Thus, the benefits of alcohol in countering atherosclerosis are observed with even substantial daily consumption, but if all health considerations are assessed, then a J-shaped curve indicates that a daily consumption of one to three 12-ounce servings of regular strength (4.0–5.5% ABV) beer is optimum. Frequency of consumption is at least as important as quantity, with daily moderate intake giving more benefit than infrequent moderate intake (Fig. 10.1).

Numerous studies have shown that all alcoholic beverages are equally advantageous in countering the risk of atherosclerosis, with Klatsky (2001) stressing that ethanol is the key ingredient. Alcohol favorably impacts the balance of "good" versus "bad" cholesterol in the body and it also reduces the risk of blood clotting.

Hypertension and Stroke

Beer consumption has been claimed to be associated with increased blood pressure. However, it has been reported that the blood pressure of nondrinkers is higher than in those consuming 10–20 grams of alcohol per day (one or two 12-ounce regular strength beers). Hypertension is a significant risk factor for stroke, but it has been observed that there is a reduced risk of stroke for light to moderate drinkers and it is only when drinking is heavy (>six beers per day) or at a binge level that the risk of stroke is significant.

Digestive System

The bacterium *Helicobacter pylori* induces gastric and duodenal ulcers but the organism is inhibited by alcohol, and moderate consumers of beer have a lower risk of infection with *Helicobacter pylori* than abstainers. Additionally, those consuming alcohol in moderation—and especially daily—develop fewer gallstones, while moderate drinking also reduces the risk of developing diabetes.

Reproductive System

There appears to be no relationship between alcohol consumption and fertility. Hops are rich in phytoestrogens, but the amounts entering beer are very low and the hormonal status of men should not be threatened. This is why it is likely not valid to make health claims for beer in respect of the potential anticancer impact of such materials.

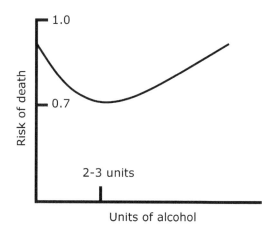

Figure 10.1. The impact of alcohol consumption on the risk of death, in a J-shaped curve. Unit of alcohol is 12 ounces of regular strength (4.0–5.5% ABV) beer or 6 ounces of wine. (Reprinted from Bamforth, 2008)

What Happens in the Brain?

Alcohol increases the effect of the body's naturally occurring neurotransmitter GABA (gamma amino butyric acid). Neurotransmitters are substances that chemically connect the signals from one nerve to the next, allowing a signal to flow along a neural pathway. An inhibitory neurotransmitter (alcohol) reduces this signal flow in the brain. This explains how alcohol depresses both a person's mental and physical activities. By way of comparison, cocaine does the opposite by producing a general excitatory effect on the nervous system.

Source: eMedicineHealth, 2010.

It may be that a barley carbohydrate promotes prolactin secretion and therefore milk production in the female, but others claim that alcohol consumption slightly reduces milk production.

Brain and Cognitive Function

There is a supposed J-shaped link between alcohol consumption and cognitive function, with moderate drinkers performing significantly better than abstainers or heavy drinkers. Moderate drinking is associated with a reduced risk of dementia and improved cognitive function in the elderly.

Hangovers are likely caused by a buildup of acetaldehyde formed through the oxidation of ethanol and perhaps by other aldehydes formed from other alcohols. Migraines may also be induced by biogenic amines found in relatively small quantities in beer but in more significant quantities in certain wines and cheeses.

Kidney and Urinary Tract

Beer is rather more diuretic than is water, and fresh beer promotes urination to a greater extent than does stale beer. Some beers should be avoided by sufferers of gout because they can contain significant quantities of purines. Beer is superior to water in "flushing out" the kidneys, thereby lessening the risk of kidney stones.

Deleterious Impacts of Beer on Health

As discussed above, while moderate consumption of beer and alcohol (two to three 12-ounce servings of regular strength beer a day) is associated with overall decreases in risk of death, there are clearly health risks of heavier alcohol consumption. In addition, binge drinking carries clear adverse health effects. While most adverse effects of alcohol consumption are observed with heavy consumption, it would be remiss not to address the effects of this overconsumption on health. Additionally, a recent study suggests that even moderate consumption may be associated with breast cancer.

Although alcohol may be good for your health in moderation, it can also be harmful. It depends on how much you drink, your age, and other factors.

Excess alcohol can increase the risk of:
Liver disease
High blood pressure
High blood fats (triglycerides)
Heart failure
Stroke
Fetal alcohol syndrome
Certain cancers

People who should not drink include:
Pregnant and breast-feeding women
People at risk for certain cancers
People with family histories of alcohol abuse
Children and adolescents
People taking medications that can interact with alcohol
People with health conditions such as liver problems or ulcers
Anyone requiring coordination to perform a task
People who have a history of pancreatitis

Source: Zelman, 2005.

Gastrointestinal

Alcohol is a leading cause of cirrhosis and end-stage liver disease, which carries a high risk of death. In addition to cirrhosis, fatty liver can be induced by alcohol, and acute alcoholic hepatitis (acute inflammation of the liver) also can produce significant illness and even death from liver failure. Both of these are associated with heavy alcohol use and abuse.

There are two major causes of pancreatitis in the Western World: gall stones and alcohol. While moderate alcohol consumption decreases the risk of gall stones, heavy alcohol use increases the risk of pancreatitis. In its most severe form, pancreatitis can be fatal.

Cancer

The literature is contradictory on the link between alcohol consumption and cancer. For every study that draws a correlation between alcohol consumption and a particular form of cancer, there is another that finds either no link or even a protective impact of moderate drinking. However, a recent large, observational study of 1.2 million women showed a link between any alcohol consumption and breast cancer in particular. While this is an observational study, the large number of subjects raises concern for a link between breast cancer and alcohol consumption at any level. Several smaller studies have also suggested this link.

There have been several recent reports of beer components that may provide anticancer value to beer, e.g., Yoshikawa et al. (2002) found pseudouridine in many beers and demonstrated its antimutagenic activity. Actually pseudouridine seemed to account for only 3% of the antimutagenic impact of beer.

Cardiovascular

Moderate beer consumption does lead to lower overall risk of death of heart disease. On the other hand, heavy alcohol use is associated with hypertension and with the abnormal heart rhythm of atrial fibrillation. Indeed, the later is known as "holiday heart", with new onset of atrial fibrillation associated with heavy drinking during holiday periods. Heavy drinkers also may suffer from cardiomyopathy, or weakening of the heart muscle. This may be because of the direct toxic effects of high levels of alcohol and compounded with poor nutrition often seen with alcohol abuse.

Alcohol Metabolism and the Liver

Unlike food, alcohol does not need to be digested to be absorbed into the blood stream. About 20% of alcohol is absorbed directly into the blood in the stomach, about 20% is broken down by alcohol dehydrogenase enzymes (ADH) in the stomach, and about 10% is expelled in breath and urine. The remainder enters the bloodstream in the upper intestines and circulates through the body until it reaches the liver. However, liver cells are the only cells in the body that produce enough ADH to appreciably oxidize alcohol. The liver prefers to metabolize fatty acids but will break down alcohol first, allowing the fatty acids to accumulate until the alcohol is metabolized. Heavy drinking can cause the buildup of fat cells in the liver. A fatty liver is the first stage of liver deterioration in heavy drinkers and can impair nutritional uptake in the body. The fat reduces the liver's ability to absorb oxygen and nutrients. With prolonged abuse, these conditions eventually cause the second stage of deterioration in which liver cells die and form fibrous scars, known as fibrosis. Abstinence and good nutrition can help regenerate some new liver cells, but in the final stage of liver disease, known as cirrhosis, the damage is least reversible.

Source: HealthCheck Systems, 2010.

Brain and Cognitive Function

Acute alcohol intoxication reduces hand-eye coordination and cognitive recall. In its most severe form, acute intoxication leads to respiratory depression and death.

Chronic, heavy alcohol use is also clearly associated with some forms of dementia (Wernicke-Korsakoff syndrome) and loss of dendrites (the connecting "branches" of neurons, or nerve cells). Magnetic resonance imaging (MRI) scanning of normal brains and those of alcohol abusers show atrophy, or loss of brain tissue, with heavy alcohol use. This is likely a direct toxic effect of alcohol on neurons. In the peripheral (body-wide) nervous system, alcohol abuse can lead to neuropathy, or damage to sensory

Blood Alcohol Content

In October 2000, the federal government passed a law mandating that all states enact laws lowering the legal driving blood alcohol content (BAC) to 80 milligrams/deciliter (mg/dL) (i.e., 0.08%) by October 2003 or face the penalty of withholding 2% of their federal highway construction funds. The following scale details the expected effects of alcohol at various BACs. There is a tremendous variation from person to person, and not all people exhibit all the effects. This scale would apply to a typical social drinker.

- 50 mg/dL (0.05%): Loss of emotional restraint, vivaciousness, feeling of warmth, flushing of skin, mild impairment of judgment
- 100 mg/dL (0.10%): Slight slurring of speech, loss of control of fine motor movements (such as writing), confusion when faced with tasks requiring thinking, emotionally unstable, inappropriate laughter
- 200 mg/dL (0.20%): Very slurred speech, staggering gait, double vision, lethargic but able to be aroused by voice, difficulty sitting upright in a chair, memory loss
- 300 mg/dL (0.30%): Stuporous, able to be aroused only briefly by strong physical stimulus (such as a face slap or deep pinch), deep snoring
- 400 mg/dL (0.40%): Comatose, not able to be aroused, incontinent (wets self), low blood pressure, irregular breathing
- 500 mg/dL (0.50%): Death possible, either from cessation of breathing, excessively low blood pressure, or vomit entering the lungs without the presence of the protective reflex to cough it out

Source: eMedicineHealth, 2010.

nerves, in the feet and hands. Again, this is likely a toxic effect of alcohol on nerve cells.

Reproduction

Any type of alcohol consumption during pregnancy carries a risk of fetal alcohol syndrome, a constellation of neurological delays in children exposed to alcohol while in the womb. There are currently no accepted safe levels of alcohol consumption during pregnancy.

Conclusion

In summary, moderate beer consumption is associated with a decreased risk of death from all causes. The biggest contributor to this statistic is likely due to a decreased risk of death from atherosclerosis (heart attack). Alcohol may also have beneficial effects on other organ systems as well. In this regard, the U.S. Department of Agriculture, in the latest "Food Pyramid", recommends that those who choose to drink alcoholic beverages "do so sensibly, and in moderation. Limit intake to one to two drinks per day for women or two to three per day for men. Avoid drinking before or when driving, or whenever it puts you or others at risk."

Conversely, heavy alcohol use and abuse carries an increased risk of sickness and death, particularly from gastrointestinal disease. Certainly, performing activities requiring high levels of cognitive skill (i.e., driving a car) should not be done while under the acute effects of excessive alcoholic beverages, of any source.

Finally, the beneficial effects of alcohol consumption are as equally valid for consumers of beer as they are for consumers of wine or spirits. Overall, moderate consumers of beer may be expected to experience the same positive health effects as those who drink wine.

Selected References

Bamforth, C. W. 2004. Beer: Health and Nutrition. Blackwell Science Ltd., Oxford, United Kingdom.

Bamforth, C. 2008. Grape vs. Grain: A Historical, Technological, and Social Comparison of Wine and Beer. Cambridge University Press, New York.

eMedicineHealth. 2010. Alcohol intoxication. Alcohol intoxication signs and symptoms. www.emedicinehealth.com/alcohol_intoxication/page2_em.htm. WebMD Inc., New York.

HealthCheck Systems. 2010. Alcohol and your health. www.healthchecksystems.com/alcohol.htm. HealthCheck Systems, Inc., Brooklyn, NY.

Klatsky, A. L. 2001. Alcohol and cardiovascular diseases. Pages 517-546 in: Alcohol in Health and Disease. D. P. Agarwal and H. K. Seitz, eds. Marcel Dekker, New York.

Preedy, V. R., ed. 2008. Beer in Health and Disease Prevention. Academic Press, London.

United States Department of Agriculture (USDA). 2005. Nutrition and Your Health: Dietary Guidelines for Americans, Part D: Science Base, Section 8: Ethanol. www.health.gov/DIETARYGUIDELINES/dga2005/report/HTML/D8_Ethanol.htm.

Wright, C. A., Bruhn, C. M., Heymann, H., and Bamforth, C. W. 2008a. Beer and wine consumers' perceptions of the nutritional value of alcoholic and nonalcoholic beverages. Journal of Food Science 73(1):H8-H12.

Wright, C. A., Bruhn, C. M., Heymann, H., and Bamforth, C. W. 2008b. Beer consumers' perceptions of the health aspects of alcoholic beverages. Journal of Food Science 73(1):H12-H17.

Yoshikawa, T., Kimura, S., Hatano, T., Okamoto, K., Hayatsu, H., and Arimoto-Kobayashi, S. 2002. Pseudouridine, an antimutagenic substance in beer towards N-methyl-N'-nitro-N-nitrosoguanidine (MNNG). Food and Chemical Toxicology 40:1165-1170.

Zelman, K. M. 2005. Blood pressure and alcohol: Should you or shouldn't you? How drinking affects your health. WebMD Weight Loss Clinic—Feature. WebMD Inc., New York.

Chapter 11:
Beer and Regulation

Art DeCelles

This chapter introduces owners and employees to basic laws and legal issues that govern the beer industry. Breweries, distributorships or wholesalers, restaurants, bars, and other retail outlets are subject to numerous regulations and face significant risks for noncompliance. For business owners, their investment and reputation are jeopardized if they do not fulfill their legal obligations. For employees, their careers in the beer industry, or any other industry, can be permanently impaired by a criminal citation or lawsuit. To protect against these risks, a working knowledge of laws and legal principles applicable to the beer industry is essential. Industry professionals should know where to find reliable sources of information. Basic sources of law include written criminal and business laws and administrative regulations. In routine matters, state regulatory agencies, law enforcement officials, or insurance companies are often good starting points for advice. For more complex issues, an attorney should be consulted.

Beer distributors and retailers hold at least one government-issued license, and many hold more than one. In addition, these licenses are subject to suspension or revocation for violations of a wide range of laws that apply to the conduct of owners, managers, and every employee. Legal liability can also arise from negligence by management or employees in conducting their business.

In areas not explicitly required by the law, self-regulation by industry members throughout the chain of commerce has been important in areas such as advertising practices and prevention of underage drinking (e.g., The Beer Institute Advertising and Marketing Code, Appendix D).

To get a perspective on the laws governing the production, sale, and consumption of alcohol in the United States, a brief history lesson is helpful. On July 4, 1789, President Washington signed the second bill enacted by the newly formed United State Congress, which levied a duty on imported beer, evidencing that beer taxation and the regulations to enforce collection are as old as the republic. Prohibition banned the manufacture, sale, transportation, and importation of alcoholic beverages in the United States between 1920 and 1933. These bans spawned illegal production and distribution networks and widespread indifference or even contempt for the law. In the words of an ardent but thoughtful opponent of Prohibition, "The law was in conflict with deep-seated habits and fundamental concepts of personal liberty" (Fosdick, 1956, p. 252). After a long and intense national debate, Prohibition was repealed in 1933 by the adoption of the Twenty-first Amendment to the United State Constitution. Most modern laws are based on policies adopted after the repeal of Prohibition.

The Twenty-first Amendment also led to the establishment of an intricate system of federal and state regulation of beer and other alcoholic beverages that was designed to ensure temperance, industry integrity, controlled markets, fair competition, and payment of federal and state taxes. Congress addressed commercial activities that occurred in interstate and foreign commerce, while each state was made responsible for regulating the sale, transportation, and consumption of alcohol within its respective borders.

Beer Distribution

Since the 1930s, Congress, state legislatures, and local governments have refined alcohol policy to meet the needs of a growing and increasingly diverse population and a dynamic alcohol beverage industry. More than 2,000 brewers and beer importers were operating in the United States in 2009. They range from small local brewpubs to large national brewers producing millions of barrels annually. Large brewers and beer importers generally utilize beer wholesalers or distributors to sell beer to more than 500,000 retail outlets throughout the nation. The brewer-to-wholesaler-to-retailer chain of commerce is commonly known as the three-tier system, which is established in each state and is supervised by state regulatory agencies. Exceptions exist in some states where brewers are permitted to self-distribute or own a separately licensed wholesalership. Brewpubs are able to sell to customers on their premises and, in some cases, sell packaged beer in growlers or other containers for off-premise consumption. The National Beer Wholesalers Association strongly supports the three-tier system as noted below in its 2008 description of the American beer distribution system.

> From a quality-control and product-integrity standpoint, the American beer distribution system provides retailers and consumers with peace of mind. In making sure that beer is fresh and meets quality standards, brewers, beer importers, and distributors can determine where a particular shipment of beer is in the supply chain. Because beer is a perishable product, distributors regularly rotate stock and remove old beer from retail outlets based on the coding systems established by U.S. and international brewers; they also ensure that labels and packages have not been altered or damaged.
>
> (National Beer Wholesalers Association, 2008)

Today's regulatory system is largely in the hands of states, which have generally maintained a three-tier distribution structure with extensive licensing requirements for brewers, importers, wholesalers, and retailers and with limited exceptions for brewpubs and other unique entities. State licensing systems help ensure that the entire chain of commerce is regulated and that excise and sales tax payments are paid in full and on time.

Federal requirements also apply. All brewers, regardless of size, are required to register with the U.S. Department of the Treasury Alcohol and Tobacco Tax and Trade Bureau (TTB) and to report production and make regular excise tax payments on a schedule that varies according to production volume. (Federal law exempts home brewers from these requirements.) Beer wholesalers or distributors are required to obtain a federal license, known as a basic permit.

One common approach to both state and federal regulations of day-to-day activities of brewers, importers, distributors, and retailers was the prohibition of tied houses. The term "tied house" is a reference to the fact that alcoholic beverages were sold in beer houses and public houses in England and Colonial America. The "tie" refers to the close financial and business relationships that often existed between taverns and the breweries and distilleries that supplied them. Before refrigeration, pasteurization, and bottles made beer more stable and transportable for widespread beer consumption at home, most beer was consumed in taverns, restaurants, and other on-premise retail outlets, which made retail sales of draft beer in taverns especially important outlets for brewers. Relatively small amounts were dispensed in containers (beer pails) for home consumption. To ensure that taverns carried their beer, brewers often gave financial assistance to tavern owners to open, expand, or maintain their pubs. In exchange for this assistance, taverns would be "tied" to the brewer and only carry the brands of beer produced by the brewery providing their business financing or other material assistance in the form of free products, fixtures, and merchandise.

Prohibition advocates argued that generous credit terms and other financial assistance, gifts, and services corrupted retailers because they would reciprocate by exclusively selling the products of a supplier that had given them favorable treatment. While some historical evidence indicates that this concern was greatly exaggerated, tied houses were blamed for a proliferation of saloons that were indebted to brewers and distillers and for businesses that engaged in unscrupulous practices to boost alcohol sales from the late nineteenth century until Prohibition.

Tied house prohibitions were intended to limit brewers, distillers, and wholesalers from establishing close business relationships with retail establishments. The idea behind these laws is to prevent the integration of retail outlets with wholesalers and brewers. The prevailing thought was that removing financial and other ties between the tiers would relieve pressure on the owners of retail outlets to engage in the practices that were prevalent prior to Prohibition. A federal tied house law and analogous laws in each state impose licensing and financial disclosure requirements, along with restrictions on business relationships among brewers, distributors, and retail outlets.

Significant variations and exceptions exist among state laws, but typical tied house laws restrict or sometimes ban the extension of credit or lending of money to retailers by brewers or wholesalers, investment in the business of a retailer, and the making of rebates or the giving of any other financial or material assistance of value to a retailer. Beyond direct or indirect financial assistance, the laws also ban or limit the value or quantity of items brewers or wholesalers can provide to retailers. Detailed laws and administrative regulations govern common items, such as signs, glassware, and even coasters. Over time, many tied house laws have been modified to accommodate new business structures, such as brewpubs, which combine the roles of brewer and retailer.

Exceptions to older laws made by legislatures, interpretations of judges, or guidance from regulatory agencies pose a challenge for businesses seeking clear legal definitions of prohibited activities. Because of numerous modifications over many decades, tied house laws and other laws governing business relationships in the alcohol beverage industry have become lengthy and complex. Even the policy goals or rationale behind changes made many years ago are not always clear, which poses challenges for industry members and regulators alike. Yet serious financial or even criminal penalties exist for violations.

In situations in which the owner or manager of a retail outlet is negotiating any type of agreement with a brewer, distiller, or wholesaler, consultation with an attorney or advice from state regulatory agencies is the best way to avoid inadvertent violations. Many practices that are common in other food and beverage sectors, such as quantity discounts and provision of free samples, signs, and advertising specialties, are banned or limited in various alcohol beverage regulations. Likewise, personal gifts, such as tickets to sporting events and dinners, may also be restricted.

Sales to Consumers

In addition to establishing the structure of the distribution system and regulating business relationships, Congress and the states have enacted numerous laws and regulations that apply to retail sales to consumers. From a business planning and risk management perspective, laws implementing the minimum purchase age and laws prohibiting sales to intoxicated persons are extremely important. These laws pose two levels of risk to businesses and employees at the point of sale, whether it is at a store, event, restaurant, brewpub, bar, or tasting room.

The first level of risk is that an employee will violate a state's criminal law by making a sale or providing alcohol to a minor or a person exhibiting signs of intoxication. These illegal sales can result in arrest, substantial fines, license suspension or revocation, and even jail time in an extreme case.

In addition to prosecution for a criminal violation, a second level of risk, known as civil liability, can result from an improper sale. Financial penalties, known as damages, can be imposed by a judge or a jury after a lawsuit stemming from illegal sales to minors or intoxicated persons. Such lawsuits may be filed by an individual who was illegally served or someone who was harmed by the actions of a minor who was illegally served or of an intoxicated person of any age.

This area of the law is often referred to as dram shop liability. (Dram shop is an old term that refers to a place that sells alcoholic beverages. A dram was a unit of measure used in Britain and many of its former colonies, and shops often measured and dispensed alcoholic beverages to individuals from barrels into smaller containers for home consumption.) Tremendous variation exists among states for liability for injuries caused by a minor or an intoxicated adult who purchases or is served alcoholic beverages at a commercial establishment. Anyone involved in the sale of alcoholic beverages to the public should know what the legal standards are in their state. Server and seller training programs establishing steps to prevent illegal sales, such as adopting consistent policies for checking identification or having a means of safe transportation for an intoxicated customer, are beneficial to prevent problems and to properly respond to situations that might arise with intoxicated patrons. Industry managers or employees who move to a position in another state should always inquire carefully to find out their obligations and potential liability at their new location.

Owners and managers should be aware that the same legal risks apply to fellow employees who consume alcoholic beverages during or after working hours. For a retail outlet selling beer, separate policies must address illegal sales to customers and alcohol consumption by employees.

The risk of a criminal conviction, civil liability, and loss or suspension of a license can be mitigated in several ways. The employee policies referenced above are a starting point, and they should be based on the law of the state where a business is located. Server and seller training programs are also beneficial to prevent problems and to properly respond to situations that might arise with intoxicated patrons. Some states may reduce penalties on a first offense for businesses and individuals when employees have completed server training and when they have taken reasonable steps to prevent illegal sales, such as adoption of consistent policies for checking identification or having a means of safe transportation for an intoxicated customer.

Self-Regulation of Beer Advertising and Marketing Activities

Beyond formal laws and regulations, another valuable resource that has served the brewing industry well for many years is the Beer Institute Advertising and Marketing Code. Because the beer industry is subject to extensive government regulations at the federal, state, and local levels, alcohol advertising is often scrutinized by law enforcement officials, advocacy organizations, and others. For decades, brewers have formulated and updated voluntary advertising and marketing codes to demonstrate to the public that the industry is sensitive to social concerns and that advertising and marketing practices are directed toward adult consumers of legal drinking age. The first voluntary beer industry code was the Brewers Code of Practice, adopted by the United Brewers Industrial Foundation in 1937. Over time, the code has been updated and refined and is now known as the Marketing and Advertising Code. While written specifically for self-regulation of brewers, the principles of the code provide guidance for advertisers and all beer industry professionals. A complete copy of the code is included in Appendix D, but its basic principles can be summarized as follows:

- Beer advertising should not suggest directly or indirectly that any of the laws applicable to the sale and consumption of beer should not be complied with.
- Beer industry professionals should adhere to contemporary standards of good taste applicable to all commercial advertising and consistent with the medium or context in which the advertisement appears.
- Advertising themes, creative aspects, and placements should reflect the fact that beer industry professionals are responsible corporate citizens.
- Beer industry professionals strongly oppose abuse or inappropriate consumption of their products.

Helpful Sources of Information

A brief background on common sources of legal information will enable the reader to learn and to keep up to date on their legal responsibilities. In the United States, Congress, state legislatures, and local legislative bodies (e.g., city councils and county boards) enact laws. At the state and federal levels, laws are compiled into standardized codes, which are usually indexed or searchable online. Government agencies or officials are authorized to implement or enforce laws. Those agencies or officials must adopt more detailed regulations, policies, or procedures to carry out the intent of the laws in a consistent and workable manner.

TTB and its predecessor federal agencies (i.e., the Bureau of Alcohol, Tobacco and Firearms and the Alcohol and Tobacco Tax Division of the Internal Revenue Service) have amended federal regulations over the years to reflect changes in the marketplace, and agency officials provide informal guidance on recurring enforcement issues. The agency's website provides access to this information.

Federal regulations are published in a single series, known as the Code of Federal Regulations (CFR). State regulations are also generally compiled in a single publication, although the titles and organization vary significantly. The CFR and state regulatory publications include all agencies, so a wide range of information is available on alcohol beverage control policies as well as on other important issues that arise for businesses. Other guidance on policies and procedures is found in a number of publications, such as instructions for completing applications and forms, agency pamphlets, and educational materials.

With the Internet, finding the text of laws, regulations, and policy guidance is relatively easy. Many Internet sites also enable users to contact administrative and enforcement personnel with questions via e-mail.

Common Legal Tasks and Issues

- Obtaining the required licenses or permits to legally produce or import beer
- Obtaining the required licensees or permits to distribute or sell beer at the brewer, importer, wholesaler, or retail levels
- Obtaining federal Certificates of Label Approval (COLA) and state approval where required for each brand and container size produced by a brewer
- Establishing and maintaining a system to pay state and federal excise taxes and to file appropriate returns with TTB and all state and local taxing authorities
- Compliance with federal, state, and local regulations to ensure sanitation and all aspects of product safety and integrity
- Compliance with laws establishing each state's beer distribution system
- Education of retail establishments and their staff on how to avoid service to persons under age 21 or to intoxicated persons and on associated civil and criminal liability

Business owners must have an understanding of legal issues to effectively guide and protect their operations from serious penalties or financial liability. Laws and regulations also apply directly to individual employees of establishments that sell or serve alcoholic beverages. Each employee should therefore have an understanding of laws and regulations that corresponds to his or her responsibilities in a business that sells beer or other alcoholic beverages.

Selected References

Beer Institute (BI). www.beerinstitute.org. BI, Washington, DC. (This site includes information on self-regulation of advertising and marketing, industry responsibility initiatives, new legislative and regulatory developments, progress in combating underage drinking and alcohol abuse, and reports on significant litigation.)

Fosdick, R. B. 1956. John D. Rockefeller, Jr.: A Portrait. Harper Brothers, New York.

National Beer Wholesalers Association (NBWA). 2008. NBWA-Brewers Legislative Conference Background Paper on the Three-Tier System. NBWA, Alexandria, VA.

National Conference of State Liquor Administrators (NCSLA). http://ncsla.org/states.htm. (An organization of state alcohol beverage control officials that maintains a website with links to agencies in all fifty states.)

United States Department of the Treasury, Alcohol and Tobacco Tax and Trade Bureau (TTB). www.ttb.gov. TTB, Washington, DC. (This site includes information on all aspects of federal regulation of brewers.)

United States Department of the Treasury, Alcohol and Tobacco Tax and Trade Bureau (TTB). Basic Mandatory Labeling Information for Malt Beverages, Vol. 3. www.ttb.gov/beer/bam.shtml. TTB, Washington, DC.

Appendix A
Summary of the Modern Brewing Process

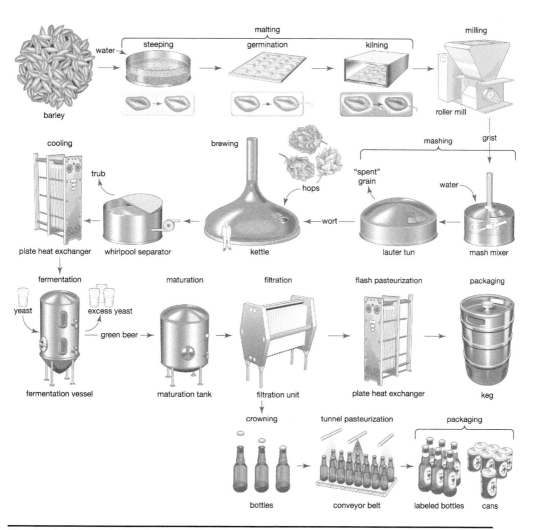

(Reprinted, with permission, from *Encyclopedia Britannica*, © 2010 by Encyclopedia Britannica, Inc.)

Appendix B:
Ideal Gas Pressure

Volume of Carbon Dioxide (CO$_2$) Based on Pounds per Square Inch Gauge and Temperature (at Sea Level)[a,b]

Temp.		Pounds per Square Inch Gauge (psig)														
°C	°F	1	2	3	4	5	6	7	8	9	10	11	12	13	14	15
−1	30	1.80	1.91	2.02	2.14	2.25	2.37	2.48	2.60	2.71	2.83	2.94	3.05	3.17	3.28	3.40
−1	31	1.75	1.87	1.98	2.09	2.20	2.31	2.43	2.54	2.65	2.76	2.87	2.98	3.10	3.21	3.32
0	32	1.71	1.82	1.93	2.04	2.15	2.26	2.37	2.48	2.59	2.70	2.81	2.92	3.03	3.14	3.24
1	33	1.68	1.78	1.89	2.00	2.10	2.21	2.32	2.43	2.53	2.64	2.75	2.85	2.96	3.07	3.17
1	34	1.64	1.75	1.85	1.95	2.06	2.16	2.27	2.37	2.48	2.58	2.69	2.79	2.90	3.00	3.10
2	35	1.61	1.71	1.81	1.91	2.02	2.12	2.22	2.32	2.43	2.53	2.63	2.73	2.83	2.94	3.04
2	36	1.57	1.67	1.77	1.87	1.97	2.07	2.17	2.27	2.37	2.48	2.58	2.68	2.78	2.88	2.98
3	37	1.54	1.64	1.74	1.84	1.93	2.03	2.13	2.23	2.33	2.43	2.52	2.62	2.72	2.82	2.92
3	38	1.51	1.61	1.70	1.80	1.90	1.99	2.09	2.18	2.28	2.38	2.47	2.57	2.67	2.76	2.86
4	39	1.48	1.58	1.67	1.76	1.86	1.95	2.05	2.14	2.24	2.33	2.43	2.52	2.61	2.71	2.80
4	40	1.45	1.55	1.64	1.73	1.82	1.92	2.01	2.10	2.19	2.29	2.38	2.47	2.56	2.66	2.75
5	41	1.43	1.52	1.61	1.70	1.79	1.88	1.97	2.06	2.15	2.24	2.33	2.43	2.52	2.61	2.70
6	42	1.40	1.49	1.58	1.67	1.76	1.85	1.93	2.02	2.11	2.20	2.29	2.38	2.47	2.56	2.65
6	43	1.37	1.46	1.55	1.64	1.72	1.81	1.90	1.99	2.07	2.16	2.25	2.34	2.43	2.51	2.60
7	44	1.35	1.44	1.52	1.61	1.69	1.78	1.87	1.95	2.04	2.12	2.21	2.30	2.38	2.47	2.55
7	45	1.33	1.41	1.50	1.58	1.66	1.75	1.83	1.92	2.00	2.09	2.17	2.26	2.34	2.43	2.51
8	46	1.30	1.39	1.47	1.55	1.64	1.72	1.80	1.89	1.97	2.05	2.13	2.22	2.30	2.38	2.47
8	47	1.28	1.36	1.45	1.53	1.61	1.69	1.77	1.85	1.94	2.02	2.10	2.18	2.26	2.34	2.43
9	48	1.26	1.34	1.42	1.50	1.58	1.66	1.74	1.82	1.90	1.98	2.06	2.14	2.22	2.30	2.38
9	49	1.24	1.32	1.40	1.48	1.56	1.64	1.71	1.79	1.87	1.95	2.03	2.11	2.19	2.27	2.35
10	50	1.22	1.30	1.38	1.45	1.53	1.61	1.69	1.76	1.84	1.92	2.00	2.08	2.15	2.23	2.31
11	51	1.20	1.28	1.35	1.43	1.51	1.58	1.66	1.74	1.81	1.89	1.97	2.04	2.12	2.20	2.27
11	52	1.18	1.26	1.33	1.41	1.48	1.56	1.63	1.71	1.78	1.86	1.94	2.01	2.09	2.16	2.24
12	53	1.16	1.24	1.31	1.39	1.46	1.54	1.61	1.68	1.76	1.83	1.91	1.98	2.05	2.13	2.20
12	54	1.15	1.22	1.29	1.37	1.44	1.51	1.59	1.66	1.73	1.80	1.88	1.95	2.02	2.10	2.17
13	55	1.13	1.20	1.27	1.35	1.42	1.49	1.56	1.63	1.71	1.78	1.85	1.92	1.99	2.07	2.14
13	56	1.11	1.18	1.26	1.33	1.40	1.47	1.54	1.61	1.68	1.75	1.82	1.89	1.96	2.04	2.11
14	57	1.10	1.17	1.24	1.31	1.38	1.45	1.52	1.59	1.66	1.73	1.80	1.87	1.94	2.01	2.08
14	58	1.08	1.15	1.22	1.29	1.36	1.43	1.49	1.56	1.63	1.70	1.77	1.84	1.91	1.98	2.05
15	59	1.07	1.13	1.20	1.27	1.34	1.41	1.47	1.54	1.61	1.68	1.75	1.81	1.88	1.95	2.02
16	60	1.05	1.12	1.19	1.25	1.32	1.39	1.45	1.52	1.59	1.65	1.72	1.79	1.86	1.92	1.99
16	61	1.04	1.10	1.17	1.24	1.30	1.37	1.43	1.50	1.57	1.63	1.70	1.76	1.83	1.90	1.96
17	62	1.02	1.09	1.15	1.22	1.28	1.35	1.41	1.48	1.54	1.61	1.68	1.74	1.81	1.87	1.94
17	63	1.01	1.07	1.14	1.20	1.27	1.33	1.40	1.46	1.52	1.59	1.65	1.72	1.78	1.85	1.91
18	64	1.00	1.06	1.12	1.19	1.25	1.31	1.38	1.44	1.50	1.57	1.63	1.69	1.76	1.82	1.89
18	65	0.98	1.05	1.11	1.17	1.23	1.30	1.36	1.42	1.49	1.55	1.61	1.67	1.74	1.80	1.86

(continued on next page)

[a] Volume of carbon dioxide = [4.85 × (psi + 14.7)] / Fahrenheit + 12.4.
[b] Note: Gauge pressure should be increased by 1 psi for every 2,000 feet of altitude above sea level.

Volume of Carbon Dioxide (CO_2) Based on Pounds per Square Inch Gauge and Temperature (at Sea Level) *(continued)*

Temp.		Pounds per Square Inch Gauge (psig)													
°C	°F	16	17	18	19	20	21	22	23	24	25	26	27	28	29	30
−1	30	3.51	3.63	3.74	3.85	3.97	4.08	4.20	4.31	4.43	4.54	4.66	4.77	4.88	5.00	5.11
−1	31	3.43	3.54	3.65	3.77	3.88	3.99	4.10	4.21	4.32	4.44	4.55	4.66	4.77	4.88	5.00
0	32	3.35	3.46	3.57	3.68	3.79	3.90	4.01	4.12	4.23	4.34	4.45	4.56	4.66	4.77	4.88
1	33	3.28	3.39	3.49	3.60	3.71	3.81	3.92	4.03	4.13	4.24	4.35	4.45	4.56	4.67	4.78
1	34	3.21	3.31	3.42	3.52	3.63	3.73	3.84	3.94	4.05	4.15	4.25	4.36	4.46	4.57	4.67
2	35	3.14	3.24	3.35	3.45	3.55	3.65	3.76	3.86	3.96	4.06	4.16	4.27	4.37	4.47	4.57
2	36	3.08	3.18	3.28	3.38	3.48	3.58	3.68	3.78	3.88	3.98	4.08	4.18	4.28	4.38	4.48
3	37	3.01	3.11	3.21	3.31	3.41	3.50	3.60	3.70	3.80	3.90	4.00	4.09	4.19	4.29	4.39
3	38	2.95	3.05	3.15	3.24	3.34	3.44	3.53	3.63	3.72	3.82	3.92	4.01	4.11	4.21	4.30
4	39	2.90	2.99	3.09	3.18	3.27	3.37	3.46	3.56	3.65	3.75	3.84	3.93	4.03	4.12	4.22
4	40	2.84	2.93	3.03	3.12	3.21	3.30	3.40	3.49	3.58	3.67	3.77	3.86	3.95	4.04	4.14
5	41	2.79	2.88	2.97	3.06	3.15	3.24	3.33	3.42	3.51	3.61	3.70	3.79	3.88	3.97	4.06
6	42	2.74	2.83	2.92	3.00	3.09	3.18	3.27	3.36	3.45	3.54	3.63	3.72	3.81	3.90	3.99
6	43	2.69	2.78	2.86	2.95	3.04	3.13	3.21	3.30	3.39	3.48	3.56	3.65	3.74	3.83	3.91
7	44	2.64	2.73	2.81	2.90	2.98	3.07	3.16	3.24	3.33	3.41	3.50	3.59	3.67	3.76	3.84
7	45	2.59	2.68	2.76	2.85	2.93	3.02	3.10	3.19	3.27	3.35	3.44	3.52	3.61	3.69	3.78
8	46	2.55	2.63	2.72	2.80	2.88	2.96	3.05	3.13	3.21	3.30	3.38	3.46	3.55	3.63	3.71
8	47	2.51	2.59	2.67	2.75	2.83	2.91	3.00	3.08	3.16	3.24	3.32	3.40	3.49	3.57	3.65
9	48	2.47	2.55	2.63	2.71	2.79	2.87	2.95	3.03	3.11	3.19	3.27	3.35	3.43	3.51	3.59
9	49	2.43	2.50	2.58	2.66	2.74	2.82	2.90	2.98	3.06	3.14	3.21	3.29	3.37	3.45	3.53
10	50	2.39	2.46	2.54	2.62	2.70	2.77	2.85	2.93	3.01	3.09	3.16	3.24	3.32	3.40	3.47
11	51	2.35	2.43	2.50	2.58	2.65	2.73	2.81	2.88	2.96	3.04	3.11	3.19	3.27	3.34	3.42
11	52	2.31	2.39	2.46	2.54	2.61	2.69	2.76	2.84	2.91	2.99	3.07	3.14	3.22	3.29	3.37
12	53	2.28	2.35	2.43	2.50	2.57	2.65	2.72	2.80	2.87	2.94	3.02	3.09	3.17	3.24	3.31
12	54	2.24	2.32	2.39	2.46	2.53	2.61	2.68	2.75	2.83	2.90	2.97	3.05	3.12	3.19	3.26
13	55	2.21	2.28	2.35	2.43	2.50	2.57	2.64	2.71	2.78	2.86	2.93	3.00	3.07	3.14	3.22
13	56	2.18	2.25	2.32	2.39	2.46	2.53	2.60	2.67	2.74	2.81	2.89	2.96	3.03	3.10	3.17
14	57	2.15	2.22	2.29	2.36	2.43	2.49	2.56	2.63	2.70	2.77	2.84	2.91	2.98	3.05	3.12
14	58	2.11	2.18	2.25	2.32	2.39	2.46	2.53	2.60	2.67	2.74	2.80	2.87	2.94	3.01	3.08
15	59	2.09	2.15	2.22	2.29	2.36	2.43	2.49	2.56	2.63	2.70	2.76	2.83	2.90	2.97	3.04
16	60	2.06	2.12	2.19	2.26	2.32	2.39	2.46	2.53	2.59	2.66	2.73	2.79	2.86	2.93	2.99
16	61	2.03	2.09	2.16	2.23	2.29	2.36	2.43	2.49	2.56	2.62	2.69	2.76	2.82	2.89	2.95
17	62	2.00	2.07	2.13	2.20	2.26	2.33	2.39	2.46	2.52	2.59	2.65	2.72	2.78	2.85	2.91
17	63	1.97	2.04	2.10	2.17	2.23	2.30	2.36	2.43	2.49	2.55	2.62	2.68	2.75	2.81	2.88
18	64	1.95	2.01	2.08	2.14	2.20	2.27	2.33	2.39	2.46	2.52	2.58	2.65	2.71	2.77	2.84
18	65	1.92	1.99	2.05	2.11	2.17	2.24	2.30	2.36	2.43	2.49	2.55	2.61	2.68	2.74	2.80

Appendix C:
Beer Flavor Wheel

(Used, by permission, from the American Society of Brewing Chemists)

Appendix D

BEER INSTITUTE

ADVERTISING
AND
MARKETING CODE

JANUARY 2006 EDITION

Introduction

Beer is a legal beverage meant to be consumed responsibly. Its origins are ancient, and it has held a respected position in nearly every culture and society since the dawn of recorded history.

In the United States, beer is a mature product category with broad cultural acceptance and a history of memorable and distinctive advertising, that because of its humor and creativity, has long been a favorite among American adult consumers. Advertising and marketing materials are legitimate efforts by brewers to inform consumers of the particular styles and attributes of numerous beers and other malt beverages that are available. Brewer advertising and marketing also foster competition, persuade adult consumers of legal drinking age to try particular brands, and maintain customer loyalty.

Brewers should employ the perspective of the reasonable adult consumer of legal drinking age in advertising and marketing their products, and should be guided by the following basic principles, which have long been reflected in the policies of the brewing industry and continue to underlie this Code:

- Beer advertising should not suggest directly or indirectly that any of the laws applicable to the sale and consumption of beer should not be complied with.

- Brewers should adhere to contemporary standards of good taste applicable to all commercial advertising and consistent with the medium or context in which the advertising appears.

- Advertising themes, creative aspects, and placements should reflect the fact that brewers are responsible corporate citizens.

- Brewers strongly oppose abuse or inappropriate consumption of their products.

(The Beer Institute Advertising and Marketing Code reprinted, by permission, in its entirety)

The term "beer" as used in this Code, covers all types of malt beverages including, but not limited to, beers, ales, porters, stouts, flavored malt beverages, and various specialty products. The production, distribution, and sale of beer in the United States are subject to extensive laws and regulations, enforced by federal, state, and local governments. Federal and state laws establish a three-tiered distribution system for beer. The first tier is composed of brewers and beer importers, which are referenced throughout this Code as "brewers." The second tier is made up of wholesale distributors, and the third tier includes a wide range of licensed retail outlets, at which beer is sold to consumers. Companies in each tier of this distribution system are required by law to maintain their commercial independence. The Beer Institute encourages all with whom brewers do business to adhere to the law, as well as this voluntary Advertising and Marketing Code.

Guidelines

1. These guidelines apply to all brewer advertising and marketing materials, including Internet and cyberspace media. In applying these guidelines, creative elements are to be considered in the overall context of the advertisement or marketing materials. Humor, parody, satire, and all other advertising themes and devices should be readily identifiable as such by reasonable adults of legal drinking age.

   These guidelines do not apply to educational materials or televised, printed, or audio messages of a non-brand specific nature; nor to materials or messages designed specifically to address issues of alcohol awareness, abuse, drunk driving, underage drinking, or over-consumption.

2. Beer advertising and marketing materials should portray beer in a responsible manner:

   a. Beer advertising and marketing materials should not portray, encourage, or condone drunk driving.

   b. Although beer advertising and marketing materials may show beer being consumed (where permitted by media standards), advertising and marketing materials should not depict situations where beer is being consumed rapidly, excessively, involuntarily, as part of a drinking game, or as a result of a dare.

   c. Beer advertising and marketing materials should not portray persons lacking control over their behavior, movement, or speech as a result of consuming beer or in any way suggest that such conduct is acceptable.

   d. Beer advertising and marketing materials should not portray or imply illegal activity of any kind by an individual prior to, during, or after the individual consumes, purchases, or is served beer, unless the portrayal or implication of illegal activity is a basic element or feature of a parody or spoof and is readily identifiable as such.

e. Beer advertising and marketing materials should not portray beer drinking before or during activities, which for safety reasons, require a high degree of alertness or coordination.

f. Retail outlets where beer is served or sold portrayed in advertising should not be depicted as unkempt or unmanaged.

3. Brewers are committed to a policy and practice of responsible advertising and marketing. As a part of this philosophy, beer advertising and marketing materials are intended for adult consumers of legal drinking age. Advertising or marketing materials should avoid elements that appeal primarily to persons under the legal drinking age. Advertising and marketing materials appeal primarily to persons under the legal drinking age if they have special attractiveness to such persons beyond their general attractiveness for persons above the legal drinking age.

a. In considering whether beer advertising and marketing materials appeal primarily to persons under the legal drinking age, brewers should take into account the following elements among others:

- Symbols
- Language
- Music
- Gestures
- Entertainers or celebrities
- Cartoon characters
- Groups or organizations

b. Beer advertising and marketing materials should not depict Santa Claus.

c. Beer advertising and marketing materials shall only be placed in magazines, on television, or on radio where at least 70% of the audience is expected to be adults of legal drinking age. A placement will be considered reasonable if the audience composition data reviewed prior to placement met the percentages set forth above. What constitutes a reasonable basis for placement depends on the medium and available data for that medium. Buying guidelines for the implementation of this section will be distributed in conformance with the dissemination provisions of this code. The brewer placing advertising or marketing materials in magazines, on television, or on radio shall conduct periodic after-the-fact audits, at least semi-annually where possible, of substantially all of its placements. If a brewer learns that a placement did not meet the Code standard, it will take steps to prevent a reoccurrence. These steps may include, but are not limited to: investigating exceptions; canceling placements on programs with unacceptable audience composition; reallocating purchases to a different and acceptable time slot; contacting the media outlet/station with regard to placement errors or possible reporting errors; reemphasizing audience composition requirements with media buyers and media outlets; and continued monitoring of a program or time slot to determine whether buys should be canceled or reallocated.

d. Models and actors employed to appear in beer advertising and marketing materials should be a minimum of 25 years old, substantiated by proper identification, and should reasonably appear to be over 21 years of age.

e. Beer should not be advertised or marketed at any event where most of the audience is reasonably expected to be below the legal drinking age. This guideline does not prevent brewers from erecting advertising and marketing materials at or near facilities that are used primarily for adult-oriented events, but which occasionally may be used for an event where most attendees are under age 21.

f. No beer identification, including logos, trademarks, or names should be used or licensed for use on clothing, toys, games or game equipment, or other materials intended for use primarily by persons below the legal drinking age.

g. Brewers recognize that parents play a significant role in educating their children about the legal and responsible use of alcohol and may wish to prevent their children from accessing Internet web sites without parental supervision. To facilitate this exercise of parental responsibility, Beer Institute will provide to manufacturers of parent control software the names and web site addresses of all member-company web sites. Additionally, brewers will require disclosure of a viewer's date of birth at the entry to their websites and will post reminders at appropriate locations in their web site indicating that brewer products are intended only for those of legal purchase age. These locations include entrance into the web site, purchase points within the web site, and access into adult-oriented locations within the web site, such as virtual bars.

4. Beer advertising and marketing materials should not make the following exaggerated product representations:

a. Beer advertising and marketing materials should not convey the impression that a beer has special or unique qualities if in fact it does not.

b. Beer advertising and marketing materials should make no scientifically unsubstantiated health claims.

c. Beer advertising and marketing materials may portray beer as a part of personal and social interactions and experiences, and a brand may be portrayed in appropriate surroundings, as a superior choice to compliment a particular occasion or activity. Beer advertising and marketing materials should not, however, claim or represent that individuals cannot obtain social, professional, educational, athletic, or financial success or status without beer consumption.

d. Beer advertising or marketing materials should not claim or represent that individuals cannot solve social, personal, or physical problems without beer consumption

5. Beer advertising and marketing materials:

   a. Should not contain language or images that are lewd or indecent in the context presented and the medium in which the material appears.

   b. May contain romantic or flirtatious interactions but should not portray sexually explicit activity as a result of consuming beer.

6. Beer advertising and marketing materials should not contain graphic nudity.

7. Beer advertising and marketing materials should not employ religion or religious themes.

8. Beer advertising and marketing materials should not disparage competing beers.

   a. Comparisons or claims distinguishing competing beers should be factual.

   b. Beer advertising and marketing materials should never suggest that competing beers contain objectionable additives or ingredients.

9. Beer advertising and marketing materials should not disparage anti-littering and recycling efforts. Beer advertising and marketing materials should not show littering or otherwise improper disposal of beer containers, unless the scenes are used clearly to promote anti-littering and/or recycling.

10. College marketing

    Beer advertising and marketing materials on college and university campuses, or in college-owned media, should not portray consumption of beer as being important to education, nor shall advertising directly or indirectly degrade studying. Beer may be advertised and marketed on college campuses or at college-sponsored events only when permitted by appropriate college policy.

    a. On-campus promotions/sponsorships

       1) Brewer sponsored events: Brewer sponsorship of on-campus events or promotions at on-campus licensed retail establishments shall be limited to events conducted in accord with this Code, state law, and applicable institutional policies. In their content and implementation, company on-campus promotions and sponsorships shall not encourage the irresponsible, excessive, underage, or otherwise illegal consumption of beer.

       2) Branded products: Beer-branded promotional products such as key chains, clothing, posters, or other tangible goods designed to promote specific beer brands, are intended only for adults of legal drinking age. Distribution of these items will therefore take place only at licensed retail establishments or where distribution is limited to those over the legal drinking age, and otherwise conforms to applicable laws and institutional policies.

3) <u>Tastings</u>: Tasting events at which product samples are provided should occur at licensed retail establishments or where distribution is limited to those over the legal drinking age, or otherwise conforms to applicable laws and institutional policies.

b. Brewer sales representatives.

Brewer sales representatives who undertake sales calls on or near a college campus must be adults of legal drinking age, and shall conduct sales activities in conformity with this Code.

11. Billboards

Billboard advertisements by brewers shall be located at least 500 linear feet from established and conspicuously identified elementary or secondary schools, places of worship, or public playgrounds.

12. Product placement

Movies and television programs frequently portray consumption of beer and related signage and props in their productions. Brewers encourage producers to seek approval before using their products, signage, or other props in artistic productions. While producers sometimes seek prior approval from brewers, the final artistic and editorial decisions concerning product portrayal are always within the exclusive control of the movie or television producers.

With regard to those producers who seek brewer approval or those brewers who seek placement opportunities, product placement will be guided by the following principles:

a. <u>Case by Case Approval</u>: Brewers will approve or reject product placement in specific projects or scenes on a case by case basis, based upon the information provided by the movie or television program's producers.

b. <u>Portrayal of drinking and driving</u>: Brewers discourage the illegal or irresponsible consumption of their products in connection with driving. Consistent with that philosophy, brewers will not approve product placement where the characters engage in illegal or irresponsible consumption of their products in connection with driving.

c. <u>Underage drinking</u>: Brewers discourage underage drinking and do not intend for their products to be purchased or consumed illegally by people below the legal drinking age. Consistent with that philosophy, brewers will not approve product placement which portrays purchase or consumption of their products by persons who are under the legal drinking age.

d. <u>Primary appeal to persons below the legal drinking age:</u> Brewers discourage underage drinking and do not intend for their products to be purchased or consumed illegally. Consistent with that philosophy, brewers will not approve product placement where the primary character(s) are under the legal drinking age or the primary theme(s) are, because of their content or presentation, specially attractive to persons below the legal drinking age beyond the general attractiveness such themes have for persons above the legal drinking age.

e. <u>Portraying alcoholism/alcohol abuse</u>: Brewers do not want their products to be abused. Consistent with that philosophy, brewers will not approve product placement where characters use their products irresponsibly or abusively or where alcoholism is portrayed, unless the depiction supports a responsible-use message.

f. <u>Measured media:</u> Brewers will not request or approve a product placement in any measured media unless the placement is consistent with the Buying Guidelines that accompany this Code and at least 70% of the audience is reasonably expected to be adults of legal drinking age.

Code Compliance and Dissemination

Each member of the Beer Institute is committed to the philosophy of the Code and is committed to compliance with the Code. When the Beer Institute receives complaints that an advertisement or marketing practice is inconsistent with a provision of the Code, the Institute's longstanding practice is to promptly refer such complaints in writing to the member company or to non-member brewers for review and a response. To facilitate this process, the Beer Institute maintains a toll-free number (1-800-379-2739) and a web site at www.beerinstitute.org.

If the proponent of a complaint is dissatisfied with the response received from a Beer Institute member or a non-member brewer, further consideration may be requested by the Beer Institute Code Compliance Review Board. The Board is composed of individuals with a variety of experience who are independent of the brewing industry. The Board will review complaints from the perspective of the reasonable adult consumer of legal drinking age and decide whether or not such complaints identify advertisement(s) or marketing material(s) that are inconsistent with one or more of the guidelines in the Code. Board decisions will be posted on the Beer Institute web site.

Copies of this code shall continue to be given to brewery employees, wholesale distributors, and outside agencies whose responsibilities include advertising and marketing beer, as well as to any outside party who might request it.

Beer Institute
122 C Street, N.W., Suite 350
Washington, DC 20001-2150
202-737-2337

Glossary

acetaldehyde—a precursor compound in the production of ethanol in alcoholic fermentation with an apple, pumpkin, or latex-paint-like aroma, often present in young, immature beer

acetic acid—an acid produced by *Acetobacter* bacteria from ethanol in the presence of oxygen. The acid found in vinegar.

adjunct—any nonmalt source of starch used in brewing, usually from raw grains, especially unmalted corn, rice, wheat, and barley, or any source of sugar, including beet or cane sugars

aeration—the dissolving of air in wort to supply oxygen to support yeast health and reproduction

alcohol by volume (ABV)—a measure of alcohol content expressed as a percentage of alcohol volume per volume of beer

alcohol by weight (ABW)—a measure of alcohol content expressed as a percentage weight of alcohol per volume of beer. Because alcohol weighs less than water, ABW is approximately 80% of the equivalent amount of alcohol expressed as alcohol by volume (ABV), i.e., 5% ABV ≈ 4% ABW. (*see* alcohol by volume)

ale—beer brewed using top-fermenting yeast that ferments at high temperatures

alkalinity—a type of water hardness, expressed as parts per million of calcium carbonate. It is used to determine a water supply's impact on the mash. (*see* pH)

alpha acid—a hop resin that contributes bitterness to beer through a process called isomerization, which occurs during wort boiling (*see* isomerization)

amino acids—organic nitrogenous building blocks of protein that are important in yeast nutrition and are supplied by malt

amylase—a malt enzyme that breaks down starch into fermentable sugars and nonfermentable dextrins

aperitif—beverage containing alcohol that is enjoyed before a meal because the alcohol stimulates the appetite

Appellation d'Origine Contrôlée—an official regional designation. No producer outside of the appellation may describe their product with the appellation name, e.g., Champagne, Bordeaux, Burgundy, *gueuze*, *Kölsch*, and *Berliner Weisse*.

aseptic filtration—fine filtration in which microorganisms are removed. It is sometimes used in beer as an alternative to pasteurization. (*see* pasteurization)

astringency—a drying mouthfeel supplied by tannins, usually extracted from malt husks. It is typically an undesirable attribute in beer caused by improper mashing/lautering techniques.

attenuation—the reduction of dissolved sugars in wort to alcohol and carbon dioxide during fermentation

attenuation limit—a measure of the fermentability of wort. When the extract in wort contains a low percentage of fermentable sugars, the wort is said to have a "low" limit of attenuation, which results in a sweeter finish. When the extract in wort contains a high percentage of fermentable sugars, the wort is said to have a "high" limit of attenuation, which results in a dryer finish. Given equal concentrations of extract, high-limit-attenuation beers are higher in alcohol content.

autolysis—death of yeast cells usually due to a lack of nutrients, which is followed by cell decomposition. If left in contact with beer, the dead cells can contribute meaty and brothy flavors.

bacteriostatic—a substance that is inhibiting to bacteria; antibacterial

barrel—in the United States, a volume of 31 gallons

beer clean—glassware that contains no oil or soil residues

beer engine—a traditional dispense method using a hand-operated pump connected to a cask from which beer (ale) is pulled. It uses no driving gas pressure and the beer is naturally slightly carbonated.

beer gas—the balanced mix of nitrogen and carbon dioxide that pushes beer from the keg to the faucet and prevents over- and undercarbonation from occurring

beer ready—(*see* beer clean)

beer stone—an accumulation of mineral and organic scale deposits

beta glucan—a gummy carbohydrate in barley that can carry over into beer through the mash

body—perceived fullness and mouthfeel of beer contributed primarily by colloidal protein substances and by dextrins, oils, and other compounds

boiling wort—a process in which wort is boiled to sterilize, clarify, volatize unwanted flavor compounds, concentrate the wort, develop color and flavor, and isomerize hop bitter acids

bottom fermentation—fermentation by *Saccharomyces pastorianus* (i.e., lager yeast), which has a tendency to settle below the surface at the end of fermentation

Brettanomyces—genus of wild yeast typically considered a beer spoiler but sometimes valued by producers of sour beer (e.g., lambics and Flanders ales) or by producers of certain traditional English ales (e.g., stock ale and porter) or Belgian beers for its tangy acidity and rustic character

bright beer—beer that has been filtered

bung—a wooden or plastic stopper used to plug the filling inlet hole of a keg or cask

butt—a cask that contained 108 imperial gallons

Campaign for Real Ale (CAMRA)—a movement begun in Great Britain to preserve traditional cask-conditioned ales

caramelization—the darkening of sugar and the production of flavor compounds due to the heating and oxidation of simple sugars

caramel malt—(*see* crystal malt)

carbonate—a salt dissolved in water that increases alkalinity (*see* alkalinity)

cask-conditioned ale—a traditional type of British ale that matures in a cask

chill haze—the haze formed when beer is chilled as soluble proteins and polyphenols lose solubility at low temperatures

chocolate malt—a type of dark malt that develops burnt toast and chocolate-like flavors through roasting

conditioning—maturation of beer flavor after primary fermentation, which may include natural carbonation through the entrapment of carbon dioxide derived from secondary fermentation

conversion—the breakdown of starches into sugars by malt enzymes during mashing

crowning—the capping of bottles that have been filled with beer. The crowning machine crimps the crown around the top or "finish" of the bottle, providing a secure enclosure.

crystal malt—a sweet caramel-tasting malt created by heating moist malt to convert the starch to sugar and then applying various degrees of heat through roasting to create color and caramel flavors

decoction mashing—a method of mashing in which part of the mash is boiled and then returned to the main mash to raise the whole mash temperature. It is used to convert undermodified malt or to create deeper wort color and malty flavors.

dextrins—unfermentable sugars produced during mashing

diacetyl—a buttery-tasting compound produced by yeast during fermentation that is reduced to a nonflavored compound during beer conditioning. It can be an indicator of a young, immature beer that needs maturation or one in which the presence of beer-spoilage bacteria have produced it.

digestif—beverage containing alcohol that is enjoyed after a meal because the alcohol is thought to aid digestion

dimethyl sulfide (DMS)—a cream corn or cooked cabbagelike flavor compound found in pale malt that is volatized during boiling. It may also be produced by beer-spoilage bacteria.

dry hopping—the process of adding hops to the fermenter, conditioning tank, or cask to create a fresh-hop aroma in beer, especially English-style ales

efficiency—in mashing, the effectiveness of converting the mash into soluble extract (*see* extract)

endosperm—the food store of the barley corn containing mostly starch (and lesser amounts of other carbohydrates and protein) that is converted to extract during mashing

enzymes—protein-based organic catalysts that effect changes in the compounds they act on. In mashing, enzymes convert starches to sugars and reduce complex proteins to simpler forms, including amino acids essential to support yeast during fermentation.

essential oil—aromatic oils found in hops that add spicy and herbal flavors to beer. It is volatile and can be removed during the wort boiling phase.

esters—aromatic and fruity aroma compounds produced by yeast during fermentation through the combination of an alcohol and acid. The amount and type of esters is very yeast-strain dependent. Warm fermentation, high wort gravity, and low wort aeration tend to increase the ester content in beer.

ethanol—the main alcohol produced by fermentation

European Brewery Convention (EBC)—the scientific and technological arm of brewers of Europe

extract—the constituents of malt that are dissolved in wort, primarily sugars converted from starch by enzymatic action during mashing

false bottom—the slotted base of a mash or lauter tun that sits a few centimeters above the real bottom. The mash rests on the false bottom, forming a filter bed that acts to clarify the wort as the wort flows through it for collection in the kettle.

fermentation—the process in which yeast converts sugar into ethanol and carbon dioxide along with various other lesser amounts of flavor compounds (e.g., esters, phenols, fusel alcohols, and acids) and less consequential by-products

filtration—the process of removing from beer the solids that cause turbidity, particularly protein-tannin haze complexes and yeast

final gravity—the specific gravity of beer after fermentation has converted sugar to alcohol. Because the density of alcohol is lower than the aqueous sugar solution, the final gravity is lower than the original gravity.

finings—agents used to clarify beer by attracting haze particles, which precipitate out of suspension. Common finings include gelatin, bentonite, silica gel, polyvinyl polypyrrolidone (PVPP), and isinglass.

firkin—a 9-imperial-gallon (11-U.S.-gallon) cask used for the production of cask-conditioned real ale

first runnings—the volume of "first wort" that flows out of the lauter tun before the addition of sparge water. They are higher in extract than are the later worts recovered through sparging.

foam—the stable protein-hop complex that forms a head (or bubbles) on beer

fobbing—uncontrolled foaming

fusel oils—(*see* higher alcohols)

German Purity Law—(*see Reinheitsgebot*)

germination—seed growth initiated by moisture and appropriate temperature

glucose—a simple, fermentable sugar

grain bill—the recipe for the total grains and adjuncts used in the brewhouse. It normally contains a base malt, specialty malts, and adjuncts, such as rice, corn, or corn syrup

gravity—the amount of wort extract (*see* specific gravity)

green beer—young beer that has not undergone complete maturation and conditioning (*see ruh*)

grind—the degree to which malt is milled

grist—crushed malt to which hot water is added for mashing

growler—a glass jug (usually one-half gallon) for "to-go" sales that is used by brewpubs. It is typically filled with draft beer at the tap and sealed with a screw top.

gruit—any number of herbs, spices, or other botanicals used to flavor beer. It was largely replaced by hops by the end of the Middle Ages.

gueuze—a blend of 1-, 2-, and 3-year-old lambics. The *Appellation d'Origine Contrôlée* requires that the weighted average age of the lambics must be at least 1 year, the oldest at least 3 years, and the mixture must have undergone refermentation on the yeast.

gypsum—calcium sulfate (naturally present in Burton-on-Trent water) used by many brewers to adjust their water's mineral content and pH balance

haze—insoluble tannin-protein compounds, starch, yeast, or other nonsoluble particles visible in beer. The primary purpose of filtration is to remove this haze and produce bright beer. (*see* bright beer)

head retention—the ability of the foam head on beer to remain stable. Protein and hop bitter acids improve head retention by increasing the stability of bubble walls that hold beer gases. Nitrogen bubbles form more stable foam than carbon dioxide bubbles.

headspace—the gas-filled volume above the beer in a bottle

higher alcohols—alcohols with a more complex molecular structure than ethanol, also called fusel oils. They are typically more aromatic and found in greater amounts in ales and high-alcohol-by-volume beers.

hop—a perennial vine that produces flowers, or cones, containing resins that contribute bitterness (alpha acids) and aroma (essential oils) to beer. Considered to be the "spice of beer".

hopback (or hop jack)—a vessel for hot wort clarification that employs hops as a filter bed to remove trub. It can also be employed to impart hop flavor and aroma through the addition of fresh hops.

husk—the outer protective covering of barley that is important in providing the filterability of the mash during sparging. It also contributes harsh astringency to beer if mashing/sparging is conducted improperly.

hydrometer—a floating glass spindle used to measure the specific gravity of wort or beer based on the principal that the spindle sinks deeper into low-density liquids than into high-density liquids

infusion—single-temperature mashing (as opposed to multiple-temperature rests) in which a single charge of hot water is mixed with the grist. This is the traditional mashing method used in the United Kingdom when using well-modified malts. (*see* rest)

international bitterness unit (IBU)—measurement unit to express the bitterness of beer based on the milligrams of hop iso-alpha acids dissolved in 1 liter of beer expressed as parts per million

isinglass—a gelatinous substance obtained from the swim bladder of fish used as a traditional fining agent in the production of British ales, especially cask ale

isomerization—the chemical change that occurs in hop alpha acids brought about by heat during wort boiling that makes these bitter acids soluble in wort and more pleasingly bitter

kettle—a vessel for boiling wort

kilning—the process of drying malt after germination to remove unwanted vegetable flavors, develop color, increase flavor, and stabilize the kernel for storage

krausen—the foam head on fermenting beer caused by escaping carbon dioxide produced during fermentation

krausening—the process of adding fermenting wort to fermented beer to mature the flavor and naturally carbonate the beer

lacing—the foam left clinging to the inside walls of a glass as the beer is emptied

lactic acid—an acid produced by certain bacteria, especially *Lactobacillus* bacteria

Lactobacillus—genus of bacteria that is typically considered a beer spoiler but is employed intentionally in the production of *Berliner Weisse* and certain Belgian ales to create a characteristic sourness

lager—beer brewed using bottom-fermenting yeast at low temperatures

lagering—the process of maturing lager beer with an extended cold-conditioning period

lauter tun—a brewing vessel with a false bottom that allows for the separation and recovery of clarified wort from the mash by allowing the formation of a filter bed formed from the insoluble grain husks and residual particles. The addition of sparge water after the first wort has been drawn off helps maximize recovery of the extract from the grain.

lautering—the separation of clear wort from the residual grain used in mashing

lees—the yeast sediment that collects at the bottom of a bottle-conditioned beer

light struck—the character of beer exposed to ultraviolet light, which causes the creation of a skunky aroma from a chemical altering of the hop alpha acids and sulfur compounds in the beer

liquor—brewing water

lupulin—bitter resin in hops

Maillard browning—the chemical reaction between amino acids and sugars when exposed to heat that produces toasted, caramel, and roasted flavor compounds (known as melanoidins) found in many foods and in malt after kilning. It also occurs with wort during the kettle boiling process. Similar to caramelization. (*see* caramelization)

maltose—a fermentable sugar (disaccharide or two glucose molecules) found in wort produced during mashing through the enzymatic conversion of malt starch

mash—a mixture of hot water and grist

mash tun—a brewing vessel where mashing takes place

maturation—postfermentation conditioning of young beer during which time young beer flavors are reduced, mellowed, or both

melanoidins—(*see* Maillard browning)

modification—the change of barley into malt during controlled germination. It includes the softening of the endosperm and the rendering of complex molecules into more soluble ones during mashing. Highly modified malts are converted into extract more easily than undermodified malts.

mouthfeel—sensations in the mouth caused by chemical or physical stimulus, such as the heat of chili peppers or the tingle of carbon dioxide bubbles

must—the unfermented crushed grapes used to make wine

nitro—short for nitrogenated beers, usually Irish stout and English bitter ales. Nitro faucets and widget cans and bottles mimic the low-carbon dioxide, cascading, breakout pours from a beer engine.

noble—the classic European hop varieties contributing light flowery aromas and flavors

original extract—the beginning extract (i.e., sugar concentration) of wort before fermentation metabolizes the sugars into alcohol and carbon dioxide. It is one parameter for estimating the final alcohol content of beer.

original gravity—the specific gravity of wort before fermentation (*see* specific gravity)

oxygen—beneficial nutrient for brewer's yeast that is added to the wort prior to the start of fermentation. However, it is undesirable in finished beer because of its staling effect on flavors.

parti-gyle—an old method of mashing in which the first extract-rich wort runnings were used to brew strong beer, the second less-rich runnings were used to brew an ordinary beer, and the third least-extract-rich runnings were used to brew a weak beer

pasteurization—procedure for heating beer to kill spoilage microbes and thereby extend shelf life. The beer may be heated in the bottle or can by hot water spray (tunnel pasteurization) or heated by a heat exchanger before packaging (flash pasteurization). (*see* shelf life)

pH (potential of hydrogen)—a measure of hydrogen ions in solution to indicate the acidity/ alkalinity of a liquid. A pH of 7.0 is neither acidic nor alkaline. A pH greater than 7.0 is alkaline and a pH less than 7.0 is acidic.

phenolic—descriptor of a variety of flavors in beer, including 1) medicinal or plastic flavors from packaging materials or cleaning compounds or the by-products of certain microbes; and 2) spicy clove, nutmeg, and vanilla flavors produced by brewer's yeast.

pitching—the process of adding yeast to wort to start fermentation

plate heat exchanger—equipment for cooling or heating liquids flowing through it using a countercurrent of a chilled liquid such as water or glycol

Plato—unit of measurement of the extract (i.e., sugar) concentration in wort expressed as degrees, which represents the percentage weight of sucrose in a solution. A solution measured at 12°Plato contains 12% sugar by weight or 12 grams of sugar in 100 grams of solution. Similar to degrees Balling but a more accurate measure.

ppm—parts per million; milligrams per liter

primary fermentation—the initial step in the fermenting process in which the yeast added to the wort converts it into alcohol, carbon dioxide, flavors, and other compounds. At its end, the young, or *ruh*, beer is immature in flavor and usually proceeds to a maturation step.

primings—sugar added to fermented beer, especially in the cask or in bottle conditioning, to produce carbonation through secondary fermentation

racking—the process of transferring beer or wine from one vessel to another .

Reinheitsgebot—German Purity Law of 1516 that allows only malted barley, water, hops, and yeast in the production of beer

rest—the time the mash sits at a specific temperature to allow the malt enzymes activated at that temperature to convert the malt starches into sugar. Depending on the malt and mash regimen used, single- or multiple-temperature rests may be used.

ruh (rūh)—young, immature, or green beer (in German)

runnings—(*see* first runnings *and* parti-gyle)

saccharification—the process of starch breakdown (conversion) into sugars by amylase enzymes

Saccharomyces cerevisiae—yeast used in ale fermentation

Saccharomyces pastorianus—yeast used in lager fermentation

secondary fermentation—the continuation of fermentation after the rapid primary fermentation process that reduces the "unfinished" products from that phase into more desirable compounds. The rate of flavor maturation is dependent upon temperature, the composition of the young beer, and the style to which it is brewed. The process is relatively slow and can be conducted in a tank, bottle, or cask. When there is residual sugar present and the carbon dioxide generated from it through fermentation is not allowed to escape, the beer is naturally carbonated. (*see* primary fermentation)

session beer—a beer, usually of mild alcohol strength (3.5 to 4.5% alcohol by volume [ABV]), that is consumed in multiple pint "sessions" at the pub

shelf life—the average number of days at 70°F (21°C) that a beer retains an acceptable flavor profile, which is determined by tasting analysis

solera—a continuous blending system, used for sherry, composed of three layers of barrels. The oldest sherry is in the bottom barrels, the middle-aged sherry is in the middle layer, and the youngest sherry is added to the top layer. As the oldest sherry is drawn out of the bottom layer, the middle-layer sherry is blended in to top off the bottom barrels and the younger sherry is drawn down to the middle barrels. More fresh, young sherry is then added to the top-layer barrels.

sparge—hot water added during lautering to rinse out the extract from the mash (*see* lautering)

sparkler—a restrictor nozzle that fits onto the swan neck of the beer engine and serves to aerate the ale as it is pulled from the cask into the glass, generating a thick head of foam

spear—the tube in a keg used for filling and emptying

specific gravity—a measure of wort strength based on the relative density of wort compared with that of pure water. Water has a specific gravity of 1.000. Wort with a specific gravity of 1.048 is 1.048 denser than water.

spent grain—the grist remaining after mashing and wort separation. It is a highly valued by-product of the process and used as cattle feed.

staling—the process by which beer loses its fresh flavor, usually by exposure to oxygen

standard reference measure (SRM)—a measure of wort or beer color

starch—the carbohydrate food source of plants found in the endosperm of malt. It is converted to sugar by enzymatic action during mashing.

starter—a quantity of yeast usually grown from pure culture yeast to a sufficient cell count that is capable of initiating fermentation in a batch of wort

steeping—barley is immersed (steeped) in moderate-temperature water to raise it moisture content from 12 to approximately 45%. Steeping involves an alternate series of immersion and air rests across 2 days to initiate growth in preparation for the next step in malting, which is germination.

sunstruck flavor—the skunky flavor created when hopped beer is subjected to sunlight or ultraviolet light

swan neck—a long, arched tube extending from the beer engine that delivers beer into the glass

tannin—a substance in barley (especially husks) or other plants that may create astringency or beer haze when bound to malt protein (*see* astringency)

top fermentation—fermentation by *Saccharomyces cerevisiae* (i.e., ale yeast), which has a tendency to rise to the surface during fermentation

trub—wort solids, consisting primarily of coagulated protein and polyphenols from malt and hops, that precipitate during boiling (hot trub) and after chilling (cold trub)

turbidity—haze found in wort or beer

vertical tasting—when different years or vintages of the same product are consumed side by side to experience the flavor changes produced by aging

vinous—relating to wine. Vinous flavor notes would be common with wine flavor and aromatic notes.

volatilization—the removal of flavor compounds, especially dimethyl sulfide and hop oils, by steam distillation during wort boiling

water hardness—the amount of calcium and magnesium ions in water. Carbonate hardness ($CaCO_3$, chalk) is typically detrimental in brewing at very high levels, while noncarbonate hardness ($CaSO_4$, gypsum, and $CaCl_2$, calcium chloride) can be considered beneficial.

water softening—a process for removing water hardness

whirlpool—a round tank in which wort is pumped in a circular flow to cause the sedimentation of the trub into the center. The clarified hot wort is then decanted from the trub as it is removed to the wort cooler. (*see* wort cooler)

widget—an insert containing carbon dioxide gas for creating foam in nitrogenated beer upon opening, mimicking a nitro or beer engine pour (*see* nitro)

wild yeast—any type of non-brewer's yeast. An unwanted yeast type considered a beer spoiler, except in lambic brewing.

wort—an extract containing liquid produced by mashing that is fermented to produce beer

wort cooler—a countercurrent flow heat exchanger that is used to lower the temperature of hot wort to the yeast pitching temperature and facilitates the precipitation of cold trub (*see* trub)

Index

abbey ales. *See* Trappist and abbey ales
"abbey" beer, 49
acetaldehyde, 30, 187, 194
Acetobacter, 52
acid cleaners, 167
acidity
    beer flavor and, 180
    cutting oils and richness with, 127–128
    neutralization by salt, 128
acute alcohol intoxication, 195–196
Adams, Samuel, 7
adjuncts
    defined, 137
    sugar, 139
    uses of, 137–138
advertising, industry self-regulation in, 203
Advertising and Marketing Code, 203, 213–220
aeration, of the wort, 153
aging. *See also* conditioning
    of barley wines, 32, 93
    barrel aging, 6, 31–32, 93, 184
    controlled oxidation and beer flavor, 93
    of English old ales, 71
    of wine and whiskey, 31
airborne yeast, 148–149
alcohol
    aromatic alcohols, 125
    beer flavor and, 179
    blood alcohol content, 196
    effect on spicy heat, 128
    fusel alcohols, 28, 153, 179
    hangovers and, 194
    human discovery of, 2
    produced during fermentation, 27
    removal in brewing non-alcoholic beer, 40
    tissue absorption, 192
Alcohol and Tobacco Tax and Trade Bureau (TTB),
    200, 204
alcohol by volume (ABV)
    bière de garde, 47
    ice beer, 39
    is unrelated to beer color, 23
    light beer, 38–39
    malt liquor, 40
    sake, 42
    strong ales, 70

alcohol consumption
    deleterious effects on health, 194–196
    effects on the brain, 193–194
    health benefits, 189, 192–194
    summary, 196
alcoholic hepatitis, 194
alcohol-tolerant yeast, 41–42
aldehydes, 24, 194
ales. *See also* Belgian ales
    Belgian blond ale, 56
    Belgian sour ales, 51–55
    Belgian strong ales, 50–51
    brown ales, 15, 51–53, 61–63
    characteristics of, 46–47
    conditioning, 30, 151, 152
    farmhouse ales, 47–48
    German ales, 81, 84–87
    India pale ales, 60–61, 146
    Irish red ale, 68
    nitrogenated cans, 110
    North American, 59–63, 89–90
    pale ales, 59–60, 146
    primary fermentation time, 30
    Scottish ales, 68–69, 70, 146
    serving temperature guidelines, 116, 117
    strong ales, 50–51, 69–72
    Trappist and abbey ales, 37, 49–50, 114, 124,
        125
    wit ("white" beer), 55–56, 117, 127–128, 138
    yeast character, 28, 29–30, 153
alewives, 5
ale yeast (*Saccharomyces cerevisiae*)
    in beer fermentation, 27–28
    conditioning time, 151
    effect on beer flavor and character, 28, 29–30,
        153
    fermentation temperature, 150
    primary fermentation time, 30
    as top-fermenting yeast, 27–28, 151
alkaline cleaning solutions, 167
alkaline flavor, 187
alkaline water, effect on brewing, 132–133
alpha amylase, 19, 20
Alt, 81, 84, 86
Alt glass, 86, 113
aluminum cans, 35

amber beers
    boiling the wort increases color, 24
    decoction mashing and, 20
amber malt
    characteristics of, 137
    kilning, 15
    pairing to foods, 122–123
American barley wine, 72
American brown ale, 62–63
American *Hefeweizen* (wheat beer), 90, 146
American hops, 182
American lagers
    American light lager, 88–89, 146
    American standard lager
        bitterness, 146
        carbohydrates per serving, 39
        characteristics of, 88
        effect of storage temperature on oxidation, 96
        pale malts, 15
    brewhouse vessels, 17
    serving temperature guidelines, 117
American pale ale
    American India pale ale, 60–61
    aromatic oils from hops, 24
    characteristics of, 59–60
American stout, 67
American wheat ale, 90, 146
amylase, 19, 20
Anchor Brewing Company, 89
ancient Egypt, 2, 3, 148
ancient Greece, 4
ancient Rome, 4, 6
Anheuser-Busch, 9, 10
antioxidants, 191
aperitifs, 128–129
Appellation d'Origine Contròlée, 54
aroma
    dispense gas and, 159
    hop oils and, 139, 146–147
    pairing beer aroma to foods, 124
    sensing, 175–176
    serving beer in glassware and, 101–102
aroma hops, 145–146
aromatic alcohols, 125
aromatic oils, 24, 25, 139, 145, 146–147
aseptic filtration, 38, 158–159
astringency, pairing with richness, 126
A System keg valve, 158
atherosclerosis, 192
atrial fibrillation, 195
automatic washers, for cleaning glassware, 103

baking, compared with brewing, 30, 148
balance, in beer flavor, 178

baled hops, 142
Baltic porter, 64–65
bar code scanning, 100
barley
    as an adjunct, 139
    in the brewing process, 207
    germinating, 16
    malting, 14–16, 17
    regions grown, 4
barley malt
    as a base malt, 134–135
    malting, 14–16, 17
    qualities of, 133
barley wines
    aging, 32, 93
    American barley wine, 72
    bitterness, 146
    English barley wine, 71
    pairing to foods, 125
    serving temperature guidelines, 117
"barley wine-style ale", 72
barrel aging, 6, 31–32, 93, 184
barrier tubing, 163, 170–171
base malt
    barley, 134–135
    description of, 133–134
    high-kilned malt, 135
basic permits, 200
Bavarian beers
    Bavarian *Weizen* (wheat beer)
        bottle conditioning, 37
        characteristics of, 82
        Dunkelweizen, 83
        Hefeweizen, 78, 82–83, 90, 124, 146, 160
        history of, 81–82
        Kristall Weizen, 83
        open fermentation, 29
        Weizenbock, 83–84
    Doppelbock, 79–80, 139
    Eisbock, 80
    monastic breweries, 5
    Renaissance beer regulations, 7
    rye beer, 84
Bavarian State Brewery, 5
Bavarian *Weizen* beer glass, 113
Becher (German tumbler), 112
beer
    characteristics during the Middle Ages, 6
    cooking with, 129–130
    diversity of, 13
    as a drink of the masses, 4
    as food, 92, 119. *See also* beer and food
    health and. *See* beer and health
    influence on human development, 1

ingredients. *See* ingredients
nutritional composition, 191–192
palate cleansing, 120
pouring. *See* pouring beer
serving. *See* serving beer
thirst quenching, 119–120
beer and food
aperitifs, 128–129
beer is food, 92, 119
beer is refreshment, 119–120
digestifs, 129
effect of alcohol on spicy heat, 128
principles of pairing
contrast, 126–128
impact, 120–121
match, 121–126
regional pairings, 128
proper glassware and serving temperature, 129
salt neutralizes acidity, 128
beer and health
beer industry controversies and, 189
critically assessing the health claims data, 190–191
deleterious effects of beer on health, 194–196
nutritional composition of beer, 191–192
positive impacts of beer on health, 192–194
summary, 196
"beer barons", 8
"beer clean" glassware
cleaning methods, 103–105
testing, 105–106
beer coding, for freshness, 93–96
beer color
factors determining, 22–23
flavor and, 178–179
lightening with adjuncts, 137
beer complaints, handling professionally, 100
beer dating, for freshness, 93–96
beer displays, beer freshness and, 99
beer engines, 36, 111, 157
beer faucets, proper operation, 161–162
beer flavor
balance, 178
barrel aging and, 6, 31–32, 93, 184
body, 178
color and flavor, 178–179
conditioning and, 30
controlled oxidation during aging, 93
dispense gas and, 159–160
effect of fermentation parameters on, 28–29, 152–153
effect of serving temperature on, 117
effect of yeast on, 28, 29–30, 142–153, 182, 183
from fermentation products, 179–183

filtration and, 32
flavor groups, 180–184
flavor intensity, 179
fullness, 178, 179
hops and, 23–24, 25, 139, 140, 181–182
human perception of, 175–177
important factors in evaluating, 178
keys to building a flavor memory and vocabulary, 177–178
lightening with adjuncts, 137
mouthfeel, 178
off-flavors, 186–187
pairing to foods, 121–126
protein-caused haze and, 32
sensing taste and aroma, 175–176
spontaneous fermentation in lambic beers, 26
strength, 179
summary, 188
wheel, 186, 211
beer flavor groups
fermentation-driven beers, 182–183
flavored beers, 183–184
hop-driven beers, 181–182
malt-driven beers, 181
overview, 180
Beer Flavor Wheel, 186, 211
beer freshness
advances in, 8–9, 91–92
beer as food, 92
dispense gas and, 159–160
draft beer, 99, 157
"Four Ts" for proper handling of beer, 92
light-struck effect, 98–99
miscellaneous issues, 99–100
shelf life, 92
temperature factors, 96–97
time factors
beer dating, 93–96
effects on freshness, 92–93
first in first out, 93
sizing the beer inventory, 93
turbulence factors, 98
beer gas, 165. *See also* dispense gas
beer glassware
Belgian-style glasses, 113–115
British-style glasses, 115
cleaning methods, 103–105
drying and storing, 105
German- and continental-style glasses, 112–113
importance of, 101, 111–112
miscellaneous glassware, 115–116
reasons to use, 101–103
stout glass, 109
testing for clean glasses, 105–106

beer industry. *See* commercial brewing; U.S. brewing industry
Beer Institute Advertising and Marketing Code, 203, 213–220
Beer Judge Certification Program (BJCP), 43
beer mugs, German, 112–113
beer pumps. *See also* beer engines
    in draft systems, 164
    hand air pumps, 159
    split lines, 172
"beer ready" glassware, 103–105
beer regulations/ordinances
    Advertising and Marketing Code, 203, 213–220
    for beer distribution, 200–202
    beer industry self-regulation, 199, 203
    common legal tasks and issues, 204
    importance of understanding, 199
    in Munich, 149
    Reinheitsgebot ("Purity Law"), 7, 23, 72–73, 74, 81
    in the Renaissance, 7
    sales to consumers, 202–203
    sources of legal information, 203–204
    in U.S. history, 199–200
beer stone, 167
beer styles. *See also individual beer styles*
    Belgium and France
        Belgian sour ales, 51–55
        Belgian strong ales, 50–51
        farmhouse ales, 47–48
        other Belgian ales, 55–56
        overview, 46–47
        Trappist and abbey ales, 49–50
    England, Scotland, and Ireland
        brown ales, 61–63
        English bitter, 57–59
        India pale ales, 60–61
        Irish red ale, 68
        overview, 57
        pale ales, 59–60
        porters, 63–65
        Scottish ales, 68–69
        stouts, 65–67
        strong ales, 69–72
    Germany and continental Europe
        Bavarian *Weizen*, 37, 81–84
        bock beers, 78–81
        continental lager beers, 73–78
        German ales, 81, 84–87
        overview, 72–73
        rye beer, 84
    list of world beer styles, 44–46
    North American
        ales, 89–90

        lagers, 88–89
        other American styles, 90
        overview, 87–88
    providing descriptions of, 100
    sources of guidelines, 43
beer tasting
    steps in how to taste beer, 184–186
    taste analysis to determine shelf life, 92
    tasting progression, 184
beer taxes, in colonial America, 8, 199
Belgian ales
    adjuncts, 137–138, 139
    aging in wooden barrels, 6, 32
    Belgian blond ale, 56
    Belgian pale ale, 60
    Belgian sour ales
        Flanders sour ales, 6, 51–53
        lambics, 53–55
        overview, 51
    Belgian strong ales
        characteristics of, 50
        dark strong ale, 51
        golden strong ale, 50–51
    characteristics of, 46–47
    farmhouse ales
        bière de garde, 47–48
        saison, 48
    opening corked bottles, 108
    pairing to foods, 124
    serving temperature guidelines, 117
    specialty ales, 56
    Trappist and abbey ales
        dubbel, 49–50, 125
        overview, 49
        tripel, 50
    wit, 55–56, 117, 127–128, 138
Belgian-style glasses, 113–115
Belgium. *See also* Belgian ales
    monastic breweries, 5
Benedict, St., 5, 49
bentonite clay, 31
Berliner Weisse, 81, 86–87
Berliner Weisse beer glass, 113
best-before coding, 94, 95
best bitter, 58
beta amylase, 19, 20
beta glucan, 191
bière blanche, 56
bière de garde, 47–48
bière de Mars ("March beer"), 48
bière de printemps ("spring beer"), 48
bière de table ("table beer"), 47
bière faible ("weak beer"), 47
biogenic amines, 194

biscuit malt, 137
bitter (English bitter)
    bitterness, 146
    extra special bitter, 58–59
    ordinary bitter, 58
    overview, 57–58
    special bitter, 58
bittering hops, 145, 146
bitterness
    hop alpha acids and, 23–24, 139, 146
    hopping and, 147–148
    international bitterness units, 146, 181
    pairing to foods, 123
    pairing with richness, 127
    pairing with salt, 126
    ranges among beers, 147–148
    worldwide trends in, 148
Black Horse Tavern, 7
black malt, 136, 137
black porters, 15
blended lambics, 54–55
blond ale, Belgian, 56
blood alcohol content, 196
blood pressure, 193
bock beers
    bock, 79
    Doppelbock, 79–80, 139
    Eisbock, 80–81
    Maibock/Heller Bock, 79
    overview, 78–79
    serving temperature guidelines, 117
body
    effect of adjuncts on, 137
    flavor complexity and, 178
Bohemian pilsner, 76
boiling
    adding hops during, 146, 147
    in the brewing process, 23–25
    in decoction mashing, 20
bombers, 33–34
Bonaparte, Napoleon, 80
born-on date coding, 94, 95–96
bottle-conditioned beer
    glass size for serving, 102
    storing for freshness, 100
bottled beer
    classic pour, 107
    pilsner pour, 107
bottles
    packaging beer in, 33–35
    packing upright, 100
    in tunnel pasteurization, 38
bottom-fermenting yeast, 27–28. *See also* lager yeast
bourbon barrels, 32, 184

bourbon whiskey, 42
Bradford, William, 7
brain, effects of alcohol on, 193–194, 195–196
Bramah, Joseph, 157
brandy, 42
brandy snifter, 116
breast cancer, 195
Brettanomyces yeast
    beer flavor and, 183
    in English old ale, 70, 71
    in Flanders sour ales, 52
    in lambic fermentation, 53, 54
    in porters, 63
    in *saison*, 48
    in stouts, 65
"Brett" flavor character, 183
brewers. *See also* commercial brewing; U.S.
        brewing industry
    determining shelf life, 92
    monastic. *See* monastic breweries
    state and federal regulations of beer distribution,
        200–202
    tied houses and, 201
Brewers Association, 43
Brewers Code of Practice, 203
brewer's yeast. *See also* ale yeast; lager yeast;
        yeast
    beer fermentation and, 27–30, 148
    description of, 149–150
    oxygenation and, 150
    scientific name, 4, 27
    sugars metabolized by, 19, 150
brewhouse vessels, 16, 17, 18
brewing
    in ancient history, 2–4
    in colonial America, 7–8
    compared with baking, 30, 148
    early modern advances in equipment, 8
    grains used in, 4
    imparting hop character to beer, 146–147
    in the Middle Ages, 4–5, 6
    process of. *See* brewing process
    rise of commercial breweries in the Renaissance,
        5–7
brewing colleges, 5
brewing process. *See also* specialty brewing
    boiling, 23–25
    conditioning, 30–32
    fermentation, 27–30
    filtration, 32, 33
    key elements in, 13
    malting, 14–16, 17
    mashing, 16–21
    modern, 207

overview of the steps in, 14
packaging, 33–37
pasteurization, 38
production of a consistent product, 13
wort clarification and chilling, 25–26
wort separation, 21–23
brew kettles, 6, 17, 18, 207
"brewmaster's kitchen", 16
brewpubs
rise of in the United States, 11
serving tanks, 37
single-temperature infusion mashing, 20
brewsters, 5
bright flavors and beers, 125
British beers
brown ales
English brown ale, 62
English mild, 62
overview, 61–62
English bitter
bitterness, 146
extra special bitter, 58–59
ordinary bitter, 58
overview, 57–58
special bitter, 58
India pale ales, 60, 61
overview, 57
pale ales, 59
porters
Baltic porter, 64–65
brown porter, 63–64
overview, 63
robust porter, 64
serving temperature guidelines for ales, 117
stouts
dry (Irish) stout, 65–66
foreign extra stout, 67
imperial (Russian) stout, 66–67
oatmeal stout, 66
overview, 65
sweet stout, 66
strong ales
English barley wine, 71
English old ale, 70–71
overview, 69–70
Scotch ale, 70
British hops, 182
British-styled mash tuns, 18, 22
British-style glasses, 115
bronze kettles, 6
brown ales
amber malts, 15
British, 61–62
of Flanders, 51–53

brown glass bottles, 98
brown malt, 137
Burton-on-Trent (England)
alkaline brewing water, 132–133
brewers, 59, 60
B vitamins, 191

calcium, in brewing water, 132–133
calcium carbonate, 132
calcium chloride, 132
California common, 89
calories, 39
Campaign for Real Ale (CAMRA), 36, 57, 63, 110
cancer, 194–195
canned beer
classic pour, 107
pilsner pour, 107
serving, 103
cans
packaging beer in, 35
serving beer in, 103
in tunnel pasteurization, 38
caramel malt, 136
carbohydrates, 191
carbonation
maintaining carbonation level in draft systems, 160
natural, 31, 35, 36–37
off-flavor and, 187
serving beer in glassware and, 102
carbon dioxide
content in beer, 160
as a dispense gas, 159
ideal gas pressure for draft systems, 160–161, 209–210
loss through foaming, 33
in mixed gas systems, 164–165
natural carbonation, 31, 35, 36–37
in nitro-beer gas, 165
purity standards, 172
release during primary fermentation, 31
storage, 172
cardiomyopathy, 195
cardiovascular system, alcohol consumption and, 192, 195
Carter, Jimmy, 10
cask ale
adding hops to, 24
English bitter, 57–59
pouring, 110–111
sugar adjunct, 139
cask beer
adding hops to, 24, 147
conditioning, 35–36

dispensing, 36
  effect of aging on flavor, 93
  packaging in, 35–36
  shelf life, 36
Castra Regina, 4
Catherine II (Empress of Russia), 66
Catholic church, 5
celiac disease, 40, 192
Celis, Pierre, 56
Ceres, 4
cerevisiae, 4
Certificates of Label Approval (COLA), 204
cerveza, 4
chalices, 114
chalk, 132
champagne, 36, 127
charcoal filters, 132
Charlemagne, 4–5
chelators, 167
chicha, 138
chill haze, 97
chilling, of the wort, 26
chime, 158
China, 4
chlorine
  chlorine cleaning solutions, 167, 168
  chlorine sanitizers, 105
  removing from water, 132
chlorophenol, 187
chocolate malt, 136, 137
choker tubing, 164
Christmas ales, 71
cirrhosis, 194
Cistercians, 49
City Tavern, 7
clarification
  removal of haze during conditioning, 30–31
  of the wort, 25–26
classic pour
  bottled and canned beer, 107
  draft beer, 109
cleaning solutions (for draft systems)
  contact time in the draft line, 168–169
  mechanical action, 168
  other cleaning issues, 169–170
  proper concentration, 168
  proper temperature, 168
  selecting, 167–168
clear glass bottles, 98
clear malt base, 41
Cleopatra, 3
closed fermenters, 151
cloudy beer, 173
cocaine, 193

Code of Federal Regulations (CFR), 204
cognitive function, alcohol consumption and, 193–
    194, 195–196
"cold" filtered beer, 158–159
cold lagering, 30
cold plate draft systems, 166
cold trub, removal during chilling, 26
collagen, 31
Cologne (Germany), 84–85, 86
colonial America
  beer taxes, 8, 199
  brewing in, 7–8
color. *See* beer color
commercial brewing
  advances in beer freshness, 91–92. *See also* beer
      freshness
  areas of self-regulation, 199, 203
  in colonial America, 8
  development of modern beer, 8–9
  rise of in the Renaissance, 5–7
  in the United States, 1, 9, 10, 11
complaints, handling professionally, 100
conditioning
  adding hops during, 147
  of ales, 30, 151, 152
  bottle conditioning, 36–37
  in the brewing process, 30–32
  cask conditioning, 35–36
  length of time, 151–152
conditioning tanks, 30–31
cone hops, 142
conical vertical fermenters, 151
Continental Army, 7
Continental Congress, 7
continental lager beers
  Dortmunder export, 77
  international pale lagers, 77–78
  Märzen/Oktoberfest, 15, 74–75, 146
  Munich *Dunkel*, 75
  Munich *Helles*, 77
  overview, 73
  pilsner, 76–77
  Rauchbier, 6, 78
  Schwarzbier, 75–76
  Vienna lager, 73–74
controlled oxidation, beer flavor and, 93
cooking, with beer, 129–130
cooling, 207
coolships, 25–26, 29, 53
copper kettles, 6
corked bottles, opening, 108
corn (maize)
  as an adjunct, 137, 138
  bourbon whiskey and, 42

in gluten-free beer, 40
in North American lagers, 88
regions grown, 4
corn grits, 88, 138
coronary heart disease, 192
craft beer movement, 10–11, 148
cream ale, 89–90
cream stout, 66
crowning, 207
crushing, of malt, 18–19
crystal malt, 17, 136
Czech pilsner, 76

damages, 202
dark chocolate malt, 137
dark flavors and beers, 125–126
dark/roasted malt
    brewing with alkaline water, 132
    impact on beer color and flavor, 15, 16
    pairing to foods, 122, 123
    in Scottish ales, 68
dark strong ale, 51
decoction mashing, 20–21
Degenberger family, 81
dementia, 193, 195
dextrins, 19, 39, 150
diacetyl, 30, 187
digestifs, 129
digestive system, alcohol consumption and, 193, 194
dimethyl sulfide (DMS), 24
dimpled mugs, 115
Dinkelbier, 81
direct draw draft systems, 166
direct-heated kilns, 8
dispense gas
    functions of, 159–160
    ideal pressure, 160–161
    in-line gas filters, 172
    purity, 172
    storage, 172
    types, 159
dispensing. *See* pouring beer
distilling, yeast and, 29
distribution
    distributors licenses, 199, 200
    state and federal regulations of, 200–202
    three-tier system, 200
Doppelbock, 79–80, 139
Dortmunder export, 77
double/imperial India pale ale, 61
draft beer. *See also* draft systems
    aseptic filtration, 38, 158–159
    classic pour, 109

components of modern kegs, 157–158
daily tasting for freshness, 100
freshness, 99, 157
handling and storage of kegs, 162
history of, 157
invention of dispensing with carbon dioxide, 8
draft systems
    balancing
        adjusting flow resistance, 163–164
        beer pumps, 164
        mixed gas, 164–165
        nitro-beer gas, 165
        overview, 163
    challenges in maintaining, 159
    cooling the lines, 166
    dispense gas
        functions of, 159–160
        ideal pressure, 160–161
        storage, 172
        types, 159
    equipment selection
        fittings, 170
        FOB stops, 171
        gas filters, 172
        gas purity, 172
        series kegs, 172
        split lines, 172–173
        tubing, 170–171
    hygiene and cleaning, 166–170
    off-flavor from draft line taints, 187
    portable cleaning system, 169
    proper pour, 161–162
    schematic of a typical system, 163
    trouble-shooting guide for common problems, 173
dram shop liability, 202
Dreher, Anton, 72, 73, 74
drum roasters, 17
dry beer, 10, 39
dry hopping, 145, 147, 182
dry-roasted malt, 136–137
dry (Irish) stout, 65–66
D System keg valve, 158
dubbel, 49–50, 125
Dublin (Ireland), 132
Dunkel, 75, 133
Dunkelweizen, 83
Düsseldorf (Germany), 84, 86
duvel, 50–51

80-shilling beers, 69
Einbeck (Germany), 78–79
Eisbock, 80–81
emmer, 81

Emmerbier, 81
end-stage liver disease, 194
English ales. *See also* British beers
 bitter
  bitterness, 146
  extra special bitter, 58–59
  ordinary bitter, 58
  overview, 57–58
  special bitter, 58
 brown ale, 62
 carbonation level, 160
 cask conditioning, 35–36
 India pale ale, 60
 mild, 61
 nitro-beer gas, 165
 old ale, 70–71
 open fermentation, 29
 pale ale, 59
 real ale, 24, 36
 stout pour, 109–110
English barley wine, 71
English pale ale malt, 134
"entire" beer, 63
Enzinger, Carl, 8
enzymes
 base malt as a source of, 133
 denatured in boiling the wort, 24
 factors affecting starch-converting efficiency,
  19–20
 malt enzymes, 16
 in seeds, 14
 in starch conversion, 19, 20
esters, 28, 152–153, 179–180
ethanol. *See also* alcohol
 ethanol oxidation and hangovers, 194
 produced during fermentation, 27
 tissue absorption, 192
European Union, 73, 85
evaporation, to remove alcohol, 40
expiry date coding, 94, 95
extra special bitter (ESB), 58–59

false head, 173
farmhouse ales, 47–48
faro, 55
fatty liver, 194
fermentable sugars
 dry beer and, 39
 in fermentation, 150
 in high-alcohol beer production, 41
 low-carbohydrate beers and, 39
 produced in mashing, 19–20
fermentation
 beer flavor and, 28–29, 152–153

 in the brewing process, 13, 27–30, 207
 conditioning period, 151–152
 early modern advances in, 8
 effect of temperature on, 27–29
 human control of, 2
 importance of sanitation, 28
 length of time, 30
 open, 29, 30, 151
 phases of, 150–151
 in sake production, 42
 spontaneous, 26, 53
 stopping to restrict alcohol formation, 40
 yeast and, 13, 27–30, 148, 150–152
fermentation cellars, 28
fermentation-driven beers, 182–183
fermentation flavors
 acidity, 180
 alcohols, 179
 esters, 179–180
 overview, 182–183
 pairing beer flavors to foods, 124–125
 phenolics, 180
fermentation vessel, 207
fermenters
 adding hops to, 24
 in medieval brewing, 6
 open-top, 29, 30
 stainless steel, 28–29
 types of, 151
ferulate, 191
Festbier ("festival beer"), 74
fiber, 191
filtered beers, 8
filtration
 aseptic, 38, 158–159
 in the brewing process, 32, 33, 207
 during clarification, 25
 early modern advances in, 8
 in the production of ice beer, 39
first in first out (FIFO), 93
fittings, in draft systems, 170
Flanders brown ales
 aging in wooden barrels, 31–32
 description of, 51–53
 pairing to foods, 125
Flanders red ales
 aging in wooden barrels, 6, 31–32
 description of, 51–53
 pairing to foods, 125
flash pasteurization, 38, 207
flat beer, 173
flavor. *See* beer flavor
flavor complexity, 178
flavored alcoholic beverages (FAB), 41

flavored beers
    barrel aging, 6, 31–32, 184
    flavoring agents, 183
flavored malt beverages (FMB), 40–41
"flavor houses", 41
flavor intensity, 179
flavor volatiles, 24
Flemish brown ales. *See* Flanders brown ales
Flemish red ales. *See* Flanders red ales
floating mash beds, 22
flocs, 24–25
flow resistance, adjusting in draft systems, 163–164
flutes, 115
foam
    carbon dioxide loss and, 33
    improving with adjuncts, 137
    pilsner pour, 107
    serving beer in glassware and, 102
foam collar, glass size and, 102
fobbing, 33
FOB stops, 171
food. *See* beer and food
food pairing principles
    contrast, 126–128
    impact, 120–121
    match, 121–126
"Food Pyramid", 196
forced-air draft systems, 166
foreign extra stout, 67
"Four Ts", 92
framboise lambic, 184
Franklin, Benjamin, 7
Free Mash Tun Act (Great Britain), 57
French beers
    bière blanche, 56
    bière de garde, 47–48
    bière de Mars ("March beer"), 48
    bière de printemps ("spring beer"), 48
    bière de table ("table beer"), 47
    bière faible ("weak beer"), 47
    petite bière ("small beer"), 47
fruit lambics, 55
fruits, flavoring beers with, 183
Fuggles hops
    in extra special bitter, 58
    in *saison*, 48
    in *tripel*, 50
fullness, in beer flavor, 178, 179
fusel alcohols, 28, 153, 179

G. H. Lett Brewery, 68
gamma amino butyric acid (GABA), 193
gall stones, 194

gas blenders, 165
gas filters, 172
gas pressure, ideal, 160–161, 209–210
gastrointestinal system, alcohol consumption and, 193, 194
gelatin, 31
George Killian beer, 68
The George Tavern, 7
German-continental beer styles
    Bavarian *Weizen*
        bottle-conditioning, 37
        characteristics of, 82
        Dunkelweizen, 83
        Hefeweizen, 82–83, 90, 124, 146, 160
        history of, 81–82
        Kristall Weizen, 83
        Weizenbock, 83–84
    bock beers
        bock, 79
        Doppelbock, 79–80, 139
        Eisbock, 80–81
        Maibock/Heller Bock, 79
        overview, 78–79
    characteristics of, 73
    continental lager beers
        Dortmunder export, 77
        German *Pils*, 76–77, 81, 85
        international pale lagers, 77–78
        Märzen/Oktoberfest, 15, 74–75, 146
        Munich *Dunkel*, 75
        Munich *Helles*, 77
        overview, 73
        pilsner, 76–77. *See also* pilsners
        Rauchbier, 6, 78
        Schwarzbier, 75–76
        Vienna lager, 73–74
    German ales, 81
        Alt, 86
        Berliner Weisse, 86–87
        Kölsch, 84–86
        overview, 84
    glassware for, 112–113
    Reinheitsgebot ("Purity Law") and, 7, 23, 72–73, 74, 81
    rye beer, 84
German immigrants, influence on North American beer styles, 87, 88
German *Pils*, 76–77, 81, 85
German-style glasses, 112–113
Germany. *See also* German-continental beer styles
    decoction mashing, 20
    history of yeast in, 149
    hop cultivation, 140
    hop production, 144

lager brewing in, 72
mit Hefe (beer with yeast), 37
Naturtrüb (unfiltered beer), 32
noble hops, 146
Reinheitsgebot ("Purity Law"), 7, 23, 72–73, 74, 81
Vorläufiges Biergesetz ("Provisional Beer Law"), 72
germination, 8, 14–15, 16, 17, 41, 207
germination beds, 16
glass, as a packaging material, 34–35
glass bottles
    opening a bottle with cork and cage, 108
    protection from light, 98
    serving beer in, 103
glucose, 19, 150
gluten-free beer, 40
glycol-brine solutions, 26
glycol chilled draft systems, 166
goblets, 114
golden strong ale, 50–51
Goldings hops, 58
gout, 194
grain husks
    milling, 19
    in wort separation, 21
grains
    malting, 14–16, 17
    nonmalted, 137, 138–139
    spent after wort separation, 23
    used to make beer, 4
grand cru, 50
Great Britain. *See also* British beers
    Campaign for Real Ale, 36, 57, 63, 110
    Free Mash Tun Act, 57
    single-temperature infusion mashing, 20
"green" beer, 152, 207
Green Dragon Tavern, 7
green glass bottles, 98
green woodruff syrup, 87
grist, 207
Groll, Joseph, 76
gruit, 140
gruit extraction, 6
G System keg valve, 158
gueuze
    description of, 54–55
    faro, 55
    fruit lambics, 55
    pairing to foods, 125
guilds, 6
Guinness, Arthur, II, 67
Guinness Brewery, 63, 65, 66, 67
Guinness gas, 165

gypsum, in brewing water, 132–133

Hancock, John, 7
hand air pumps, 159
hangovers, 194
Hanseatic League, 78
Hansen, Emile Christian, 8, 72, 149
"hard" lemonade, 41
Harvard University, 8
Harwood, Ralph, 63
haze
    beer flavor and, 32
    removal during conditioning, 30–31
    removal during filtration, 32
head retention test, 106
heart disease, alcohol consumption and, 192, 195
heather ale, 68
Hefeweizen
    American, 90
    bitterness, 146
    carbonation level, 160
    characteristics of, 82–83
    pairing to foods, 124
Hefeweizen Rauchbier, 78
Helicobacter pylori, 193
Helles, 75, 77
Helles export, 77
hepatitis, alcoholic, 194
herbs, flavoring beers with, 183
high-alcohol beer, brewing techniques, 41–42
highball glass, 116
high-kilned malt, 135
high-sugar extract, 41
Himbeersirup, 87
Hodgson, George, 60
Hoegaarden brewery, 56
Hofbräuhaus, 82
"holiday heart", 195
home brewing, 10–11
hop alpha acids
    beer bitterness and, 23–24, 139, 146
    in bittering hops, 145
    dissolved during boiling, 23–24
    in fermentation, 29
    worldwide trends in, 148
hopbacks (hop jack), 18, 24, 25
hop cones, 139, 140
hop-driven beers, 181–182
hop extract, 143
hop oils
    in aroma hops, 145
    beer aroma and, 139, 146–147
    effect of heat on, 24
hopping, 147–148

hops (*Humulus lupulus*)
    alpha acids. *See* hop alpha acids
    art and science of hopping, 147–148
    beer flavor and, 23–24, 25, 139, 140, 181–182
    in the brewing process, 207
    in cask conditioning, 35, 36, 147
    cultivation, 141–143
    filtering the wort with during clarification, 25
    harvesting and drying, 142, 143
    history of, 139–141
    imparting bitterness to beer, 23–24, 139, 146
    imparting hop aroma to beer, 146–147
    international bitterness units, 181
    in medieval brewing, 6
    oils, 24, 139, 145, 146–147
    pairing the flavor of hops to foods, 123–124
    phytoestrogens, 193
    prevention of light-struck aroma with, 143
    processed products, 142–143, 144
    U.S. production, 144
    varieties, 145–146
    world growing areas, 141
    world production, 144
hordein, 192
hot-air kilns, indirect, 8
Humulus lupulus. See hops
hydrometers, 8
"Hymn to Ninkasi", 2
hypertension, 193

ice beer, 39, 81
ideal gas pressure, 160–161, 209–210
imperial pint, 102, 115
imperial (Russian) stout, 63, 66–67
importers, state and federal regulations of beer
        distribution, 200–202
Indian Queen Tavern, 7
India pale ales (IPA)
    American India pale ale, 60–61
    bitterness, 146
    double/imperial India pale ale, 61
    English India pale ale, 60
indirect hot-air kilns, 8
industrial beers, 63
Industrial Revolution, 8
ingredients
    adjuncts, 137–139
    hops, 139–148
    malt, 133–137
    water, 131–133
    yeast, 148–154
inlet mixer, 18, 22
in-line gas filters, 172
Institute of Brewing and Distilling (IBD), 42

international bitterness units (IBUs), 146, 181
international pale lagers, 77–78
inventories, sizing to maintain freshness, 93, 100
Irish beers. *See also* British beers
    Irish red ale, 68
    Irish stout
        characteristics of, 65–66
        nitro-beer gas, 165
        pouring, 109
        production of, 68
    overview, 57
isinglass, 31, 35, 36
Islam, 3–4
isomerization, 24

Jefferson, Thomas, 7
jockey box, 166

"kash", 3
kegs
    carbonation level, 160
    components of modern kegs, 157–158
    handling and storage, 162
    history of, 157
    packaging in, 35
    in series, 172
    storage time after delivery, 98
    stout pour, 109–110
keg valve systems, 158
Kellerbier ("cellar beer"), 77
Kenamun's tomb (Egypt), 2, 3
kidneys, alcohol consumption and, 194
kilns and kilning
    in the brewing process, 207
    in malting, 15–16
    in medieval brewing, 6
    modern improvements, 8
koji mold, 42
Kölsch, 81, 84–86
Kölsch glass, 86, 113
Kölsch Konvention, 85
"*Kölsch*-style" beer, 85
krausen, 29, 151
krausening, 31
kriek lambic, 184
Kristall Weizen, 83
Krug (German beer mug), 112
Kulmach (Bavaria), 80

lacing test, 106
lactic acid, 180
Lactobacillus
    in Flanders sour ales, 52
    in lambic fermentation, 53

Lactobacillus delbrueckii, 86
lactose, 66
lager brewing
    origins of, 72, 73, 149
    rise of in America, 9, 10
lagering, 30, 73. *See also* conditioning
lagers
    bottom-fermenting, 81
    cold conditioning, 30
    conditioning period, 151, 152
    continental lager beers
        Dortmunder export, 77
        German *Pils*, 76–77, 81, 85
        international pale lagers, 77–78
        Märzen/Oktoberfest, 15, 74–75, 146
        Munich *Dunkel*, 75
        Munich *Helles*, 77
        overview, 73
        pilsner, 76–77
        Rauchbier, 6, 78
        Schwarzbier, 75–76
        Vienna lager, 73–74
    effect of yeast on flavor, 28
    North American lagers, 88–89
    primary fermentation time, 30
    top-fermenting, 81
lager yeast (*Saccharomyces pastorianus*)
    in beer fermentation, 27–28
    beer flavor and, 152–153
    as bottom-fermenting yeast, 27–28, 151
    conditioning time, 152
    fermentation temperature, 150
    origins of, 149
    primary fermentation time, 30
lambics
    aging in wooden barrels, 31–32, 184
    criteria for, 54
    faro, 55
    fruit lambics, 55
    gueuze, 54–55
    overview, 53–54
    spontaneous fermentation, 26, 53
    unblended lambics, 54
La Trappe Abbey, 49
lauter tuns, 17, 20, 21, 26, 207
laws. *See* beer regulations/ordinances
leaf hops, 142
Lent, 80
Lett, George Killian, 68
licenses, for beer distributors and retailers, 199, 200
light, effects on beer, 98–99
light beer
    American consumer preferences and, 10
    brewing techniques, 38–39

light-struck aroma, use of hop extract to prevent, 143
light-struck effect
    description of, 98
    off-flavor and, 186–187
    tips to avoid, 99
limestone, 132
lipids, removal during conditioning, 31
liver, effects of alcohol on, 194
low-carbohydrate beer, 10, 39
lupulin glands, 139

magnesium, in brewing water, 132
Maibock/Heller Bock, 79
maize. *See* corn
malt
    base malt, 133–135
    coagulation of proteins by boiling the wort, 24–25
    effect of kilning on color and flavor, 15–16
    grains used in, 133
    importance to beer and beer flavor, 133, 181
    mashing process, 18–20
    milling, 18–19
    pairing malt flavors to foods, 122–123
    peated, 68–69
    process of making, 14–16, 17
    specialty malts, 135–137
    stability of, 15
malt-driven beers, 181
malt enzymes, 16, 24
malting
    in the brewing process, 14–16, 17, 207
    early modern advances in, 8
    in high-alcohol beer production, 41
malt liquor, 40
maltose, 19, 20, 150
maltotriose, 19, 150
malt proteins, 24–25
malt syrups, 41
"malt" wines, 71. *See also* barley wines
marketing
    Advertising and Marketing Code, 203, 213–220
    beer freshness and, 99
    industry self-regulation in, 203
Märzen/Oktoberfest, 15, 74–75, 146
mash, 19–20
mash beds, floating, 22
mashing
    brewhouse vessels, 16, 17, 18
    in the brewing process, 207
    decoction mashing, 20–21
    effect of temperature on sugar production, 20
    in high-alcohol beer production, 41

parti-gyle method, 70
process of, 18–20
in Renaissance brewing, 6
single-temperature infusion mashing, 20, 21
step mashing, 21
variables affecting yeast and fermentation, 152
mashing cycles, 19
mash/lauter tun, 18
mash mixer, 207
mash tuns
British-styled, 18, 22
in a large American lager brewery, 17
in medieval brewing, 6
mixing the mash in, 19
in Renaissance brewing, 6
in single-temperature infusion mashing, 21
Mass, 112–113
Massachusetts, 8
maturation, 207
Maytag, Fritz, 89
mechanical scrubbing, in draft system cleaning, 168
melanoidins, 15, 20, 24, 135
membrane separation, 40
Mesopotamia, 2, 3
metallic off-flavor, 187
Mexico, 73
microbiology, 8
microbottling machines, 33–34
microbreweries, 11
Middle Ages
brewing in, 4–5
characteristics of beer during, 6
Middle East, 2–4
migraines, 194
milk stout, 66
millet, 4
millet malt, 135
milling
in the brewing process, 207
of malt, 18–19
minerals
in beer, 191
in water, 132–133
mit Hefe ("with yeast"), 37
mixed gas
in draft systems, 164–165
split lines, 172
monastic breweries. *See also* Trappist and abbey ales
Bavarian, 79–80
Belgian, 49, 50
in the Middle Ages, 5
monochloropropanols, 192
Moortgat Brewery, 50
mouthfeel, 178

M System keg valve, 158
mugs, 112–113
multiple-temperature mashing, 21
Munich (Germany)
alkaline brewing water, 133
brewing ordinance of 1551, 149
Hofbräuhaus, 82
monastic breweries, 5
Oktoberfest, 74
Munich *Dunkel*, 75
Munich *Helles*, 77
Munich malt, 133, 135

National Beer Wholesalers Association, 200
natural carbonation
in bottle conditioning, 36–37
in cask conditioning, 35
during secondary fermentation, 31
Naturtrüb ("naturally turbid beer"), 32, 77
neurotransmitters, 193
Nigeria, 67
nitro-beer gas, 165
nitrogen
as a dispense gas, 159
in mixed gas systems, 164–165
in nitro-beer gas, 165
purity standards, 172
storage, 172
nitrogenated beer, 36, 109, 110, 165
nitrogen generators, 172
nitrosamines, 192
nitro-stout, 109
noble hops, 146
non-alcoholic beer, 40
noncarbonate calcium, 132
nonfermentable sugars, 19–20, 39, 150
nonic, 115
nonmalted grains, 137, 138–139
North American beer styles
ales
American brown ale, 62–63
American *Hefeweizen*, 90
American India pale ale, 60–61
American pale ale, 24, 59–60
California common, 89
cream ale, 89–90
other American styles, 90
overview, 89
American stout, 67
American wheat ale, 90, 146
ice beer, 81
influences on the development of, 87–88
lagers
American light lager, 88–89, 146

American standard lager, 88
brewhouse vessels, 17
overview, 88
serving temperature guidelines, 117
North American Brewers Association (NABA), 43
nose, 176–177
nutrients, in beer, 191–192
nuts, flavoring beers with, 183

oak barrels, 184
oatmeal stout, 66
oats
as an adjunct, 139
in Scottish ales, 69
off-flavors, 186–187
oils. *See also* hop oils
cutting with acidity, 127–128
Oktoberfest, 74
Mass glassware, 112–113
Oktoberfest *Märzen*, 74–75
olfactory system, 175, 176–177
open fermentation, 29, 30, 151
open-top fermenters, 29, 30
Order of Cistercians of the Strict Observance, 49
ordinary bitter, 58
organic beer, 41
osteoporosis, 191
oxidation
controlled oxidation and beer flavor, 93
microbial stability and, 96–97
oxidative staling
accumulative nature of, 97
beer freshness and, 92
effect of temperature on, 96–97
from oxygen intrusion during filtration, 32
turbulence and, 98
oxidized flavors, 186
oxidized wines, 93
oxygen, yeast metabolism and, 150, 153

packaging
bottle conditioning, 36–37
bottles, 33–35, 207
cans, 35, 207
casks, 35–36
early modern advances in, 8
kegs, 35, 207
keys to success in, 33
serving tanks, 37
packaging date coding, 94, 95–96
palate cleansing, 120
pale ales
American pale ale, 59–60
Belgian pale ale, 60

bitterness, 146
English pale ale, 59
overview, 59
pale malt
as base malt, 133–134
kilning, 15
malt enzymes and, 16
pairing to foods, 122
pancreatitis, 194
papain, 31
parti-gyle method, 70
Pasteur, Louis, 8, 38, 72, 149
pasteurization, 8, 38, 207
Paulaner's brewery, 79–80
peat, 42
peated malt, 68–69
Pediococcus, 53
pentosan, 191
peripheral nervous system, toxic effect of alcohol
on, 195–196
pesticide residues, 192
petite bière ("small beer"), 47
pH, effect on fermentation, 29
phenolics, 180, 191
phenols, 19
phytoestrogens, 193
Pichler, Elias, 79
Pilgrims, 7
Pils, 76–77, 81, 85
Pilsen (Czech Republic), 72, 76, 133
Pils malt, 133–134
pilsner glass, 112
pilsner malt, 133–134
pilsners
bitterness, 146
Bohemian pilsner, 76
German *Pils*, 76–77, 81, 85
hop aroma, 145–146
modern advances in malting and, 8
overview, 76
pairing with rich foods, 127
pouring, 107
serving temperature guidelines, 117
Pilsner Urquell, 76
pint glasses, 102
pitch, 31
plastic bottles, 35
plastic cups, 103
plastic flakes, 31
plate-and-frame filter, 33
plate heat exchanger, 207
Plymouth Colony, 7
pneumatic beer pumps, 164
Pokal (pilsner glass), 112

polyethylene terephthalate (PET) bottles, 35
polyphenols, 39, 191
polypropylene tubing, 163
polyvinyl-polypyrrolidone (PVPP), 31
port pipes, 32
portable cleaning system, for draft systems, 169
porters
    Baltic porter, 64–65
    brown porter, 63–64
    overview, 63
    robust porter, 64
    stouts and, 65
potassium hydroxide, 167
pouring beer, 106. *See also* serving beer
    beer engines for cask beer, 36
    bottled and canned beer, 107–108
    cask ale, 110–111
    draft beer, 109, 161–162
    opening a bottle with cork and cage, 108
    stout pour, 109–110
    widgets, 110
prebiotics, 191
pressurized pot cleaning, 168
primary fermentation
    length of time, 30
    overview, 150–151
    release of carbon dioxide during, 31
priming
    in bottle conditioning, 36–37
    in cask conditioning, 35
Prohibition, 10, 87, 89, 199, 201
prolactin, 193
proteins
    coagulation by boiling the wort, 24–25
    removal during conditioning, 31
    removal in production of ice beer, 39
"Provisional Beer Law" (Germany), 72
provision beers, 47–48
pseudouridine, 195
pub glasses, 115
"Purity Law" (Germany), 7, 23, 72–73, 74, 81

Ramses (Egyptian pharaoh), 3
Rauchbier ("smoked beer"), 6, 78
real ale
    adding hops to, 24
    characteristics of, 36
    English bitter, 57–59
    pouring, 110–111
    sugar adjunct, 139
red ales. *See* Flanders red ales
Red Lion Brewery, 8
red raspberry syrup, 87
red wine, health and, 189

Reformation, 5
refrigeration
    beer freshness and, 96, 97
    early modern advances in, 9
    of kegs, 162
Reinheitsgebot ("Purity Law"), 7, 23, 72–73, 74, 81
Renaissance, 5–7
repitching, 30
reproductive system, alcohol consumption and, 193, 196
retailers
    important sources of off-flavors, 187
    licenses, 199
    state and federal regulations of beer distribution, 200–202
rice
    as an adjunct, 138
    in gluten-free beer, 40
    regions grown, 4
    in sake production, 42
rice wine, 42
richness
    cutting with acidity, 127–128
    pairing with astringency, 126
    pairing with bitterness, 127
roasted malt. *See* dark/roasted malt
roasters, 17
roasting. *See* kilns and kilning
robust porter, 64
Roggenbier, 81, 84
roller mill, 207
ruh beer, 31
Russia, 66
Russian stout, 63, 66–67
Rutledge, John, 7
rye, 4
rye beer, 81, 84

Saaz hops, 51
Saccharomyces, in lambic fermentation, 53
Saccharomyces cerevisiae, 4, 27. *See also* ale yeast; brewer's yeast; yeast
Saccharomyces pastorianus. See lager yeast
saison
    characteristics of, 48
    pairing to foods, 124–125
sake, 42
salt
    neutralization of acidity, 128
    pairing with bitterness, 126
salt test, 106
Salvator, 80
sanitation, importance during fermentation, 28
sanitizers, in hand-washing glassware, 104–105

Sanke keg, 158
Scandinavia, 64
Schneider, George, 82
Schneider brewery, 83
Schwarzbier, 64, 75–76
Schwarz Pils, 76
Scotch whiskey, 42
Scottish ales
    bitterness, 146
    overview, 68–69
    Scotch ale, 70
    Scottish export, 69
    Scottish heavy, 69
    Scottish light, 69
secondary fermentation
    natural carbonation and, 31
    overview, 151–152
Sedlmayr, Gabriel, II, 73, 74
"see, swirl, sniff, and sip" tasting, 185
seeds, germination, 14–15
series kegs, 172
serving beer. *See also* pouring beer
    beer-appropriate glassware, 111–116
    beer clean glassware, 103–105
    in bottles, cans, or plastic cups, 103
    pouring, 106–111
    reasons to use a glass, 101–103
    serving temperature guidelines, 116–117
serving tanks, 37
serving temperature
    for cask beer, 36
    effect on beer flavor and character, 117
    glassware and, 102–103
    guidelines for, 116–117
session beer, 58
"7-minute pour", 107
75/25 gas blend, 165
70-shilling beers, 69
shaker glass, 116
sheeting test, 106
shelf life, 92
Sherman, Roger, 7
Shoreditch Brewery, 63
Sierra Nevada Brewing Company, 11
silica hydrogel, 31
silicon, 191
single-temperature infusion mashing, 20, 21
six-row barley, 134, 138
six-row pilsner malt, 48
Sixty Minutes, 189
60-shilling beers, 69
smoked beer, 6, 78
snifters, 114
sodium hydroxide, 167

soft water, effect on brewing, 132–133
soluble fiber, 191
sorghum, 40
sorghum malt, 135
sour beers
    Berliner Weisse, 86–87
    Flanders sour ales, 51–53, 184
    pairing to foods, 125
sparge water, 131
sparging, 20, 21–22
sparklers, 111
Spaten brewery, 77
special bitter, 58
special B malt, 136
specialty brewing
    dry beer, 39
    flavored malt beverages, 40–41
    gluten-free beer, 40
    high-alcohol beer, 41–42
    ice beer, 39
    light beer, 38–39
    low-carbohydrate beer, 39
    malt liquor, 40
    non-alcoholic beer, 40
    organic beer, 41
    sake, 42
    whiskey, 42
specialty malts
    caramel or crystal malt, 136
    dry-roasted malt, 136–137
    overview, 135
    uses of, 133
spelt, 81
spent grains, 23, 207
spices, flavoring beers with, 183
spicy heat
    effect of alcohol on, 128
    pairing with sweetness, 127
split draft lines, 172–173
sponge cleaning, 168
spontaneous fermentation, 26, 53
S System keg valve, 158
St. Joseph's Day, 80
stainless steel tubing, 163
    in draft systems, 171
staling flavors, 186, 187
Stange glass, 86
starches
    as adjuncts, 137
    conversion to sugars in malting, 14–15
    conversion to sugars in mashing, 19–20
    in lambic fermentation, 53
starchy endosperm
    milling, 18–19

of seeds, 14–15
Starkbierzeit ("strong beer season"), 80
static line cleaning, 168–169
steam beer, 89
Steele's masher, 18, 22
steeping, 15, 207
Steinbier, 78
steins, 112, 113
step mashing, 21
sterilization, of the wort by boiling, 23
storage
    bottle-conditioned beer, 100
    effect of temperature on oxidative staling, 96
    of kegs, 98, 162
stout faucet, 109, 165
stout glass, 109, 115
stouts
    aging in old bourbon barrels, 32
    American stout, 67
    bitterness, 146
    dark malts, 15
    dry (Irish) stout, 65–66
    foreign extra stout, 67
    imperial (Russian) stout, 63, 66–67
    in Ireland, 68
    nitrogenated cans, 110
    oatmeal stout, 66
    overview, 65
    pouring, 109–110
    sweet stout, 66
strength, in beer flavor, 179
stroke, 193
strong ales
    American barley wine, 72
    Belgian strong ales, 50–51
    English barley wine, 71
    English old ale, 70–71
    overview, 69–70
    Scotch ale, 70
    serving temperature guidelines, 117
Styrian Goldings hops
    in golden strong ale, 51
    in *saison*, 48
    in *tripel*, 50
sugars
    as adjuncts, 137, 139
    concentrated by boiling the wort, 24
    conversion of starch to in malting, 14–15
    dry beers and, 39
    in fermentation, 150
    in high-alcohol beer production, 41
    low-carbohydrate beers and, 39
    metabolized by brewer's yeast, 150
    nonfermentable sugars, 19–20, 39, 150

priming with in bottle conditioning, 36–37
priming with in cask conditioning, 35
produced in mashing, 19–20, 21
sulfites, in wine, 91
sulfur, 30
Sumeria, 2, 3, 148
sump, 158
swan neck spout, 111
sweet mash, sparging, 20
sweetness, pairing with spicy heat, 127
sweet stout, 66
sweet wort. *See also* wort
    boiling, 23–25
    defined, 21
    separation, 21–23

tanks, 15, 17, 18, 24, 25, 30–31, 37, 207
tannic beers, 93
tannins, removal during conditioning, 31
taste
    sensing, 175–176
    steps in how to taste beer, 184–186
    taste analysis to determine shelf life, 92
taste buds, 176
taverns
    in colonial America, 7, 8
    "tied" to brewers, 201
"teacup effect", 25
temperature
    in automatic glassware washing, 103
    during conditioning, 30
    effect on fermentation and beer flavor, 27–29,
        152–153
    effect on sugar production in mashing, 20
    factors affecting beer freshness, 96–97
    in tunnel pasteurization, 38
thermometers, 8
three-sink method, 104–105
"three threads", 63
three-tier system, of beer distribution, 200
tied house laws, 201
tongue, taste buds and tasting, 176
top-fermenting yeast, 27–28. *See also* ale yeast
Trappist and abbey ales
    bottle conditioning, 37
    dubbel, 49–50, 125
    glassware, 114
    overview, 49
    tripel, 49–50, 124
Trappist brewing monasteries, 5
Trappistenbier, 49
trichloroanisole (TCA), 187
tripel, 49, 124
tropical stout, 67

trub
    in the brewing process, 207
    in cask-conditioned beers, 36
    removal during clarification, 25–26
    removal during fermentation, 29
TTB, 200, 204
tubing, in draft systems, 163–164, 170–171
tulip glass, 114
tumblers, 112
tunnel pasteurization, 38, 207
turbulence, beer freshness and, 98
turnover, of kegs, 162
Twenty-first Amendment (United States), 199–200
twilight, beer freshness and, 98–99
two-row barley, 134, 138

ultraviolet light, effects on beer, 98, 186–187
unblended lambic, 54
unfiltered beer
    bottle conditioning, 36–37
    characteristics of, 32
    handling and storing kegs, 162
United Brewers Industrial Foundation, 203
United States
    brewing in colonial America, 7–8
    colonial beer taxes, 8, 199
    historical overview of beer regulation in, 199–200
    hop production, 144
University of Munich, 5
unmalted grains, 137, 138–139
urinary tract, alcohol consumption and, 194
U.S. brewing industry
    consolidation of breweries, 9–10
    craft beer movement, 10–11
    economic importance of, 1
    loss of individual styles, 10
    number of breweries, 9, 10, 11
    production to meet consumer preferences, 10
    during Prohibition, 10
    rise of lager brewing, 9, 10
    rise of national breweries, 9
U.S. Department of Treasury, 200
use-by coding, 94
U System keg valve, 158

vegetables, flavoring beers with, 183
vertical tasting, 93
very-long-draw draft systems, 164
Vienna lager, 73–74
Vienna malt, 73–74, 133, 134
vinyl tubing, 163, 170
vitamins, in beer, 191
von Linde, Carl, 8–9

Vorläufiges Biergesetz ("Provisional Beer Law"), 72

Waldmeistersirup, 87
Washington, George, 7, 63, 199
water
    in the brewing process, 207
    importance to brewing, 131
    qualities affecting brewing, 131–133
water hardness, 132–133
Weihenstephan Monastery, 5
Weissbier, 82
Weisses Bräuhaus, 82
Weizen. See also Hefeweizen
    glass size for serving, 102
    open fermentation, 30
    pouring, 108
    serving temperature guidelines, 117
Weizen beer glass, 102, 113
Weizenbock, 83–84
Westmalle Monastery, 50
wheat
    as an adjunct, 138
    regions grown, 4
wheat beer
    American Hefeweizen, 90, 146
    Bavarian Weizen, 37, 81–84
"wheat bock", 83
wheat malt, 133, 135
Wheeler, Daniel, 8, 64
whirlpool separator, 207
whirlpool tank, 18, 24, 25
whirlpool technique, 25
whiskey
    aging in barrels, 31
    production of, 42
wholesalers
    important sources of off-flavors, 187
    state and federal regulations of beer distribution, 200–202
widgets, 110
Wiesn ("meadow beer"), 74
wild beer, 173
wine
    aging in barrels, 31
    as a drink of the affluent, 4
    health and, 189
    oxidized, 93
    sulfites and, 91
wine casks, 31, 32
wine glass, 116
winemaking
    influence on Belgian beers, 46
    yeast and, 29, 42

wine yeast, 29, 42
wit ("white" beer)
    characteristics of, 55–56
    pairing with rich foods, 127–128
    serving temperature guidelines, 117
    wheat adjunct, 138
wit beer glass, 115
Wittelsbacher family, 81–82
women, brewing in the Middle Ages, 5
wooden barrels and casks
    aging beer in, 6, 31–32, 93, 184
    aging of wine and whiskey, 31
wort
    adding hops to, 146, 147
    boiling, 6, 23–25
    in the brewing process, 207
    chilling, 26
    clarification, 25–26
    color increases during boiling, 24
    increasing wort strength with adjuncts, 137
    separation, 21–23
    sugars produced in mashing, 19–20
    variables affecting yeast and fermentation, 152, 153

for whiskey production, 42
wort chillers, 26, 28

yeast. *See also* ale yeast; *Brettanomyces* yeast;
    brewer's yeast; lager yeast
    alcohol-tolerant, 41–42
    in beer fermentation, 13, 27–30, 148, 150–152, 207
    beer flavor and, 28, 29–30, 152–153, 182, 183
    in bottle conditioning, 36, 37
    in cask conditioning, 35, 36
    effect of temperature on fermentation, 27–29
    history of, 148–149
    importance to brewing, 148, 153–154
    key characteristics for brewing, 152
    management of strains, 153
    modern identification of, 8
    removal during conditioning, 31
    removal during filtration, 32
    repitching, 30
    in sake production, 42
    top-fermenting and bottom-fermenting, 27–28
    in winemaking and distilling, 29, 42
    wort and mashing variables affecting, 152